Hollywood's American Tragedies

Hollywood's American Tragedies
Dreiser, Eisenstein, Sternberg, Stevens

MANDY MERCK

Oxford • New York

English edition
First published in 2007 by
Berg
Editorial offices:
First Floor, Angel Court, 81 St Clements Street, Oxford OX4 1AW, UK
175 Fifth Avenue, New York, NY 10010, USA

Berg is the imprint of Oxford International Publishers Ltd.

Library of Congress Cataloging-in-Publication Data
Merck, Mandy.
    Hollywood's American tragedies : Dreiser, Eisenstein,
Sternberg, Stevens / Mandy Merck. — English ed.
        p. cm.
    Includes bibliographical references and index.
    ISBN-13: 978-1-84520-664-2
    ISBN-10: 1-84520-664-9
    ISBN-13: 978-1-84520-665-9 (pbk.)
    ISBN-10: 1-84520-665-7 (pbk.)
    1. Dreiser, Theodore, 1871-1945. American tragedy. 2.
Dreiser, Theodore, 1871-1945.—Film and video
adaptations. 3. American literature—Film and video
adaptations. 4. Film adaptations—History and criticism.
I. Title.

    PS3507.R55A8235 2007
    813'.52—dc22   2007031194

British Library Cataloguing-in-Publication Data
A catalogue record for this book is available from the British Library.

ISBN 978 1 84520 664 2 (Cloth)
    978 1 84520 665 9 (Paper)

Typeset by Avocet Typeset, Brill Road, Chilton, Aylesbury, Bucks
Printed in the United Kingdom by Biddles Ltd, King's Lynn.

www.bergpublishers.com

Contents

Illustrations

Acknowledgements

This book could not have been written without the help and generosity of a great many people and institutions. I am particularly indebted to the Leverhulme Foundation for the research fellowship that enabled me to conduct archival studies in the United States. To Jean Cater goes my special thanks, for her kindness and support throughout the project. The University of California at Berkeley's Film Program in the Department of Rhetoric offered a Visiting Scholarship at a key moment. I'm very grateful to Judith Butler and Linda Williams for that invitation and their hospitality during my visit. Barbara Hall and the staff of the Margaret Herrick Library of the Academy of Motion Picture Arts and Sciences in Los Angeles were extraordinarily generous with their vast knowledge of the George Stevens and Paramount Collections, and very tolerant of my fledgling efforts at archival investigation. My thanks also to the UCLA Film and Television Archive for permission to view its print of *An American Tragedy*, and to the Arts Special Collections department of the UCLA Arts Library for allowing me to consult Michael Wilson's papers. Nancy M. Shawcross and her colleagues at the Annenberg Rare Book and Manuscript Library at the University of Pennsylvania offered invaluable access to the Theodore Dreiser Papers. Leslie DeLassus of the Office of the Associate Librarian at the Harry Ransom Humanities Research Center at the University of Texas at Austin guided me to relevant material in the David O. Selznick collection. I am also grateful to Michelle Harvey and the staff of the Museum of Modern Art Archives in New York, for enabling me to view the Eisenstein collection. Thanks also to Rudy Behlmer for providing the full text of a key Selznick letter.

The department of Media Arts and Dean of Arts Maire Davies of Royal Holloway, University of London, provided generous leave and kind support for this book's writing. My research student Ruth O'Donnell worked wonderfully hard on the preparation of the final manuscript. In Los Angeles Jennifer Doyle, Bill Handley, Susan Heyer, Heather Lukes and Molly McGarry housed me, fed me and sustained me during the rainiest winter in memory. My family, Helen, Betsy, Sally and Peter Merck, gave me respite up and down the West Coast. Patricia White made my visit to Philadelphia a treat and Jose Munoz, Sharon Livesey and Neil Talbot were warmly hospitable in New York. Tristan Palmer has been an exceptionally knowledgeable and enthusiastic editor.

Four other friends have lent particular support to this project. Susan Nash located invaluable US documents for me, Richard Dyer kindly read early drafts of some chapters and Laura Mulvey has been a long-suffering interlocutor in my progress to publication. And in her endless contributions to this particular Hollywood history, Nel Druce has been, quite simply, a star.

Introduction

In 2006 a macabre anniversary was observed in the United States. One hundred years earlier, a handsome young man named Chester Gillette was tried in upstate New York for the murder of his factory co-worker, Grace ("Billy") Brown. The son of Salvation Army missionaries, Gillette had left home at age 14 and worked his way across the country. By chance he encountered a wealthy uncle who offered him employment at his garment factory in Cortland, NY. There Gillette courted several women and seduced Brown, the daughter of a local farming family. After she became pregnant the couple traveled to the Adirondacks under assumed names, eventually arriving at Big Moose Lake, where Gillette rented a rowboat. On July 14, 1906, Brown's battered body was reportedly found in the lake, together with the capsized boat and a man's straw hat. The trial for her murder, with the victim's plaintive letters to Gillette read aloud in court and rumors circulating of a beautiful rival from one of Cortland's most prominent families, made national headlines. Gillette insisted that Brown had thrown herself in the water when he said he could not marry her but her head injuries, his departure from the scene and a suspiciously buried tennis racquet convinced the jury to convict him in a matter of hours. Soon afterwards, his mother arrived from the Midwest, her expenses paid by the *New York Evening Journal* and the *Denver Times* in exchange for reports on her son's fate. The condemned man maintained his innocence until his appeals were exhausted. On March 30, 1908 he was electrocuted in Auburn State Prison.

In *The People of New York v. Chester Gillette*, Theodore Dreiser saw "a crime sensation of the first magnitude, with all those intriguingly colorful, and yet morally and spiritually atrocious, elements—love, romance, wealth, poverty, death."[1] But instead of its small-town Lothario, his 1925 novel indicted American sexual hypocrisy, American religion and American justice. The resulting bestseller, hailed as the greatest novel of its generation, was an unexpected success. As one magazine put it a year later, "The whole thing contains a certain splendor because this wealth has come to Dreiser after pioneering as a realist in which time he has been hailed, reviled and suppressed, only to win a wholesale popular acclaim at last by his gloomiest tragedy of all" (Carples, 1926: 46).

That this publication was a movie magazine, announcing the sale of *An American Tragedy* to Hollywood for a record sum, was still another surprise. Although a stage adaptation of his novel enjoyed a run on Broadway, Dreiser was warned that the Hays Office would never permit its filming. Nevertheless, in pursuit of prestige for his denigrated industry, the Hollywood producer Jesse Lasky eventually gambled the then-huge sum of US$125,000 on an anti-American novel whose main character was far more a creature of events than their creator. Sergei Eisenstein would be the first to attempt a screen adaptation during his 1930 sojourn in Hollywood, producing the remarkable treatment that Paramount production chief B. P. Schulberg called "a monstrous challenge to American society" (Eisenstein, 1988h: 228). Taking a very different tack, Josef von Sternberg sought to eliminate the novel's sociological determinism in order to represent the obscure psychology of its doomed protagonist. In response Dreiser sued Paramount for its "utter misrepresentation and libelous distortion" (letter from Arthur Garfield Hays and Arthur Carter Hume to Paramount Publix Corporation, June 26, 1931, Theodore Dreiser Papers, Annenberg Rare Book and Manuscript Library, University of Pennsylvania, hereafter Dreiser Papers) of his book in a 1931 court case that became another newspaper sensation.

When, in August 2006, the *Journal News* of Westchester, New York, commemorated the centennial of the Gillette-Brown case, it recalled both the murder trial and Dreiser's lawsuit a quarter of a century later. The writer, a long-time local resident, "really didn't like Hollywood," the *Journal News* claimed, quoting his description of the movie making capital as populated by "the lowest grade of political grafters, quacks not calculable as to number or variety ... loafers, prostitutes, murders and perverts. In the bland sunshine here they multiply like germs in the canal zone." Hollywood, it continued, "didn't think so highly of Dreiser either. The studio honchos Dreiser was feuding with in 1931 cast him as 'childish,' 'a dilettante,' a man of deeply anti-American views and, more to the point, a hopelessly bad screenwriter" (Marchant, 2006).

This picture of irreconcilable opposites is not new. In its August 3, 1931 account of "Dreiser's Fight with Hollywood," the *Chicago Tribune* concluded:

> The twain never should have met, and it's Hollywood's fault that they did. The vague ambition of the producers to touch the admittedly more critical life leads it into these esthetic adventures which it will not pursue through. It may be believed by many people that the Hollywood idea of individual responsibility hits nearer the mark of probability than Dreiser's theory of social responsibility, but that's not Dreiser, and Hollywood should get its scripts from its own sources. It is not its province to insist that Hamlet's mother was his aunt.

But although Dreiser's attempt to stop Paramount from distributing Sternberg's film made Hollywood history, an exclusive focus on this battle neglects the writer's long involvement with the cinema and its capital city before and afterwards, as well as notable continuities between the novel and all three attempts to film it between 1930 and 1951.

An American Tragedy was begun in Hollywood, where the first draft of Book I, on the protagonist's youth, was completed and revised. Although Dreiser had been collecting real-life accounts of its murder story for some time, his experiences in Los Angeles seem to have catalyzed its writing. The narrative of his tragedy echoes at least one major film of the period and his characters' imaginings are influenced by them. The courtroom at its climax is specifically compared to a movie set, with the ambitious prosecuting attorney seeing himself as its star. Not only would Eisenstein and Sternberg attempt its film adaptation—twenty years later George Stevens would brave the opposition of Paramount and film it again as *A Place in the Sun*. The studio also filmed adaptations of two other Dreiser novels, *Jennie Gerhardt* (directed by Marion Gering in 1933 with *An American Tragedy* star Sylvia Sidney in the title role) and *Sister Carrie* (filmed as *Carrie* by William Wyler in 1952). Their author wrote screenplays from as early as 1914 and lived in Hollywood from 1919 to 1922 with an aspirant actress whom he later married. Despite the frustrations of his time there, his diaries are full of detail about movie life and specific films he has viewed. On leaving Hollywood in 1922, his condemnation of the industry was leavened by praise for the work of Griffith, Fairbanks and Barrymore. When he met Sergei Eisenstein in 1927 he enthused about James Cruze's *The Covered Wagon* (1923) and John Ford's *The Iron Horse* (1924)—two Hollywood Westerns, which his diary declares "as good as Potemkin" (Riggio and West, 1996: 102).

Throughout the period between Paramount's purchase of *An American Tragedy* in 1926 and its first adaptation in 1931, Dreiser took an active interest in its production, nominating Erich von Stroheim as his ideal director in a 1926 interview. Asked if the public would go to see a tragedy, he replied that the novel was "different in psychology from other American films only in so far that it shows that sometimes in the mist we live in some individuals can't pay up for their illusions. Otherwise the gilt is there, our success dreams and our love dreams, that is what I wrote about" (Carples, 1926: 107). Bitter as he was at the perceived failure of the 1931 version to attempt this, Dreiser fulsomely praised Paramount's 1933 interpretation of *Jennie Gerhardt*. In 1938 he returned to live out his days in Hollywood, characteristically complicating that gesture with his late enrollment in the Communist Party. At his funeral in 1945, Charlie Chaplin read one of his poems over his grave.

This study of Dreiser's novel and its film adaptations is a textual history, combining production study with textual analysis. Both methods tend to undermine claims to individual authorship—the production study with its interest in industrial practices, group work, financial limits and technical possibilities, the textual analysis with its emphasis on convention, ideology and unconscious signification. Moreover, these narratives (Dreiser's novel, Eisenstein's treatment, Sternberg's *An American Tragedy* and Stevens' *A Place in the Sun*) exert subtle and often unacknowledged influences on their successors and—in the case of Stevens' adaptation—on Godard's *Histoire(s) du cinéma*. Yet the question of authorship is central to this account. When Paramount purchased *An American Tragedy*, the studio proclaimed their undertaking that "the book would be filmed exactly as it is written" (Lingeman, 1990: 270–1). When Dreiser cited this promise in his injunction against the distribution of Sternberg's version, Paramount replied by claiming that he had plagiarized significant elements of his novel from newspaper accounts of the Gillette-Brown trial. Eisenstein and his English collaborator Ivor Montagu were certain that Paramount would never permit "foreigners, some even Russians, to make *An American Tragedy* in the way we were bound to make it" (Montagu, 1969: 113–14). And when NBC eliminated the transitional dissolves in *A Place in the Sun* in order to broadcast it around commercials, George Stevens declared to the Superior Court of the State of California: "I am particularly meticulous about the cutting, editing and scoring of any picture which I direct, for it is here that the director puts his impress, his hallmark, on the picture. It is in this process that his own style, his own conception, his own method becomes clear and recognizable" (January 31, 1966 declaration, *George Stevens v. National Broadcasting Company*, George Stevens Collection, Margaret Herrick Archives, Academy of Motion Pictures Arts and Sciences). In recounting such claims, this study is not endorsing them but it pays due attention to the contests over origination, ownership and interpretation that intersect this series of adaptations.

My interest in the authorship of these texts extends to the circumstances of their composition. One of the central issues of such an apparently aberrant project for Hollywood adaptation is how it came to be undertaken at all. What appeal did *An American Tragedy* have for those who commissioned its adaptation and those who undertook it? How did they regard the completed work? Such concerns demand a certain amount of biographical inquiry but this is not offered as an explication of these adaptations' unique features. If anything, they tend to resist both biographical reductionism and the broader parameters of auteur criticism. Although they may share stylistic or thematic elements with their directors' other films, they are far from characteristic works. In their varied attempts to get to grips with the novel's conflict of individual intention and other influences, these adaptations have more in common with each other than with films by the same director. Just as the conflict between Dreiser and Hollywood has been overstated, so the differences between the adaptations of his novel by a Marxist, a declared individualist and a director often described as a romantic prove to be less evident than previous accounts have suggested.

In retrospect, the quarter century between the publication of *An American Tragedy* and the release of *A Place in the Sun* is such a brief period that the thematic, institutional and individual continuities that this study will describe are not surprising. Dreiser was introduced to Jesse Lasky in 1919 by his publisher Horace Liveright, who subsequently was employed at his studio in a development role. Eisenstein first met Dreiser in 1927, Sternberg in 1929 and Lasky in 1930. Sternberg met Dreiser when the indignant author flew to Hollywood in an attempt to rewrite his script in 1931. George Stevens first read *An American Tragedy* at the time of its original publication, while establishing his own career as a cameraman and then director. He had seen and disliked Sternberg's adaptation long before he persuaded Paramount to let him try again. Despite

Stevens' insistence that he did not read Eisenstein's treatment until after making *A Place in the Sun*, its early script drafts suggest that his associate producer Ivan Moffat and screenwriter Michael Wilson did consult it. For these reasons, among others, I have recounted the encounters and collaborations that contributed to these projects.

The question of authorship is bound to occur in any study of a literary adaptation. It was never my intention to write a "novel-into-film" book, with its traditional concerns for fidelity to the writer's views or expression, its cavils with change and abridgement, its denunciations of censorship. But the film makers who attempted to bring *An American Tragedy* to the screen paid exceptional attention to both its narrative and its narration, and so must this account. And, of course, the first of the novel's adaptors, Sergei Eisenstein, was himself a considerable literary critic, who in addition to his discussion of *An American Tragedy* wrote significant commentaries on Joyce's internal monologues, Whitman's queer poetics, Zola's materialism and—most famously for film students—Griffith's debt to Dickens. Despite his disappointments in Hollywood, Eisenstein stressed the refreshing influence of his first attempts at literary adaptations there on his "directorial and dramaturgical intentions." "We must study writers," Eisenstein wrote. "And writers must study cinema" (Eisenstein, 1988i: 274).

Behind these questions of authorship lurks the entity that Dreiser regarded as the real author of his protagonist's misfortune—America. Written in its Jazz Age, filmed first in the Depression and then at the height of McCarthyism, the novel and its adaptations both constitute and are constituted by the convulsions of the nation state that is its antagonist and its theme. "I call it *An American Tragedy*," Dreiser said of his title, "because it could not happen in any other country in the world" (Bowers, 1962: 156). Both the use of the hemispheric signifier to designate a single country and the writer's certainty of that country's uniqueness attest to the paradoxical American exceptionalism of his anti-American novel. But at a time when less critical understandings of "Americanness" are exerting their devastating influence on the wider world, its dissection of those fantasies has a renewed currency. As the president of the International American Studies Association cautioned in the January 2003 issue of *PMLA*, "the United States of America is too important to be left to itself and to its myths" (Kadir, 2003: 22).

Dreiser's novel and at least two of its film adaptations, *A Place in the Sun* and the scene that quotes it in Godard's *Histoire(s) du cinéma*, offer reflexive commentaries on Hollywood's own role in American mythmaking. In *An American Tragedy* the cinema itself is made an accessory to crime when its protagonist wants to rid himself of his inconvenient lover. A "melodramatic movie" suggests a "mock marriage ... to deceive some simple country girl" (*An American Tragedy*: 458). And at the media spectacle which the trial for her murder becomes—with its vast press coverage, "the cameras clicking and whirring" (682) and a "full house" (683) in the public gallery—the District Attorney sees himself in the leading role: "Were not the eyes of all the citizens of the United

States upon him? He believed so. It was as if someone had suddenly exclaimed: 'Lights! Camera!'" (689). If Hollywood is complicit in this tragedy it has also been accused of complicity in Dreiser's narration, whose use of perspective and shifts of focus prompted Robert Penn Warren to describe it as 'the movie in our heads' (Warren, 1971: 118). In Stevens' film the cinema's guilt is intensified by the addition of a scene not found in the novel or in previous film adaptations. The hero—significantly renamed after the photographic pioneer George Eastman—befriends the ill-fated factory girl at the movies. Subsequently, Godard defended superimposing Stevens' image of Elizabeth Taylor cradling Montgomery Clift over the director's wartime film of Nazi victims by saying, "When I found out that Stevens had filmed the camps and that for the occasion Kodak had given him his first rolls of 16 mm color film, that explained to me how he could do that close-up of Elizabeth Taylor that radiated a kind of shadowed happiness" (Daney, 1991: 165). Godard appropriates Stevens' central optical effect, the overlapping dissolve, to demonstrate that Hollywood itself is "shadowed" by tragedy. Doing so he suggests why the Westchester *Journal News* was wrong to oppose Dreiser's novel to the system that filmed it. Whatever the difficulties of their production, these American tragedies are—in the many ways that this study will investigate—Hollywood productions.

Godard's historicization of Stevens' adaptation is not the only return to Dreiser's story. On the eve of the hundredth anniversary of the 1906 case, a new opera based on it was given its world premiere. Composed by Tobias Picker with a libretto by Gene Scheer, *An American Tragedy* debuted at the Metropolitan Opera in New York on December 2, 2005. The critics perceived its contemporary relevance for a society still fascinated by ambition and its price, still obsessed by sensational murder trials like O. J. Simpson's, still divided by the class stratifications represented in the production's three-tiered set, through whose levels the drowning victim sinks to her demise.

In the same month that the Met debuted its *American Tragedy*, the unlikely figure of Woody Allen revived its themes of money and murder in *Match Point*. Transferred to Britain under the auspices of the BBC, which took on the production of Allen's originally American story, the film scarcely covers its tracks by changing its social climber's name from Chester to Chris and having him wield his racquet in tennis lessons rather than lethal assault (although he does hide the murder weapon in his racquet bag). Chris reads Dostoevsky rather than Dreiser, but the counterpointing of his affair with a nagging poor girl and the comforts offered by marriage to a rich one was too reminiscent of the 1925 novel and its film adaptations for the critics to miss. Stevens' film, far better known than Sternberg's, was frequently cited, as well it should have been, since Allen not only duplicated much of its plot but also its unique scenes of a date in a cinema, an erotic encounter in a mansion's games room and a threatening telephone call that arrives during a dinner party. Most noticeably, its casting of the lead lovers duplicates Stevens' facial matching of Montgomery Clift and Elizabeth Taylor with the identically "sensual lips" (actually mentioned in the dialogue) of

Scarlett Johansson and Jonathan Rhys-Meyers. But Dreiser's indignation at the American injustice masked by its egalitarian ethos is not transferable to Britain. Both his novel's irony and its awful plausibility are sacrificed to the United Kingdom's more blatant class divisions, which would still stifle a poor tennis pro's aspirations to the country house set.

The 2005 film and opera versions followed the reissue of Dreiser's novel as a certified national classic by the Library of America two years earlier. Writing in the *New Yorker*, David Denby saluted the awkward prose stylist as "the strongest of the novelists who have written about America as a business civilization. No one else confronted so directly the sheer intractability of American social life and institutions, or dramatized with such solicitousness and compassion the difficulty of breaking free from social law" (Denby, 2003: 178). The use of the past tense here might have suggested the consignment of these themes to yesteryear had Denby not reasserted their continuing relevance in his own memoir of thwarted love, personal greed and national fantasy as his marriage, Nasdaq and the Twin Towers collapsed in the new millennium. That this alienated film critic's autobiography is bracketed by complaints about the bad movies made by a conglomerate-owned cinema industry only serves to confirm the connection with the earlier tragedy echoed in his title—*American Sucker*. As this study seeks to show, Dreiser's challenge to the country and its cinema retains its salience today.

Notes

1. Dreiser, T. (1948), *An American Tragedy*, Cleveland: World Publishing Company, p. 623. The references to *An American Tragedy* in this book are to the 1948 edition, which was consulted by George Stevens for *A Place in the Sun*.

CHAPTER 1

An American Tragedy

Not one, but thousands, after contesting with the ultra severe conditions that confront the beginner at every turn in Los Angeles, have packed their few or many remaining belongings, "snapped a picture" of the house or the room or the street in which they had dwelt, while "they tried" and then sorrowfully taken the next train out. They couldn't quite make it. The struggle was too grim. But that is a type of picture that you will never see in the movies. It didn't end happily.

Theodore Dreiser, "Hollywood: Its Morals and Manners"

In 1919 Theodore Dreiser left New York City for Hollywood. The move was an impulsive one, prompted in part by financial woes, in part by writing difficulties, in part by the reactionary mood gripping the city in the wake of the First World War—but mostly by a new romance with a young woman determined to get into pictures. At 48 Dreiser was a major American writer, the author of pioneering naturalist novels like *Sister Carrie* and *The Financier*, as well as short stories, profiles, memoirs, essays, journalism and stage dramas, but he was not a financial success. Throughout his career the economic and sexual realism of his fiction made it vulnerable to suppression. His own publisher, Frank Doubleday, effectively blocked the distribution of his first novel, a study of a steely young Midwesterner who rises from salesman's mistress to Broadway success. Doubleday had been abroad when the vice president of his company accepted *Sister Carrie* (1900) on the strong recommendation of Frank Norris, the author of realist works like *McTeague* (1899) and *The Octopus* (1901). On his return, he was appalled at the unpunished triumph of its amoral heroine and it was not until Dreiser arranged for its reissue by a different press in 1907 that it saw more than minimal US sales. *The Titan*, closely based on the life of the ruthless transport magnate Charles Tyson Yerkes, was rejected by its contracted publisher Harper & Brothers to avoid offending the Morgan Bank, which had a controlling interest in the firm. In 1914 it was published instead by the American branch of the English publisher John Lane, which also brought out Dreiser's novel *The Genius* in the following year. Described by the New York *World* newspaper as "the story of an artist who goes in for advertising and the pursuit of women" (Swanberg, 1965: 194), *The Genius* was withdrawn from sale after the

Society for the Suppression of Vice attacked it for obscenity. Despite Dreiser's extensive efforts to persuade John Lane to mount a legal challenge to the Society, it was not reissued until 1923. In the meantime the writer struggled with a novel in progress on a Quaker industrial family provisionally titled *The Bulwark*, while supporting himself with a variety of non-fiction projects ranging from memoirs to travel writing.

Not only was Dreiser poor, he was being pursued for financial support by his wife Sara, the Missouri schoolteacher he had married in 1898. A convinced and energetic opponent of monogamy, he was unfaithful to Sara throughout much of their marriage and had left her altogether by 1914, but as a Roman Catholic she refused to grant him a divorce. Meanwhile the writer enjoyed relationships with a succession of women, often simultaneously. The latest was a second cousin who had called one Saturday at his Greenwich Village apartment. Helen Richardson had grown up in Portland, Oregon, where her mother ran an actors' hotel next door to a vaudeville theater. As a stage-struck child she had longed to travel with the performers passing through the provincial city. At fourteen she acted in amateur theatricals and at sixteen married a young man with whom she formed a dance team touring cities in the Northwest. After they separated she became the secretary and mistress of an executive of the Industrial Finance Corporation in New York. When he recommended Dreiser's 1919 collection *Twelve Men*—character sketches of typical American figures including a foreman, a wrestler and, significantly, a shop front evangelist and a talented writer reduced to hackwork—Richardson read it and went to visit her cousin the author.

Richardson was twenty-five, pretty and saving up to try her luck in Hollywood. Dreiser was also drawn to the movies and had been suggested as a possible buyer of scenarios for the fledgling Mirror Films company before the War. Whether he actually took up the post is not known but he did submit a few scripts to Mirror and other studios. A letter of August 29, 1914 refers to a script titled *The Born Thief*, which "has practically been accepted by Pathé Frères" (Elias, 1959: 175). Dreiser's diaries of the period occasionally refer to the films he has seen, with a February 6, 1916 entry noting, for example, "Talk of Ince, Griffiths, movies" (Riggio, 1982: 136). (Given the date that talk may well have involved D. W. Griffith's *Intolerance* and Thomas Ince's *Civilization*, both anti-war films released in 1916 prior to the US entry into the war against Germany, a conflict that this critic of imperialist warfare and son of a German immigrant also opposed.) Moreover, his current publisher Horace Liveright was a friend of Jesse L. Lasky, a pioneering producer of "quality" films for the middle classes, whose Famous Players-Lasky studio had bought out Mirror. Within a month of meeting Helen, the writer had accepted Lasky's invitation to submit screenplays to Famous Players as well as Liveright's advance for *The Bulwark* and departed westward.

Dreiser and Richardson arrived in Los Angeles at the beginning of November. After the slump in ticket sales caused by the deadly influenza epidemic of 1918, the movies were experiencing a boom and the city was full of new arrivals attracted by the same lures that drew the couple. But on November 14 Dreiser suffered two setbacks: a telegram from Liveright arrived complaining that John Lane claimed the rights to *The Bulwark,* for which it had earlier paid $2000 in advances. On the same day the writer was turned away at the gate of Famous Players: "Don't know me," he noted tersely in his diary (Riggio, 1982: 292).

Nevertheless he continued work on his screenplays, including a story of a fugitive called *The Long Long Trail.* Submitted as a treatment narrated in the present tense rather than as a scenically divided screenplay, Dreiser's scenario follows the life of a poor boy named Richard Gard who later takes the alias "Griffen." Abandoned as an infant in an orphanage the hero suffers "the poor clothes, the routine life, the rather limited instruction provided. He views the outside with an [sic] hungry and hopeful eye" (Dreiser, 1919: 1). Eventually Richard escapes the orphanage, only to be caught and sent to a reformatory. Escaping again, he joins a gang planning the robbery of a streetcar garage. When the watchman is killed, a captured gang member accuses Richard, who has only acted as a lookout. Fleeing the city, Richard drifts across the country, educates himself and learns ranching. In New Mexico he meets a young woman named Rheta who has inherited a ranch and is impressed by his "true managerial skill" (Dreiser, 1919: 6). Then Richard is denounced to the law by a neighboring rancher. The two disappear into remote country and have a child before he is finally arrested and taken to an eastern penitentiary. As Rheta appeals to the state governor, the real killer confesses. Richard is freed and they resume their life together.

At the end of December Dreiser was finally granted an appointment with Lasky, only to be told that his submissions had been rejected. Fortunately, his memoir of his youthful *Newspaper Days* was going well, even if *The Bulwark* was not, despite Liveright's anxious inquiries. On March 12, Dreiser's diary notes Helen's suggestion that she send his screenplay *Lady Bountiful, Jr.* directly to Mary Pickford, for whom he had written the title role. Headed "a film adaptation of a proposed novel," this 20-page treatment is far more elaborate in its characterizations and settings than *The Long Long Trail.* The heroine Lois is the daughter of a Virginian "who is dark, slender, reticent" (Dreiser, 1920: 1) and musically talented. When his marriage to a society woman breaks down, he leaves his infant daughter with her wealthy mother to study singing in Europe. At fourteen, Lois travels with her mother and her second husband to Italy. During the voyage the generous girl tends to the poor passengers in steerage, including some Italian immigrants who are returning there "having failed to realize their hopeful dreams of the great America, where they believed there was no poverty" (Dreiser, 1920: 4). In Florence Lois studies the violin and becomes fast friends with a young woman vocalist named Guillito. Lois's mother dies when Lois is sixteen and she discovers that her stepfather has lost her inheritance in speculation. She returns to New York with Guillito, who has a prosperous uncle in Brooklyn. Seeking musical employment, Lois "is very soon sadly disillusioned. All the important agencies are interested in but one type of artist and that is the genius of someone who is well known and with whom they can make a great stir" (Dreiser, 1920: 10–11). Guillito is such a talent, and becomes a concert soloist with a socialite escort named Clark. To further Lois's career, she introduces her to Monsieur Roux, a Belgian opera star known to support struggling artists. Meanwhile, despite Guillito's anger and Lois's discouragement, Clark protests his love for her. Eventually Monsieur Roux confesses to Lois that he is her long lost father and invites her to live with him in Belgium. As their liner puts out to sea, Lois discovers Clark waiting for her on deck.

In his diary Dreiser described *Lady Bountiful, Jr.* as "pure hoakum—& sweet morale [sic] optimism prepared for movie sale" (March 12, 1920; Riggio, 1982: 307–8). But although Pickford wrote a note of thanks, no sale ensued. A later diary entry praises Griffith's South Seas romance *The Idol Dancer* (1920) as showing "what may be done" (June 27, 1920; Riggio, 1982: 323) but Dreiser was unable to do it. Despite the efforts of his agency, Willis & Inglis Moving Pictures and Theatrical Enterprises, occasionally abetted by Helen, his screenplays were not successful. Among his papers are several unsold scenarios, including *The Choice*, in which a young woman arrives in the West from New York, is wrongly convicted of a vice charge and goes to prison, only to later become a movie actress and the sweetheart of the judge who sentenced her. Wrongful conviction also features in *The Door of the Trap*, a script in which a wealthy man falls for a young woman who has been imprisoned for theft.

By that spring it was Helen who was earning money in the movies. Pawning her ring to buy clothes and have casting photographs taken, she quickly rose from the $7.50 extra's daily rate to $12.50. In May she got work in a film starring Charles Ray, the actor who played innocent country boys for Thomas Ince's studio. Dreiser ruefully noted that "She has made so great a hit that I am slightly jealous." In the sexual convention of the industry, she was the object of "all sorts of civilities & approaches" (May 14, 1920; Riggio, 1982: 315) from her director Jerome Storm and Ray himself, and it worried Dreiser deeply. A May 18 entry in his diary confesses that he has conceived a short story "of a jealous clerk who cannot lose his beauty bride to the movies & finally kills her & himself" (Riggio, 1982: 316). While Dreiser worked alone at home, Helen was meeting "movie actors, actresses, directors, calling [casting] directors, camera men etc" (July 14, 1920; Riggio, 1982: 330). While he fretted that they couldn't afford a car, Famous Players was sending her home by automobile after night work on a Bebe Daniels comedy in which Helen was filmed undressing behind a screen and getting into bed "in <u>tight</u> pajamas." "This sex struck country," Dreiser fumed in his diary (July 9, 1920; Riggio, 1982: 327).

Dreiser understood all too well the pressure applied to actresses in the industry to service their male employers sexually. An article he wrote for a 1921 issue of the women's magazine *McCall's* includes the example of "Sanchia," summoned one afternoon from the set "clothed in diaphanous and beribboned pajamas [sic] over which she has wrapped tightly a long blue coat of some soft cloth." Asked by her producer to join his little party that evening for "a spin and a swim," she tactfully demurs, arguing that she's had a difficult day and wouldn't be good company. The producer, however, "financially and in every other way ... appears to be her master." Waving aside Sanchia's protests, he assures her that he'll have her scenes rescheduled for later the next day, and that she should be ready at seven. "Positively," Dreiser concludes, "no Pasha addressing the seventy-third wife could have done it better" (Dreiser, 1921: 18).

Although his diary does not name the films in which Richardson won bit parts, it supplies enough details to suggest *Are All Men Alike?* (directed by Philip Rosen in 1920) as the Metro film starring May Allison on which she worked in July. In it Allison, a delicate blonde who played romantic leads, is a New York society girl fascinated by the bohemian habitués of the Greenwich Village café to which she is taken by her childhood sweetheart. Then an artist falls in love with her, a woman sues her for alienating her prizefighter's boyfriend's affections and the prizefighter wrecks her car. At the film's end she is rescued by her sweetheart and happily accepts his offer of a more sedate married life. The plotline of this film suggests something of the changes in sexual mores then being registered in the movies. Earlier films had occasionally essayed infidelity and cross-class relationships but postwar directors transformed this fare into sophisticated comedy for the middle classes. At Famous Players, Jesse Lasky encouraged Cecil B. De Mille to portray "modern problems and conditions" in movies that celebrated sexual exploration and companionate marriage in highly consumerist terms.[1] In the years directly after the War, Hollywood was relatively free from government and industrial regulation. Although a 1915 Supreme Court ruling had exempted the movies from First Amendment protection, no federal censorship bill was passed through Congress and few states had censorship boards. When the industry's moguls appeared before the Chicago Motion Picture Commission in 1918–19, they insisted that the existing criminal laws on obscenity were sufficient to protect Americans. Not until 1921, and the Fatty Arbuckle case, did calls for censorship intensify, and when they did Dreiser paradoxically played his part.

In September 1920, Dreiser recorded several notable events in his diary. Fox telephoned Helen to report for a small part, her first summons of this kind. Famous Players employed her to do publicity stunts with a group of bathing beauties in Pasadena. And then she got a week's work at Metro for the impressive sum of $90. On the set she met "Rudi," Dreiser noted, "who comes around on a black horse when not working." "Rudi" was Rudolph Valentino and the film was *The Four Horsemen of the Apocalypse* (1921). An anti-war saga that follows the grandsons of an Argentine landowner to their deaths on opposing sides in the World War, it was a breakthrough for the Latin lover. His tango scene was a sensation and the film became one of the most critically and financially successful of its time. Although Helen did not have a named part, the costumes Dreiser mentions, including a striking black lace afternoon dress, suggest that she appeared in at least three scenes, and again she was "a great hit." Director Rex Ingrams pursued her, and so did an unnamed "vamp-beauty"

(September 20–25, 1920; Riggio, 1982: 338). But as Helen became immersed in the racy world of Jazz Age Hollywood, Dreiser was withdrawing further from it. A diary entry for September 6 proclaims "work on 'An American Tragedy' till 4 p.m." (Riggio, 1982: 336).

Ragged Dick in Shadowland

Dreiser's failure in the movies clearly influenced the thematics of this novel and the recent completion of *Newspaper Days* had left him in an autobiographical cast of mind. That memoir of his youthful experiences as a journalist in the 1890s includes two notable recollections that combine sexual and material aspirations in the manner of his new protagonist. In one he recalls standing outside an avenue of mansions "envying the rich and wishing that I was famous or a member of a wealthy family, and that I might meet with one of the beautiful girls I imagined I saw there and have her fall in love with me and make me rich" (Dreiser, 1991: 475). In another he simply states "My body was blazing with the keen sex desire I have mentioned, as well as a desire for material and social supremacy" (Dreiser, 1991: 128). The melodramatic staples of newfound wealthy relatives and wrongful accusations that he employed in his film scripts would also survive into his novel, as well as the dark, slender, reticent characterization of Lady Bountiful's papa. Another influence was the pervasive religiosity of the City of Angels, where, as he wrote to H. L. Mencken, cultists and cranks abounded and one landlord regularly greeted the couple with "PRAISE THE LORD" (January 23, 1920; Elias, 1959: 266). But Dreiser's German immigrant father had also been religious, an increasingly devout Roman Catholic in the poverty that resulted from his injury and unemployment in the Midwestern wool industry, and his son had endured several years in German Catholic schools. A final stimulus may have been a much-publicized murder of 1919, in which the illegitimate son of a former US Senator killed his pregnant working-class girlfriend when she demanded that he marry her, but Dreiser had been collecting similar cases for years. All of them involved an ambitious boy who wants rid of his pregnant girlfriend when he falls for a richer girl. That August he had written to the district attorney of Herkimer County, NY, requesting transcripts of the 1906 trial of Chester Gillette for the murder of Grace Brown.

Herkimer County is in northern New York State, where the battered body of Grace ('Billy') Brown was discovered in Big Moose Lake along with an overturned rowboat and a man's straw hat. When an autopsy revealed Brown's pregnancy, a deputy interviewed her employer, the owner of a local garment factory. The deputy soon learned that she was close to the owner's nephew, Chester Gillette. The son of Salvation Army missionaries, Chester had traveled across the country as a laborer. After meeting a wealthy uncle by chance, he had been invited to take a lowly position in his factory, from whence he wooed not only

Grace Brown but the daughters of the local bourgeoisie. A search of his boarding-house lodgings revealed a bundle of Grace's letters, begging him not to abandon her to unwed motherhood. On the advice of a factory supervisor, whom Gillette had written to request a loan, the district attorney went to a lakeside resort on nearby Eagle Bay and arrested him in his tennis clothes.

Chester Gillette pleaded not guilty at his trial, testifying that when Brown threatened to expose him he had taken her to the lake to tell her that he could not marry her and persuade her to go back to her parents' farm. He explained that they had traveled there in separate railway cars to avoid the attention of their fellow workers. On the fateful day he had packed their lunch in his suitcase, to which he had attached his camera tripod and his tennis racket, and left it on the shore where they planned to return from their afternoon's boating. But when he declared that marriage was impossible, the distraught woman had jumped from the boat and his attempt to pull her from the water had upset it. After swimming for her unsuccessfully he had made for shore, abandoned the tennis racket to lighten his load and walked with his case the two miles to Eagle Bay.

In response, the prosecution argued that the victim's severe head injuries were consistent with a beating prior to entry into the water, a beating that could have been inflicted with a tennis racket. Although Brown had previously threatened suicide, Chester's failure to summon help, combined with the excavation of the buried tennis racket, convinced the jury to find him guilty of first degree murder within five hours. And as Dreiser's biographer Richard Lingeman (1990: 250) argues, "no upstate New York jury in 1906 would have let him off" after Brown's letters were read aloud by the prosecution, producing headlines like the following from the *New York World*: "COURT IN TEARS AS LOVE LETTERS BARE GIRL'S SOUL." After unsuccessful appeals to a higher court and the state Governor, Chester Gillette was executed in 1908.

Dreiser was never able to acquire transcripts of Gillette's trial, but he rapidly drafted the early chapters of his novel, sometimes referred to as *An American Tragedy* and sometimes as *Mirage*. All twenty-one deal with the youth of his protagonist, the son of a financial failure turned missionary who longs for success and social position. His name, Clyde Griffiths, retains the initials of Chester Gillette, who used aliases with his own initials on his fatal journey with Grace Brown. But in a process of softening that will continue long beyond Dreiser's version of this case, Clyde is portrayed as a sensitive child and adolescent whose aspirations result from the "psychic wound[s]" (Lingeman, 1990: 202) of teasing and privation. Very little of these draft chapters, which take Clyde to employment in a wholesale grocery firm, survives into the finished novel but the psychological vocabulary employed and the theory of subjectivity that it reveals, are significantly retained.

In the same month that he first records work on *American Tragedy*, Dreiser wrote a long letter on the subject of free will. Decrying "religious balderdash," he argues first for the cultural relativity of moral judgments and then for their neurological origins as perceptions of balance and proportion. Such perceptions, he maintains, depend on "our material existence here—not elsewhere, get that!" (September 23, 1920; Elias, 1959: 285–6). Specifically, they are described as the consequence of environmental factors on brain chemistry. The authorities he recommends to his correspondent were pioneering proponents of evolutionary biology (Ernest Haeckel) and the neurological basis of human behavior (George Crile and Jacques Loeb). Loeb's research particularly fascinated Dreiser, who read his publications and eventually secured an introduction to him in 1919. In the parlance of the time Loeb was a "mechanist," arguing that living organisms were subject to the physico-chemical laws that governed inorganic matter.[2] Consciousness he dismissed as a metaphysical concept, proposing instead his theory of "associative memory" (Loeb, 1901: 12), in which the central nervous system is said to record traces of its processes, which can be reproduced and fused together. Instituting or inhibiting those associations could "prevent wrong-doing," so long as it was done in the subject's youth, "as the time at which the penal code is enforced is usually too late for any lasting benefit. Cruelty in the penal code and the tendency to exaggerate punishments," he declared in his study of the comparative physiology of the brain, "are sure signs of a low civilization and of an imperfect educational system" (Loeb, 1901: 234). Loeb's interest was in observing the objective signs of associative memory and the conditions that determined it, anticipating his student John B. Watson's definition of psychology as "a purely objective experimental branch of natural science" aimed at "the prediction and control of behavior" (Watson, 1913: 158). Watson's behaviorism also engaged Dreiser, but so did the writings of a very different but no less determinist theorist, Sigmund Freud.

In 1918 Dreiser had met and befriended the psychoanalyst Abraham Arden Brill, the American translator of Freud's *Three Contributions on the Theory of Sex*. Freud had repeatedly revised these essays after their first publication in 1905, noting as he did so new research in biochemistry. Trained as a clinical neurologist, he had asserted the importance of endocrine chemistry in sexuality from the 1890s and in 1921 he appealed to Loeb to see in his work "connections which lead to your way of thinking" (Moers, 1969: 266). Loeb found their differences far too great to resolve, dismissing Freud's findings as wholly non-empirical and Dreiser himself decried what he regarded as their mystical tendencies. Nonetheless, psychoanalysis opened up a rich vocabulary of sexual compulsion, of concepts like sadism, repression, libido and inhibition, that—together with a notion of chemical attraction derived from Loeb—he would employ in *An American Tragedy*.

Despite their differences, these authorities offered a scientific warrant for Dreiser's profound determinism, his conviction, as he stated it to his Russian translator Sergei Dinamov in 1927, that human existence, with its economic and political problems

is an organized process about which we can do nothing in the final analysis. Of course, science, art, commercial progress, all go to alleviate and improve and ease the material existence of humanity, and that for the great mass, is something. But there is no plan, as I believe, from Christianity down, that can be more than a theory. And dealing with man is a practical thing—not a theoretical one. Nothing can alter his emotions, his primitive and animal reactions to life ... misery, weakness, incapacities, poverty, side by side with happiness, strength, power, wealth, always have, and no doubt, always will exist. (January 5, 1927; Elias, 1959: 450)

This apparent political resignation, as commentators inevitably observe, seems contradicted by Dreiser's denunciations of big business, censorship and American imperialism. His diary entry on the Bolsheviks' overthrow of the Kerensky government is a succinct "good" (November 9, 1917; Riggio, 1982: 202). But, as Richard Lingeman points out, Dreiser's enthusiasm for the Russian revolution was at that time purely verbal, although this would eventually change. His inclination to criticize rather than campaign and his cynicism about the possibility of political transformation may have stemmed from his mechanist naturalism, but the tension between his fatalism and his indignation over injustice would feed into *An American Tragedy*.

To explain the gestation of Dreiser's novel, Ellen Moers invokes Freud's description of how a powerful experience can revive memory of an earlier one and a related wish that finds fulfillment in the creative work. In illustration she offers a simple proposal—that the narrative of *An American Tragedy* represents Dreiser's desire to be with the newly met Helen Richardson rather than his wife. But the fantasy[3] that Freud discusses has a far greater resemblance to the narrative of Dreiser's novel: A poor orphan boy seeking employment imagines that he finds a job, impresses his employer, marries his daughter, becomes a director of his business and then its inheritor. The story that Freud recounted in the 1907 lecture that became "Creative Writing and Daydreaming" would have been wholly familiar to his audience. It is, as Freud indicates, a public fantasy. Rooted in folklore, its basic plot had been repeatedly elaborated in Horatio Alger's hugely influential Victorian tales of poor boys who make good, most famously his 1868 novel *Ragged Dick*.

Dick is a homeless New York bootblack of fourteen, hard working and generous, with a handsome, indeed aristocratic, appearance. Asked by a gentleman acquaintance to show his nephew around the city, Dick is given a bath and a new suit. In one of several allusions to fairy tale, the delighted boy compares himself to Cinderella. During the tour of New York clever Dick confounds a con artist and clears himself of theft. The nephew compares him to the quick-witted Aladdin and encourages him to go to school. Dick then enters into partnership with a better educated young orphan and receives lessons from him in reading, writing and mathematics. Invited to dinner by a former customer, he impresses the daughter of the house. When the two boys take the ferry to Brooklyn to search for better jobs, a child falls into the river and Dick, an excellent swimmer, rescues him. The child's father is revealed to be the wealthy industrialist James Rockwell, who rewards the hero with a well-paid job in his office.

Dreiser, like Freud's audience, was wholly conversant with this story and took several of its key motifs directly into *An American Tragedy*. Though not an orphan, his protagonist is alienated from his missionary family, and longs to meet the rich uncle who will become his patron. He too is possessed of an aristocratic appearance and exults in a succession of new suits. He enters his wealthy patron's business and his likeable demeanor proves attractive to a daughter of the bourgeoisie. A strong swimmer, he also is involved in a boating accident. Like Aladdin, he hears the voice of a mysterious spirit or "efrit," and in prison he reads the *Arabian Nights*. In writing his anti-Alger narrative, Dreiser made extensive recourse to that of Aladdin, since the tale stresses the insubstantiality of the fantasies that *Ragged Dick* happily fulfills. As William L Phillips (1963: 580–3) has observed in an influential study of *An American Tragedy*, it is suffused with terms like "visions," "apparitions," "enchanted" and, indeed, "phantasies." And the fable of the original "Ala-ed-Din" is much darker than Dick's. He begins as a lazy boy who refuses support to his mother. Taken up by a wicked sorcerer who pretends to be his rich uncle, he gains admission to a cave of jewels and greedily stuffs them into his pocket. When he glimpses the Sultan's beautiful daughter, his vision is disturbed and he is compared to a dreamer. Before the inevitable happy ending, he loses the princess, his position and his wealth, and is finally blindfolded for execution. Brill's case histories also offered a sobering reflection on the Aladdin story: as a prison psychiatrist he had treated patients with obsessions apparently derived from the *Arabian Nights* and he warned against the fantasies of omnipotence represented by the magic lamp.[4]

Dreiser's reworking of this tale may be traced to the writer's growing frustration with American realism, whose lack of imagination and epic perspective he railed against in a newspaper interview of 1921 (Moers, 1969: 277). In the previous year he had declared the nation's literature outpaced by its material growth, which—he maintained—had remained uninterpreted. "Despite many defects," he added, "the movies show more of an advance than do our current books and plays ... Some moving picture directors appear to have more brains and taste than the authors whose work they interpret" (December 26, 1920; Elias, 1959: 331). This endorsement may have been defensive, since literary colleagues like H. L. Mencken had derided his relocation to Hollywood, and it was soon to be contradicted, but a cinematic style has been attributed to *An American Tragedy* and it makes many references to the movies. Both tactics could be said to serve the novel's representation of fantasy.

In one of many ironies, however, Dreiser's "movie in our heads," as Robert Penn Warren (1971: 118) would describe the narration of *An American Tragedy*, would not be completed in Hollywood. By April 1921 he had completed his first draft of the novel's opening chapters, which he then revised that summer. During the same months he followed up his article for *McCall's* with a four-part series, "Hollywood: Its Morals and Manners," for *Shadowland*, a short-lived arts magazine that anticipated *Playboy* in combining essays and interviews by the likes of Frank Harris and Janet Flanner with photographs of scantily clad starlets. Like the *McCall's* piece, the *Shadowland* series focuses on the travails of the aspirant actress, clearly employing the stories that Richardson brought home from the set. But the magazine's bohemian interest in sex encouraged a lengthier exposition of the studios' exploitation of women, from the calculations of the casting couch to naturalist touches about the beginner's payment for costumes, make up and hairstyling. As Dreiser observes, the bit-part players of the day had to supply these themselves, at not a little expense. The long hours, workless rainy days, non-unionization, and near-prostitution of "literally hundreds of girls and women" (Dreiser, 1987: 78) made a sorry, if suitably salacious, story. Moreover, its publication coincided with the trials of the comedian Roscoe "Fatty" Arbuckle for the rape and manslaughter of a Hollywood extra named Virginia Rappe in a San Francisco hotel room. Arbuckle was acquitted in his final trial, but after two which ended with hung juries and all the attendant scandal, his career—and Hollywood's respite from intensive regulation—were finished. Although Dreiser had deliberately cut all mention of the case, as well as the "bungalow with orgy attachment in the hills" (February 22, 1921; Elias, 1959: 353) promised in a letter touting this series, he did include an ill-judged appeal to "all those high-salaried and comfortable vice-snoopers, who are even now so busily engaged hailing before the courts of the land respectable publishers, to say nothing of serious authors whose only crime is that they seek via admirable letters to set forth pictures of the social state of the time ... [to bring] to light" the prevailing conditions in the industry (Dreiser, 1987: 80). The series appeared monthly between November 1921 and February 1922. By January Dreiser learned of the studios' displeasure when the editor of *Photodramatist* cancelled a commission. In reply the furious writer pronounced the moguls "muddle-brained braggarts or fat lechers, or both, and all they know is the commercial—not the artistic or creative side of their problem" (December 8, 1921; Elias, 1959: 387).

   The *Shadowland* articles not only intensified Dreiser's estrangement from the film industry—they also contributed to the clamor for its reform that resulted in the appointment of the former Republican Party national chairman Will Hays to chair the newly formed Motion Picture Producers and Distributors of America. The ensuing control of sexual transgression in the industry's representations as well as its performers' behavior would make it even more difficult for Hollywood to film any of Dreiser's works, including the novel that he had begun there.[5] By the autumn of 1922, three years after meeting Richardson and leaving New York, he was preparing to return. Helen's work in the movies had not yielded larger roles, and Dreiser's diary complains of seeing "no very clear way out of money troubles or that I am making any real artistic headway" (September 11, 1922; Riggio, 1982: 394). In a farewell interview with the *Los Angeles Sunday Times*, he declared "There is no art in Los Angeles and Hollywood. And there never will be" (Ryan, 2005: 74). He conceded the achievements of Griffith, Fairbanks and Barrymore but dismissed Chaplin, De Mille and Helen's recent director Allan Dwan (for whom, his diary indicates, she was a small-part player, and an object of erotic pursuit, in the 1922 production of Fairbanks' *Robin Hood*). He challenged the reporter to name any American film that compared with *The Cabinet of Dr Caligari* (Robert Wiene, 1919) or the German work of Ernst Lubitsch. Significantly, the director's *Sumurun* (*One Arabian Night*, 1920), the story of a sheik who wants to add dancing girl Pola Negri to his harem, was among the titles he praised. Lubitsch had just arrived in Hollywood and Dreiser expressed hopes that he would have a "constructive influence. But will he be allowed to have his own way, to carry out his ideals? I am skeptical. We are not an artistic nation. All we care about is to be rich and powerful" (Ryan, 2005: 75–6). In an observation that suggests the classical roots of in his work-in-progress on America, he declared the United States "a continuation of old Rome. The Roman knew two things—money-getting and war. Any knowledge of art he learned from the Greeks" (Ryan, 2005: 76).

At the behest of the remarkably sympathetic journalist, who found the writer "except for his dislike of Los Angeles, full of sanity and honest vision" (Ryan, 2005: 78), Dreiser's denunciation of the city expanded into a diatribe about Rome's debt to Athens and the lack of opportunities anywhere in America for the contemporary equivalents of Sappho, Dante, Michelangelo and Shakespeare. On the question of returning to Hollywood, he was pessimistic. Asked if he would ever write a book about studio life, he replied with what became the final sentence of the interview: "Pause and expletives, 'Not I'" (Ryan, 2004: 78).

A Crime Sensation

In late October Dreiser returned to New York with Helen Richardson. After some months spent untangling his publishing contracts, Liveright bought out the titles claimed by John Lane and Harper and offered the writer $4000 a year through 1927 in exchange for his backlist and a substantial schedule of future publications. One of these was the novel begun in Hollywood. Dreiser's diary entries for January 1923 record visits to both Brill and Loeb, whose different determinisms would combine to doom his protagonist. In February he and Helen watched an African wildlife documentary at the Lyric Theatre. "Am impressed," he noted, "with the terror of death in which every animal appears to live" (February 3, 1923; Riggio, 1982: 397). At the end of June, the couple motored upstate to view the scenes of the Gillette-Brown case. They stayed in the town where a garment factory still operated, by then making men's shirts rather than women's skirts. In the countryside they met a farmer who had known Grace Brown's father. They rowed on the lake where she drowned and talked to the guide who found her body. But, significantly for the future of its film adaptation, much of the research for *An American Tragedy* was conducted in print, the pages of the New York *World* and the pamphlet of Brown's letters.

In a strategy that would elicit much critical debate (and a lawyer's allegation of plagiarism) Dreiser created his fable of the workings of fantasy from non-fiction sources, at times duplicating the printed ones almost word for word. Mencken's deprecating introduction to a posthumous edition of the novel attributes its documentary derivation to Dreiser's respect for facticity, a realist's insistence on presenting things as they actually happened. "When he sent some character into an eating-house for a meal it was always some eating-house that he had been to himself, and the meal he described in such relentless detail was one he had eaten, digested and remembered" (Mencken, 1948: 8). In following his sources so closely, the novelist opened his work to accusations of banality, incoherence, repetition and downright theft. But as Mencken admits, his version of Chester Gillette's story is at once a "literal reporting" and a vast elaboration, extending to over 800 pages divided into three books.

The first begins with the protagonist's unhappy youth as the uneducated child of impoverished evangelists who run a mission in a Kansas City slum. From his adolescence Clyde Griffiths is "as vain and proud as he [is] poor" (*An American Tragedy:* 27). Good looking, attentive to his dress, fascinated by pretty girls and contemptuous of manual labor, he gets a job as a bellboy at a luxury hotel. There he discovers the louche pleasures of its fashionable customers, as well as those of the hotel staff. When his mother begs a contribution from his earnings for a worthy cause, Clyde learns that his sister Esta has been made pregnant and abandoned. Although he has visited a brothel with the other bellboys, her plight only intensifies his disdain for his family. Reluctantly surrendering an extra five dollars a week to his mother, he reserves most of his money for the department store assistant he's pursuing, who promises bliss for the price of a beaver jacket. Then a winter's outing with her and his friends ends with their borrowed Packard crashing after hitting a child. Desperate to avoid jail, Clyde escapes by crawling away from the scene through the snow.

Book Two opens three years later, in the upstate New York town where Clyde's uncle owns a factory making the detachable men's shirt collars of the period. Samuel Griffiths has met his nephew in a hotel in Chicago, to which he has absconded to avoid prosecution. Although still a bellboy, the twenty-year-old Clyde has acquired sufficient polish to impress his uncle, who duly offers him a job in his factory. There his cousin Gilbert, disdaining the youth he so closely resembles, assigns him to the basement precincts of the shrinking room, where cloth is soaked in boiling water. Shunned by his relations, the lonely youth languishes until his uncle decides that the post is too menial for a Griffiths and makes him supervisor of a roomful of women stamping sizes on the collars. Among them is Roberta Alden, whose prettiness and modest demeanor distinguish her from her peers, many of whom are from immigrant families. Although forbidden to associate with the factory's female workforce, Clyde begins to court Roberta after encountering her one weekend at a local lake. He encourages this daughter of strict farming stock to move to less supervised lodgings and eventually pressures her to let him spend the night.

Meanwhile Clyde retains his social ambitions. A chance encounter with Sondra Finchley, the daughter of another wealthy local family met on his sole visit to the Griffiths home, leads to an offer of a lift in her chauffeur-drive car. Piqued at the disdain Clyde's cousin Gilbert shows her, Sondra decides to take up his handsome relation instead, forcing his family to do likewise. Received into town society at last, Clyde pursues Sondra and neglects "Bert." Then he learns that she is pregnant. When drugstore remedies fail, Clyde makes inquiries and is given the name of a doctor reputed to have helped out someone from a locally prominent family. But the physician refuses the pleas of this poorer woman and she begs Clyde to honor his promise not to desert her. Hoping to convince her that marriage on his salary is impossible, Clyde stalls. His relationship with Sondra prospers and he is invited to the lakeside resort where local society spends its summer holidays.

A headline in the local paper catches Clyde's eye, and he reads of an incident in which an unidentified woman, but not her male companion, has been discovered drowned in a Massachusetts lake. As he prepares for bed that evening, he is struck by the suggestion that such an accident could solve his dilemma. But the very thought appalls him, seeming in itself "a crime in his heart" (*An American Tragedy*: 476). He resolves to suppress it and finally goes to sleep, but wakes from a dream of entrapment between a horned beast and a nest of snakes. When the desperate Roberta threatens to reveal their relationship, Clyde's temptation becomes personified as the persuasive voice of "the genii at the accidental rubbing of Aladdin's lamp—as the efrit emerging as smoke from the mystic jar in the net of the fisherman" (*An American Tragedy*: 501). Suggesting a trip to a remote lake discovered with Sondra, he proposes to Roberta that they marry and honeymoon there. At their destination Clyde signs the register Clifford Golden and then rows Roberta out on the water for a prenuptial picnic. Reaching a distant point he stops on the pretext of taking a photograph, but the conflict between his desire to act and his fear to do so paralyzes the weak-willed youth. His expression registers such torment that Roberta draws near to take his hand. Moving to ward her off, Clyde inadvertently strikes her face with his camera and his apologetic reach towards her capsizes the boat, which again hits her head. As she screams for help, the voice of temptation returns, insisting that a moment's hesitation will do what Clyde has been unable to. Roberta sinks beneath the surface and he swims to shore.

Book Three details the discovery of a letter in the dead girl's pocket to her mother announcing her marriage. Pursued by a politically ambitious district attorney, Clyde is identified and Roberta's letters are discovered in his room. A final piece of incriminating evidence is furtively added by the assistant district attorney, who attaches two of Roberta's hairs to the camera after it is brought up from the lake. To the horror of his uncle's family, Clyde becomes the star of "a crime sensation of the first magnitude, with all of those intriguingly colorful, and yet morally and spiritually atrocious, elements—love, romance, wealth, poverty, death" (*An American Tragedy*: 623). Disabused of her romantic fantasies, Sondra confesses her involvement to her father, who pulls political strings to keep her name out of the proceedings. The Griffiths are forced to defend their honor by funding the defense, unwittingly employing a firm who support the party opposed to the district attorney's. When Clyde finally tells the truth about the drowning to his sympathetic lawyer (who in his youth surmounted a similar dilemma with the aid of a wealthy father) he fears that the jury will not believe him. Determined to undermine the opposition's election chances, he and his colleague concoct a different story—that on the journey to the lake Clyde was moved by Roberta's plight and decided to marry her after all, only for her to drown in a genuine accident.

The case reaches the national press and, via that, Clyde's parents, who are advised by his lawyers to remain in the Midwest. During a lengthy trial that reviews his life story and the evidence against him, including his romance with "the rich and beautiful Miss X" (*An American Tragedy*: 691), he cowers under cross-examination. Although the judge instructs the jury that failure to rescue the victim of a genuine accident is not a crime, they swiftly convict Clyde of murder in the first degree. Samuel Griffiths abandons him and he sends for his mother, who raises funds for an appeal by giving public lectures on the merits of his case. Taken by train to a state prison, Clyde discovers that he has become a celebrity, a "daring and romantic, if unfortunate figure" (*An American Tragedy*: 811) to the crowds who throng the stations he passes through. As he waits in the death house he is befriended by a charismatic minister, to whom he eventually discloses his confused feelings that day at the lake. Told that Clyde hoped that Roberta's drowning would enable him to be with Sondra, the Reverend McMillan sorrowfully concludes, "In your heart was murder then" (*An American Tragedy*: 854). When Clyde's appeal fails, McMillan accompanies his mother to petition the state governor for clemency but, convinced of Clyde's guilt, he offers no statement in his defense. Instead, he helps the condemned man write a final testament proclaiming his faith in Christianity. After witnessing Clyde's terrible execution, McMillan is sick with regret but recovers to pray with his mother. At the novel's conclusion she and her family are back preaching on the streets of another American city, accompanied by the small son of Clyde's sister.

The Movie in Our Heads

In titling this story Dreiser over-ruled Liveright, who feared the term "tragedy" was too depressing. After considering alternatives naming doomed classical heroes—Icarus, Orion, Xion—the author retained his original choice, significantly arguing for its national rather than generic suitability: "I call it *An American Tragedy* because it could not happen in any other country in the world" (Bowers, 1962: 156). By the 1920s the national designation of its cultural commodities was no innovation for a country whose intellectuals had been debating the characteristics of the Great American Novel since the *Nation* nominated *Uncle Tom's Cabin* for that accolade in 1868.[6] Such titling upholds the very

American exceptionalism to which this novel makes its own ironic contribution. But even as it conveys the epic scope and ambition of its national naming, Dreiser's vast and contradictory narrative complicates this designation, being, as Eisenstein complained, "99 per cent a statement of facts and one per cent atti- tude towards them" (Eisenstein, 1988h: 228). As critics (and film makers) would later ponder, what constitutes the "Americanness" of this tragedy? The "emotional casualties, inevitably female, of a mobile society" or "the formation and damnation of the boy Clyde" (Moers, 1969: 213–4)? The false allure of consumer culture or the unjust barriers to the pleasures it provides (Michaels, 1987: 18–19; Jameson, 1991: 200–17)? Class restrictions or the lack of "caste- based exclusiveness" (Eisenstein, 1988h: 229) that encourages Clyde's hopes for a union with Sondra? Religious fanaticism (Cohen, 1977: 246–7) or the failure to observe the commandments?

However Dreiser might assess the influence of such allegedly national phe- nomena on his protagonist, there are further contradictions in his identification of them with his fate. Clyde is an "individual," with a particular physical consti- tution, psychology and biography, whose very Catholic examination of con- science (notwithstanding his family's evangelical Protestantism) raises the responsibilities of "free" will at the novel's conclusion. But he is also a generic subject of the country's commodity culture, sexual hypocrisy, religious mystifi- cation, social snobbery, political manipulation and economic avarice. The novel knowingly exposes the logic of typification that makes him want to be more like other boys and then destroys him in a tragedy named as national in its origin and extent. When it comes to social status, the "old mass yearning for a likeness in all things" (*An American Tragedy*: 18) that troubles Clyde in his boyhood is transmuted into an equally mass yearning for distinction: "true to the standard of the American youth, or the general American attitude toward life, he felt himself above the type of labor which was purely manual" (26). Here his belief in his superiority to ordinary work is itself revealed as conformity. For what Dreiser's Americans hold in common is a reluctance to regard themselves as common, to do "all the commonplace things" (26), to be anything other than "one of those interesting individuals who looked upon himself as a thing apart" (27).

To these national characteristics the novel adds still another American dimen- sion—its popular culture. After the austerity of his mission childhood, the pro- tagonist (significantly named Griffiths) enthusiastically takes up the fashions, dances and especially the cinema of the early 1920s. At the Kansas City hotel where he works his first object of admiration is a bellboy called Doyle—"so very good-looking, so trim of figure, easy and graceful of gesture ... and his hair cut and brushed and oiled after a fashion which would have become a moving- picture actor" (60–1). When Clyde lies in bed thinking of the shop assistant who manipulates his affections, "she would flicker before him as upon a screen" (115). In the small industrial city of his uncle's factory, the movies are the unmarried workers' alternative to church socials and there are repeated allusions to the town's theatres and their current fare, to Charlie Chaplin and the "snappy" (217) picture at the Mohawk. Applying for a job at the factory, Roberta is described as one of "the extras or try-outs" (265), whereas Sondra will later realize that Clyde sees her as "a star, a paragon of luxury and social supremacy" (396). When Clyde wants to fob Roberta off, a "melodramatic movie" suggests a "mock marriage ... a fake minister and witnesses combining to deceive some simple country girl" (458). And when she believes that they will wed at last, she plans to wear "a flowered gray taffeta afternoon dress, such as she had once seen in a movie" (467). The blow that disables her is struck, not by a tennis racket, but by Clyde's camera; and at the media sensation that the trial for her murder becomes—with "the cameras clicking and whirring" (682) and a "full house" (683) in the public gallery—the politically ambitious prosecutor seizes his opportunity: "Were not the eyes of all the citizens of the United States upon him? He believed so. It was as if someone had suddenly exclaimed: 'Lights! Camera!'" (689). Finally, when his mother's attempts to fund Clyde's appeal with a series of pulpit lectures is stymied by church opposition, she secures free premises from "a Jew who controlled the principal moving picture theater of Utica—a sinful theater" (823) as she had warned her son from childhood.

All these allusions suggest this novel's cinematic origins, but some point to specific precursor texts. Naming his protagonist after a director he particularly admired (with the addition of the unpronounceable final "s", another decision to which Liveright objected), Dreiser more than hints at a recent melodrama whose heroine declares herself "an ignorant girl betrayed through a mock marriage." D. W. Griffith's *Way Down East* (1920) was one of the most financially successful films of its decade. The narrative elements it shares with *An American Tragedy* begin with a poor cousin who travels to a city to seek financial support from her rich relatives. Like Clyde she is at first snubbed and like Roberta she is then wooed by a well-dressed man of superior social standing. Dependant on his family's money, her seducer insists on secrecy and arranges a marriage ceremony whose illegitimacy he only reveals when she later announces her pregnancy. Again, like Clyde, he is by then pursuing another woman and offers her money to have the baby elsewhere. Here the storylines diverge but other similarities abound, not least the centrality of a scripture-quoting mother and the dramatic threat of drowning for the heroine. And like *An American Tragedy*, *Way Down East* is a vast work that proceeds at a stately pace, marking, as Dreiser's novel does, the dramatic changing of the seasons in the northeastern United States. Opening the film, a title offers an observation that Dreiser's might have cited in his lifelong defense of sexual "varietism": "Today's woman brought up from childhood to expect ONE CONSTANT MATE possibly suffers more than at any moment in the history of mankind, because not yet has the man-animal reached this high standard, except perhaps in theory."

Way Down East is not the only Griffith film to which *An American Tragedy* is indebted. The "Modern Story" section of *Intolerance* features a young mill worker. He too courts a pretty working class woman and sulks when, citing her religious views, she refuses to invite him into her apartment. Later he is wrongly accused of murder and convicted on circumstantial evidence. When his initial appeal to the state governor fails, a minister leads him to the gallows, where he is strapped, hooded and positioned over the trap door. Among other themes that will be echoed in Dreiser's novel are the hypocrisy of the industrial bourgeoisie, who use the profits exploited from the workers to campaign against their recreations, and the incompetence of the defense lawyer at the murder trial.

Although Eisenstein never drew a comparison between Dreiser's novel and Griffith's films, he wrote about both, the latter in his essay on the director's debt to Dickens. Here he identifies the key to *Way Down East's* success into the 1920s,[7] the persistence "alongside the hurtling motor cars, the flying steamboats and the racing tickertapes and production lines" of "a traditional, patriarchal, provincial America." The opposition represented in *Way Down East's* parallel montage of village life in rural New England and the smartly dressed predators of the bridge-playing bourgeoisie was intensified by industrialization: "America the provincial and America the ultra-dynamic" (Eisenstein, 1996: 195). Intensified but commingled, as Eisenstein discovered on his visit to the United States, for the antimacassar under the radiogram and the sermons broadcast on it attested to the Victorian sensibility retained in the Jazz Age. These observations offer an important perspective on what has been described as the film aesthetic in *An American Tragedy*. Where the work of Dreiser's contemporaries Joyce and Woolf has prompted discussion of the literary cinematic in terms of modernism's avant-garde, his novel invokes what Miriam Hansen has described as the movies' interwar registration of modernity's impact on "vernacular" culture, the everyday culture of mass production and mass media.[8]

Asserting the modernity of American melodrama, Linda Williams stresses the continuing relevance of its production of pathos, or sympathetic sorrow, through scenarios of wounded innocence. Where tragedy reconciles the spectator to the inevitability of suffering, melodrama is driven by "a moral, wish-fulfilling impulse toward the achievement of justice that gives American popular culture its strength and appeal" (Williams, 1998: 48). From the nineteenth century its basic formula is "the virtuous but humble maiden pursued by the more powerful villain and defended by the humble hero" (Williams, 1998: 68)—the plot of *Way Down East*. Dreiser knew this formula well. He encountered it regularly in the cinema and attempted versions of it in his film scenarios. But in *An American Tragedy* he rewrites it, making Clyde both the humble hero of his upward progress through Lycurgus society and the more socially powerful villain who seduces Roberta and lets her drown. The reader is offered no cathartic reconciliation to his punishment but neither is his trial a spectacle of innocence proved. It is, however, a spectacle, a mass mediated event staged on a film set.

Robert Penn Warren was the first critic to claim a filmic style for *An American Tragedy* in a 1962 essay aimed at rehabilitating Dreiser's critical reputation. Challenging those who would attribute the novel's power to its documentary sources, Penn Warren (1971: 113) argues that it contrasts these with "the anguishing inwardness" of Clyde's story. The identification compelled by the latter narrative is said to be periodically relieved by a more detached presentation of the story's wider context, via what Penn Warren (119) describes as a rhythmic "shifting [of] perspectives". Although Penn Warren (119) insists he is referring to "an angle of interest", such as factory organization or missionary life, rather than optical point of view, he follows much literary criticism in eliding these meanings of "perspective." Thus the ending of Book II, in which Clyde is seen walking away from the lake through the dark woods and its succession by the geographic description that opens Book III, is said to be achieved via a reverse tracking shot, a cut and a pan across the landscape: "Dreiser jerks back his camera from that lonely figure and begins Book III by withdrawing into magisterial distance for a panoramic sweep of the lens" (116). Similarly, when Clyde is first locked in his cell and throws himself on to his cot in despair, Penn Warren (1971: 117) perceives a sharpening of "focus" in this "movie in our heads" (118).

Following Penn Warren, Ellen Moers (1969: 232) attributes this "camera-like technique" both to the Hollywood site of the novel's conception and to the attention given to Clyde's eyes via repeated "closeup[s]." In the successive specular regimes of religious ritual, luxury hotel service, factory supervision, athletic display, society dances and prison incarceration, Clyde is repeatedly described as both the subject and the object of the look. At sixteen his eyes are "black and rather melancholy at times" (27) but "deep and rather appealing" (40). His beseeching glance attracts helpful advice from an otherwise irritable drugstore manager and his nervous expression elicits kindness from a prostitute: "I like your eyes. You're not like those other fellows. You're more refined, kinda" (80). Roberta loves Clyde's "beautiful face, his beautiful hands. His eyes" (320) Sondra is charmed by their "admiring, pleading light" (336) and later tells him "My sweetum is so good-looking. Everybody thinks so—even the boys" (593).[9]

When Clyde first sees Sondra he is agonized by the fear "that he was destined not even to win a glance from her. It tortured and flustered him. At one moment he had a keen desire to close his eyes and shut her out—at another to look only at her constantly—so truly was he captivated" (243). Desiring to see and be seen, Clyde combines the erotic impulses of voyeurism and exhibitionism. His gaze has an almost feminine appeal but he also looks in a more conventionally masculine manner. At the luxury hotel where he becomes a bellboy, "a mirror over the mantel" reveals a roomful of partying youth at which he stares "even while pretending not to" (57). His desk in the stamping room is "in a corner commanding a charming river view" (258) as well as one of Roberta, whom he will "study and admire and by degree proceed to crave" (278). When he becomes angry with her for refusing to let him spend the night, his "dark eyes" are "hard ... with the mingled pain and unrest and dissatisfaction and determination that had been upon him all day" (327). And on the fateful day at the lake their pupils grow "momentarily larger and more lurid" (530).

Dark-eyed, beautiful and intense, Clyde is characterized in a cinematic style that Dreiser was in a position to know about, that of "Rudi" Valentino, whose marketing to a mass female spectatorship was then reversing the conventional erotics of the cinematic gaze. Like the star, Clyde attracts the rapt visual attention of both immigrant factory girls and the wealthy daughters of their employers. As in Hansen's description of Valentino, he too combines sexual ambiguity and social marginality, albeit without the star's "ethnic and racial otherness" (Hansen, 1991: 253). Clyde himself prefers the native-born women in the stamping room for the reticence he shares with them, but like Valentino, he could be said to suffer the tragic consequences for American manhood of the wrong shade of limelight.

In addition to *An American Tragedy's* arguable use of camera perspectives and indisputable attention to the protagonist as the subject and object of intradiegetic spectatorship, its prose style has been described as cinematic by Keith Cohen (1977: 240-5). Each of its three books opens with a series of verbless descriptions typical of dramatic stage setting. Book I:

Dusk—of a summer night. And the tall walls of a commercial heart of an American city of perhaps 400,000 inhabitants—such walls as in time may linger as a mere fable. (15)

Book II:

The home of Samuel Griffiths, in Lycurgus, New York, a city of some twenty-five thousand inhabitants midway between Utica and Albany. (165)

Book III:

Cataraqui County extending from the northernmost line of the village known as Three Mile Bay on the south to the Canadian border, on the north a distance of fifty miles. (537)

Such fragmented sentences, with their use of participles like "extending" rather than verbs, can anticipate or suspend action and prolong dramatic moments. Together with the novel's characteristic use of conjunctions such as "and" and "yet" to open sentences (a conspicuous device in the *Arabian Nights*), this style can create the connective equivalence of the montage progression, as Eisenstein will suggest in his marginal sketches of the lake scene or, as Sternberg and Stevens will later develop it, the dissolve. In the former a perceived intellectual similarity motivates the juxtaposition of shots, in the latter a character's fantasy. The passage Eisenstein illustrated offers two close-ups of Clyde: "His wet, damp, nervous hands! And his dark, liquid, nervous eyes, looking anywhere but at her" (529). If, by the force of the conjunctive "and" as well as the rhyming repetition of the two verbless descriptions, the hand is made equivalent to the eye, then, as Reverend McMillan will later declare, the intention signaled by the latter may be morally equivalent to the action committed by the former.

But if Clyde's eyes have the power to turn his wishes into deeds, the irony of this scene on the lake (and so much of his life) is that he is not, finally, their doer. The effective actor will be the victim herself, whose perceptions these are, but in narrative circumstances and a syntactical style that troubles any clear attribution of agency. In the previous paragraph Roberta protests that she is tired and urges Clyde to return to shore: "And Clyde, assuring her that presently they would— after he had made one or two more pictures of her in the boat with those wonderful trees—that island and this dark water around and beneath her" (529). In this sentence and those that follow, Dreiser uses free indirect discourse to present first Clyde's spoken reassurance and then Roberta's anxious observations of him in a style combining elements of his direct speech ("those wonderful trees"), her unspoken thought ("'His wet, damp, nervous hands!'") and an "objective" third person narration ("Clyde, assuring her that presently they would"). Employed since Jane Austen to blur the thoughts of narrators and characters, the free indirect was by the 1920s being radically rewritten by Woolf and Joyce in stream of consciousness narrations. Such inner speech, albeit in a more conventional syntax, is also the medium of Clyde's deliberations about his dilemma, since his homicidal wishes cannot be spoken aloud. Dreiser's solution, a series of debates between Clyde and a literalized "devil's whisper" (476), that of the genii or efrit, moves at times beyond the monologous free indirect to passages of internal dialogue:

"I will not hit her. That would be too terrible ... too vile."

"But a little blow—any little blow under such circumstances would be sufficient to confuse and complete her undoing. Sad, yes, but she has had an opportunity to go her own way, has she not? And she will not, nor let you go yours." (503)

These multiple modes of subjective narration might have proved more adaptable to the intertitles of silent film (which often alternate between first and third person) than to the synchronized dialogue that followed. The problem of how to retain the novel's attempts to represent inner speech in a sound film would engage not only Eisenstein, who longed to film *Ulysses*, but the writers of *A Place in the Sun*.

The Story that Cost $93,000

An American Tragedy was published in December 1925, late for the Christmas trade, in a $5 two-volume edition. Anticipating hostile notices, Dreiser left for Florida before publication. On January 9, he received a telegram in Fort Lauderdale announcing "amazing" reviews and "excellent" sales. The *Nation* would hail his book as "the greatest American novel of our generation" and H. G. Wells pronounce it "one of the very greatest novels of this century" (Lingeman, 1990: 261–2). In March Horace Liveright and a fledgling dramatist named Patrick Kearney outlined a stage adaptation of four acts and twelve scenes.[10] Kearney's contract gave him 35 per cent of any motion picture rights, with Liveright claiming 50 per cent as the play's producer. When Dreiser objected, Liveright withdrew his claim, agreeing to receive nothing if the film rights were sold for $30,000 or more before the play opened.

Although the publisher hoped to capitalize on the book's success with a theatrical run, he was highly skeptical of its film prospects. Lasky's readers had rejected the novel prior to publication and Liveright wrote Dreiser that "tremendous pressure would have to be brought on Hays to let him pass it, and then the theme is such that it's rather unlikely that any company who would make a good picture out of it would care to go on it" (Lingeman, 1990: 268). But when a New York *World* columnist predicted that a Hollywood adaptation "if courageously treated would make the greatest film yet produced" (Martin, 1927), the East Coast office of Famous Players took notice. On March 17 Lasky and his assistant Walter Wanger met Dreiser and Liveright at the Ritz. The novelist later recalled asking Lasky why he wanted to buy the film rights and the mogul replying that such a prestigious sale would "make a gesture" (Lingeman, 1990: 269) against the then prevalent denigration of the industry. After an angry argument between Dreiser and Liveright about what, if anything, the publisher was owed prior to the opening of the play, Lasky agreed to pay $90,000, of which $10,000 went to Liveright. The studio issued a press release announcing that they had paid a record sum for the novel and "given a guaranty to Mr Dreiser that the book would be filmed exactly as it is written" (Lingeman, 1990: 271).

The studio's assurance became part of the publicity for the adaptation, with the *Los Angeles Times* reporting at the end of March that "it was only under that condition that Dreiser consented to sell the film rights." The paper also reported that D. W. Griffith had been selected by the studio to direct, despite his reluctance to work "in the hurried way that they approve" (Klumph, 1926: 23). By July the director Monta Bell had become the likely nominee, and he described the difficulties of casting the film:

Consider the crime that Griffiths commits—the horrible nature of the murder— and then consider whether or not it would have been possible to tell the story any differently than it was told and yet retain the sympathy for Griffiths. In the picture version we hope to portray the leading character in the same very sympathetic light, and for that reason he must appear at the beginning of the story as a normal and to a degree very lovable human character. Almost, perhaps, what we consider in pictures now a "straight hero." (Schallert, 1926: C19)

The August *Motion Picture Magazine* headlined an interview with Dreiser as "The Story That Cost $93,000—With the Understanding That the Author Is to

Approve the Scenario." In it the writer plumped for Erich von Stroheim as director, citing his *Greed* (1924) as "one of the momentous things in any medium" and his grasp of "the psychology of America ... our fairy tale avoidance and dislike of reality, materialism, self-indulgence, a good time, dancing and having a swell time, all this fan-tan is ours." Noting the rumors that Griffith would be chosen, Dreiser agreed that the epic film maker could "picture the sweep" of the novel, but cautioned that he didn't want "a sentimental melodrama made of it, or a stylized tragedy." "Dreiser likes the movies," *Motion Picture* proclaimed; "he is not afraid that they can't picture his novels, but he is going to keep a grip on his works until he sees the scenario" (Carples, 1926: 46–107).

Despite its Hollywood sale, *An American Tragedy* was unofficially banned in Boston, where the pro-censorship Watch and Ward Society opposed its distribution. To challenge the ban (and generate new interest in the novel) Liveright's partner Donald Friede journeyed to the city the following year, sold a copy of the novel to a Watch and Ward agent and had himself arrested. At the trial the district attorney read aloud several sections of the book, including the passages in which Clyde visits a brothel and those in which he attempts to arrange an abortion for Roberta. Clarence Darrow testified for the publisher, arguing that not all literature should be tailored for the feeble minded and the very young, but the prosecutor summed up by asking the jury if they would want their fifteen-year-old daughters to read the passages he had recited in court. They duly found the publisher guilty of obscenity, a verdict later upheld by the Massachusetts Supreme Court: "there is nothing essential to the history of the life of its principal character that would be lost if these passages were missed which the jury found were indecent, obscene, and manifestly tending to corrupt the morals of youth" (*Massachusetts v. Friede* (1930), cited in De Grazia, 1991: 138).

A few months later Dreiser received an invitation to attend the November celebrations of the tenth anniversary of the Bolshevik revolution. The Soviet authorities, he was told, regarded him as "the outstanding literary intelligence in America" (Swanberg, 1965: 325). Eager to investigate this social experiment, Dreiser was reluctant to confine his visit to the festivities and bargained for a longer stay and the right to travel where he wished. On October 19, 1927, he left for Moscow.

Notes

1. See Higashi, S. (2002), "The New Woman and Consumer Culture," in J. M. Bean and D. Negra (eds), *A Feminist Reader in Early Cinema*, Durham: Duke University Press, p. 301.
2. See Seltzer, M. (1992), *Bodies and Machines*, New York: Routledge, for a sustained discussion of the mechanization of organic life and the organicization of industrial production in naturalist discourse.

3. My spelling of the noun "fantasy" and the adjective "fantasmatic" throughout this text proceeds from the criticism by Jean Laplanche and Jean-Bertrand Pontalis of the widespread use of "ph" for unconscious fantasies and "f" for daydreams. They argue persuasively that this distinction is not Freudian. See Laplanche, J. and Pontalis, J.-B. (1986), "Fantasy and the Origins of Sexuality," in V. Burgin, J. Donald and C. Kaplan (eds) *Formations of Fantasy*, London: Methuen, 19–20 and 32, footnote 40).

4. In 1919 Dreiser read about Freud's untranslated work on fairy tale, as well as Brill's own views of the genre, in Brill, A. A. (1914), *Psychanalysis [sic], Its Theory and Practical Applications*, Philadelphia: W. B. Saunders. See Moers, E. (1969) *Two Dreisers*, New York: Viking Press, footnotes 21 and 31: 351–2.

5. See Kenaga, H. (2006), "Making the 'Studio Girl,'" *Film History*, 18, pp. 129–39.

6. See Merck, M. (2007), "Introduction," *America First: Naming the Nation in US Film*, London: Routledge.

7. In 1923, *Way Down East* came second, after *The Four Horses of the Apocalypse*, in the favorite film category of an American high school students' poll. See Koszarski, R. (1990: 29).

8. Compare Hansen, M. (2000), "The Mass Production of the Senses: Classical Cinema as Vernacular Modernism," in C. Gledhill and L. Williams (eds), *Reinventing Film Studies*, London: Arnold, pp. 332–50 with Hankins, L. (1993), "'Across the Screen of My Brain': Virginia Woolf's 'The Cinema' and Film Forums of the Twenties," in D. Gillespie (ed.), *The Multiple Muses of Virginia Woolf*, Columbia, MO: University of Missouri Press, pp. 148–79.

9. The vulnerability of handsome young men like Clyde to a male erotic gaze is made clear when he is warned in the hotel of "a certain type of social pervert, morally disarranged and socially taboo, who sought to arrest and interest boys of their type" (*An American Tragedy*: 58–9).

10. The play, starring Morgan Farley, Katherine Wilson and Miriam Hopkins, opened in New York on October 11, 1926 and ran for 216 performances.

CHAPTER 2

A Monstrous Challenge to American Society

America has not understood montage as a new element, a new opportunity.
Sergei Eisenstein, "Béla Forgets the Scissors"

On November 16, 1927, Dreiser met Sergei Eisenstein. The director received the author with tea and cakes at his Moscow home, a room decorated, *Dreiser's Russian Diary* recalls, with "a fantastic bulls eye in a series of convolutions in color on the ceiling, a placard advertising a new cream separator above his desk, and kino photos on the wall" (Riggio and West, 1996: 100). Both men knew something of the other's work. Dreiser had seen *The Battleship Potemkin* (1925), which had premiered in the US in December of the previous year, to far greater plaudits than it received in the Soviet Union. His own novels, with their dissection of American capitalism, its robber barons and working-class victims, were esteemed by the Soviet authorities who had invited him to tour the country and during his visit the state press agreed to publish all his works. But neither the Russian nor the American was without reservations about the other. Eisenstein would later describe *An American Tragedy* as "not a class-based work from our point of view," although one "that has every chance of being counted as a classic of its time and place." Unlike Zola's novels, which he read and reread before filming *Strike* (1925), *October* (1928) and *The Old and the New* (1929), or Joyce's, whose "direct emergence of the theme through powerfully effective raw material" and close-up detail he deemed highly cinematic, what he knew of Dreiser's, he later confessed, was acquired the night before meeting him (Eisenstein, 1988c: 96). Dreiser, for his part, arrived with a list of American films he thought "as good as *Potemkin*" (Riggio and West, 1996: 102)—the influential Westerns *The Covered Wagon* (James Cruze, 1923) and *The Iron Horse* (John Ford, 1924) and the ethnographic documentaries *Nanook of the North* (Robert J. Flaherty, 1922), *Grass* (Merian Cooper, Ernest B. Schoedsack, Marguerite Harrison, 1925) and *Chang* (Ernest B. Schoedsack, 1927)—and took care to record that Eisenstein hadn't seen them.

In this unpropitious atmosphere, the author inquired about the funding and organization of the film industry in the Soviet Union and learned that it was a branch of the Department of Education. "There is strict control as in

America," he notes, "only here it is political whereas in the U.S. it is moral."
Eisenstein offered a brief outline of his cinematic practice, stressing his avoidance of detailed shooting scripts and professional actors in favor of making
"daily life itself a drama" (Riggio and West, 1996: 101), an aim he illustrated
with his work-in-progress on agricultural collectivization, then titled *The
General Line*. To Dreiser, who opens his memoir of his visit with a robust declaration of his individualism, the contrarian's position he assumed (to an exaggerated degree) throughout his tour, Eisenstein's commitment to a cinema of
collective protagonists and analytical exposition was doomed. His diary summarizes his defense of the narrative of the individual, "his private trials, terrors
& delights, since only through the individual could the mass & its dreams be
served and interpreted" (Riggio and West, 1996: 102). Eisenstein—who for
some time had compared his opposition to singular protagonists and personal-
ized plotting with the critics' "personification of cinema in the *individualized
shot*" (Eisenstein, 1988b: 79)—would not agree. Indeed, he declared his
interest in filming Marx's *Capital*, a project for which he had begun drafting
notes during the previous month: "OCTOBER ... led to a complete departure
from the factual and anecdotal ... Here's a point of contact already with completely new film perspectives and with the glimmers of possibilities to be realized in CAPITAL, a new work on a libretto by Karl Marx. A film treatise"
(Eisenstein, 1976: 3–4).

The following day Dreiser viewed excerpts from the director's current projects, including scenes from *The General Line* and sequences from *October*, then
nearing completion of its first version. The revolutionary drama he pronounced
"exciting, *but not so moving*" (Riggio and West, 1996: 104), but *The General Line*,
with its rich detailing of rural life, including a religious procession, a model dairy
and the incident in which the impoverished peasant Marfa is refused the loan of
a horse for her plowing by a prosperous farmer, interested him far more. The fat
"kulak" and his fatter livestock, he noted, were reminiscent in their primitive
luxury of feudal barons. Although Dreiser detailed nothing of the film's formal
strategies—beyond the juxtaposition of a plump farm wife and the figure of a
whirling pig—his engagement with *The General Line* anticipated his approval of
Eisenstein's adaptation of *An American Tragedy*, in which certain narrative and
stylistic aspects of the earlier film would be brought to bear on its narrative of
the individual, the mass and its dreams.

Dreiser returned to the United States in January 1928. Eisenstein would
arrive there in June 1930. In the ensuing period he negotiated the complexities
of completing *October* and *The General Line* in the increasingly turbulent politics
of the Soviet Union while exploring opportunities to work with sound. As early
as 1922, he had set out his position on its use in the cinema, deploring early
French attempts to synchronize images and recorded sound naturalistically.
Significantly, the same article, co-written with Sergei Yutkevich, celebrates the
leading Hollywood stars of the period as an opposing force to this illusionism,
via their highly stylized star personas: "Mary Pickford, the ideal Anglo-Saxon

woman, the heroine of improbably adventure films, Douglas [Fairbanks] the sportsman and optimist" (Yutkevich and Eisenstein, 1928: 31). Four years later, Warner Brothers inaugurated "scored feature" production by adding a music and effects track to *Don Juan* (Alan Crosland, 1926). In October 1927, the studio debuted the first "talkie," whose acoustic track had been recorded simultaneously with the image, *The Jazz Singer* (Alan Crosland, 1927). In France, where theatrical technology enabled a rapid conversion to sound, the "talkie" or *film parlant* briefly coincided with the scored feature or *film sonore*. Together with René Clair and Abel Gance, Eisenstein recorded his advocacy of the latter, with its potential autonomy of the two separately recorded elements.

As commentators have since observed, the development of synchronized dialogue tended to reassert a humanist integration of the actor's persona while actually restricting the technical possibilities of sound recording.[1] The 1928 "Statement on Sound," co-signed by Eisenstein, his assistant Grigori Alexandrov and the director Vsevolod Pudovkin, was issued long before such technology was feasible in the USSR, where by 1930 only two theaters in the entire country were equipped to play audio tracks and the first domestically produced sound feature was not exhibited until 1931.[2] Nevertheless, the statement warned that it could become a double-edged sword. Used naturalistically, sound was predicted to become a commercially exploitable attraction to film-goers eager to experience the "'illusion' of people talking, objects making a noise, etc." (Eisenstein, 1988d: 113). More worrying would be the next stage, when synchronized dialogue could encourage cinema to become filmed theater, with all its high cultural limitations. For Eisenstein, the former stage director who gloried in the cinema's capacity for *montage*—the combination of conflicting elements of image, text and sound to powerful emotional and intellectual effect— synchronized filming raised the prospect of regression to a pre-modernist aesthetic of representational transparency and cognitive stasis.

But sound also offered the opposite possibility. Employed independently, in contradiction to a film's visual elements, sound could resolve problems of signification intractable to the further elaboration of the image track. (Here the statement's allusions to "fantastic montage constructions, provoking a fear of abstruseness and reactionary decadence" (Eisenstein, 1988d: 114) registers the increasing Soviet opposition to visual experiment in this consumerist period of the New Economic Plan, when foreign imports dominated the Russian cinema and socialist realism loomed on the horizon.) Invoking musical terminology, the statement urges the "contrapuntal" and "discordant" use of sound to create a new orchestration of acoustic and visual elements. Where the naturalist soundtrack would threaten the internationalism of cinema, forcing it into multiple language versions, remakes and eventual dubbing, the contrapuntal sound film was advocated to escape the national markets that had confined the theatre and offer "an even greater opportunity than before of speeding the idea contained in a film throughout the whole globe, preserving its world-wide viability" (Eisenstein, 1988d: 114).

There were clear precedents for the use of sound that Eisenstein championed, even in Hollywood. Walt Disney's Mickey Mouse animations were celebrated by the director for their non-naturalistic accompaniment of a gesture with an acoustic "association or pure equivalence" (Eisenstein, 1988g: 200–1). The 1929 MGM black musical drama *Hallelujah* used exaggerated off-screen sounds for its chase sequence and overlapped individual speech with a vocal chorus, "the jazz ecstasy of African Methodists" that Eisenstein said "enchanted" its director, King Vidor (Eisenstein, 1933: 100). The same year saw the opening of Paramount's *Applause* (Rouben Mamoulian), which like many early sound features—among them, the 1929 ventriloquism drama *The Great Gabbo* (James Cruze) and Sternberg's early films with Dietrich—employs a performance setting to notable acoustic effect, inflecting dressing room intimacies with onstage noises and making a villain's shadow speak.

By June 1929, Eisenstein had concluded that "the entire future of cinema lies with sound" (Bergen, 1999: 156). To study its technology, it was necessary to leave the Soviet Union for Hollywood, and the warm reception there for *Potemkin* made this possible. After viewing the film at private screenings prior to its US opening, a MGM associate producer named David Selznick described it to his supervisor Harry Rapf as "unquestionably one of the greatest motion pictures ever made." Eschewing the issues of the film's politics and commercial prospects, he urged the studio's executives to "view it in the same way that a group of artists might view or study a Rubens or a Raphael" and consider employing "the man responsible for it, a young Russian director named Eisenstein." "The picture has no characters in an individual sense; it has not one studio set; yet it is gripping beyond words—its vivid and realistic reproduction of a bit of history being far more interesting than could any film of fiction; and this simply because of the genius of its production and direction" (Behlmer, 1972: 9).

Pickford and Fairbanks themselves enthused about the film after viewing it at a special showing in Berlin en route to Moscow, where they met Eisenstein and promised to bring him to their studio, United Artists. Two years later the head of Universal, Carl Laemmle Sr., was urged to hire Eisenstein by his advisor and production assistant Seymour Stern, while Joseph Schenck, the Russian-born president of United Artists, followed up his stars' invitation by negotiating for Eisenstein's services with Sovkino, the Soviet film production trust, during a tour of its new Moscow studio.

In June 1929, Eisenstein declared his hope to travel to the United States to add sound to *The General Line*, then being revised for its debut under a new title, *The Old and the New*. Changes afoot in the Soviet line on agricultural collectivization, from the official encouragement that had motivated the project initially to the coercive policy that proceeded from Stalin's first five-year plan, mandated additional filming and re-editing. Having completed this, Eisenstein secured leave from Sovkino with his two main collaborators, his assistant director Grigori Alexandrov and the cameraman Eduard Tisse. In August, the trio journeyed to Berlin to introduce *The Old and the New*. There Eisenstein learned that Schenck's invitation to United Artists had fallen through but the three Russians remained in Western Europe to pursue other opportunities. Their adventures over the next nine months—meeting the major progressive figures in the fields of film, literature and fine art, dining at Parisian cafes and Cambridge high tables, investigating bookshops and brothels, harried all the while by anti-Bolshevik authorities who censored their screenings and threatened them with deportation—have been much chronicled, most wonderfully by Eisenstein himself. This account will be confined to their route from Russia to *An American Tragedy*.

In September, Eisenstein, Alexandrov and Tisse took *The Old and the New* to the First International Congress of Independent Cinematography in La Sarraz, Switzerland, where it was screened with Bunuel's *Un Chien Andalou*, Dreyer's *The Passion of Joan of Arc*, Man Ray's *L'Étoile de Mer*, and other major avant-garde works of the period. Convened by the critic and political journalist Robert Aron to establish a non-commercial co-operative of international experimental film making, it was attended by a distinguished delegation that included the directors Walter Ruttmann, Hans Richter and Alberto Cavalcanti, the film theorist Béla Balázs and the *Revue du Cinema* founder Jean-Georges Auriol. Also present was a young Englishman, the writer and fledgling film-maker Ivor Montagu. A member of the wealthy banking family, Montagu had traveled to the Soviet Union twice and translated Pudovkin, who had recommended him to Eisenstein. Together with the literature scholar Jack Isaacs, Montagu attended La Sarraz as a delegate of the Film Society, founded in London to show international and experimental films not distributed in the United Kingdom. As a Russian speaker he could communicate with Alexandrov and Tisse, who did not share Eisenstein's facility with languages. As a wit he relished the director's mockery of the conference's "elevated and enervating atmosphere of high polite discussion" (Montagu, 1969: 14). By its end he had befriended the trio and extended an invitation to the director to lecture in London as the guest of the Film Society.

After La Sarraz, Eisenstein explored a variety of production opportunities while writing and lecturing. In Zurich he was asked to film a documentary advocating the legalization of abortion, a commission he delegated to Tisse. The finished work—*Fraüennot-Fraüengluck* (*Women's Joy is Women's Woe, 1930*) —centers on the pregnant mother of a poor family forced to seek an illegal abortion, a theme to which Tisse and Eisenstein would soon return. Meanwhile in Berlin, Eisenstein re-met Emil Jannings, whom he had briefly encountered three years before when he and Tisse had first visited to learn about new developments in film technique and German production methods. Jannings cherished hopes of persuading Eisenstein to star him in a film about Catherine the Great's lover, Prince Potemkin—"a second Potemkin" (Eisenstein, 1995: 327), Eisenstein wryly observed, and not the last he would be asked to make.[3] The actor introduced him to Josef von Sternberg, then directing him in *The Blue Angel*. Invited to view the rushes, Eisenstein noted with disapproval the director's multiple takes, probably necessary because the film (whose synchronized vocal effects, including whistling, singing and classroom recitation, are so conspicuous) was being made in two versions, German and German-English. Nevertheless, Eisenstein clearly thought that Sternberg squandered time and he would later complain about his slow shooting after watching him on the set of *Morocco* (1930).

Still seeking a route to Hollywood, Eisenstein lunched in Berlin with Luigi Pirandello, who had received an invitation to work with Paramount, the former distribution company that had merged with Famous Players-Lasky. To Eisenstein's disgust ("How old-fashioned! What self-plagiarism!"—Eisenstein, 1995: 46), the playwright expatiated on the possibility of a Pirandellesque film in which the onscreen characters rebel against the will of the projector, although he did not accept the studio's invitation. But among the guests at lunch was a representative of a trade delegation who knew Otto H. Kahn, a New York banker, art patron and member of the Paramount board. In addition to its acquisition of prestigious literary and theatrical properties, Paramount was distinguished for its employment of sophisticated European talent, including stars like Pola Negri, Maurice Chevalier, Emil Jannings and Marlene Dietrich. Ernst Lubitsch, Rouben Mamoulian and Sternberg were among its directors. The studio that sought the services of Pirandello seemed Eisenstein's best hope of an entrée to Hollywood.

While his European sojourn continued, broader politics events were transpiring that would radically affect his production aspirations. During the summer of 1929, a contract dispute between the major studios and the Actors' Equity Association led a former army officer named Frank Pease to form an anti-union group called the Character Actors Association. In October, the stock market crash initiated a depression monitored anxiously by studio executives, whose own share holdings were affected long before ticket sales were. In December Stalin announced the "Great Turn" to the forced collectivization of agriculture in the Soviet Union; and in the April following, another Pease front organization, the Hollywood Technical Directors Institute, sent a telegram to President Hoover and all the US state governors denouncing Universal's newly released anti-war film, *All Quiet on the Western Front* (Lewis Milestone, 1930).

Internal Speech

In November and December 1929, Eisenstein made two visits to England. There he appeared at a Film Society screening of *Potemkin* (which would remain banned for public exhibition in the country until 1954) on a double bill with John Grierson's documentary of herring fishermen, *Drifters*. He also gave a hugely influential series of lectures for the Society, referencing the major subjects of his writing in the period, among them Japanese *kabuki* theater, Charles Dickens, Emile Zola and James Joyce. In the preceding year Eisenstein had studied *Ulysses* during a holiday between the completion of *October* and the resumption of filming on *The Old and the New*. The novel's "exceptionally musical prose" incited his interest in an acoustic counterpoint commensurate with the visual counterpoint of montage. Its stream-of-consciousness narrative offered an alternative to filmed dialogue—one that had captivated the director in his language studies: "that very same sensuous linguistic canon of prelogic, with which we ourselves speak when we talk to ourselves—our internal speech" (Eisenstein, 1983: 213). In Paris Eisenstein had several meetings with Joyce, whose increasing blindness did not stifle his interest in *Potemkin* and *October*. Later the novelist would permit his interpreter Stuart Gilbert to draft a scenario based on *Ulysses*, for which he regarded Eisenstein and Walther Ruttmann, the German director of *Berlin— Symphony of a Great City*, as the only possible directors.[4]

In Paris between visits to England, Eisenstein was shown Joyce's scheme for *Ulysses*, which he had also given to Gilbert. This detailed outline locates each of the book's episodes in the actual geography of Dublin, transformed from the individual to the universal city through a symbolism of bodily coherence and the stages of human life. In one critic's view, the scheme's orchestration of correspondences was a factor in Eisenstein's subsequent movement from an aesthetics of fragmentation and contradiction to the holistic organicism of his later theories. But the schematic synedoches of *Ulysses* also perform the part-for-whole substitution through which individual protagonists may represent larger social forces.[5] The peasant co-operator Marfa had already become one such protagonist in the revision of *The Old and the New*, apotheosized in the film's final sequence reprising her image from different episodes of its narrative. Hollywood would encourage the creation of others.[6]

Soon after hosting Eisenstein's visit to England, Ivor Montagu set off for the United States, on behalf of his own ambitions in film production and those of Eisenstein and "the boys," as he referred to Alexandrov and Tisse. A banker uncle furnished him with a loan and a letter to Paramount president Adolph Zukor, a dedicated gambler whom he had met in a Riviera casino. Producer Basil Dean offered an introduction to David Sarnoff, the head of the Radio Corporation of America, whose cinematic sound system was used by its studio subsidiary RKO. H. G. Wells and George Bernard Shaw, who had already promised Eisenstein options on *The War of the Worlds* and *The Devil's Disciple*, also provided references. Armed with these credentials, and sufficient family connections to secure a dinner invitation from the then New York state governor Franklin Delano Roosevelt, Montagu met Zukor in Paramount's New York headquarters and received a letter commending him to the studio's West Coast production executives. He also met Paramount's Head of Production, Jesse Lasky, about to embark on a visit to Europe, and mentioned the option on *The War of the Worlds*. Lasky promised to see Eisenstein in Paris.

After a speculative discussion with David Sarnoff on the future of sound, Montagu departed to Hollywood, supplied with yet another letter of introduction. There he sought out the Paramount hierarchy, meeting its Head of West

Coast Production and overall number three after Zukor and Lasky, Benjamin
("B .P.") Schulberg. Asked for an opportunity to shadow a production and learn
American pictures, Schulberg assigned Montagu to a First World War romance
with a Moscow setting. Operating on it as a wholly ignored expert on things
Russian, Montagu was immersed in the institutional illogic and bizarre
infighting that makes his memoir of Hollywood an exceptionally funny example
of a very comic genre. Scarcely more seriously, he recorded the early reaction at
Paramount to Pease's red scare:

> Although there were no diplomatic relations in the nineteen-twenties and nine-
> teen-thirties between the USA and the USSR, the atmosphere was totally different
> then from what it afterwards became, in the McCarthy era. There were McCarthy
> precursors, as we shall later see, but by and large they were looked on as a lunatic
> fringe. Russia was not a menace. Of course one disapproved of it but one lost no
> sleep over it. (Montagu, 1969: 53)

On Eisenstein's behalf, the young Englishman accepted an invitation from the
Czech-born Universal executive Paul Kohner to discuss employing the director
with the studio's founder, Carl Laemmle, Sr. Although the aging Universal boss
seemed taken with the idea, it was quickly quashed by Laemmle, Jr., apparently
in resentment at the influence Kohner exerted over his father. Meanwhile in
Paris, Jesse Lasky had arrived with Paramount's general manager Albert
Kaufman and executive producer Richard Blumenthal to transact business at
the studio's European headquarters. Their initial proposals to Eisenstein
included films on the Dreyfus affair, the life of Zola and an adaptation of Vicky
Baum's *Grand Hotel*. Eisenstein replied with his authorized options on Wells'
The War of the Worlds, Shaw's *The Devil's Disciple* and Joyce's *Ulysses*. The
prospect of a film on black Americans was raised by the director and immediately quashed by the executives, citing the failure of Vidor's *Hallelujah*. As
Eisenstein awaited the Soviet extension of the leaves granted him, Alexandrov
and Tisse, he insisted that both men be included in any contract offered. This
increased the difficulty of the negotiations but an agreement was finally signed
on May 3, paying Eisenstein a weekly wage of $900—just sufficient to support
him and his two associates for an initial six months development period. If no
agreement could be reached on a subject, the contract could be terminated after
the first three months. If successful, the Russians were promised the possibility
of alternating production in the Soviet Union with work in Hollywood. The contract with Paramount enabled the speedy acquisition of United States' visas and,
on May 12, 1930, Eisenstein and Tisse arrived in America—"the America,"
Eisenstein later wrote, "of anti-Sovietism, of Prohibition; the imperialist
America of Hoover" (Eisenstein, 1995: 287).

The director was immediately fed into the Paramount publicity machine,
charming an Atlantic City convention of the studio's licensees on his second day
in the country and breakfasting with the New York press at the Hotel Astor. *The*

Old and the New had opened at the Cameo Theatre, a Times Square art house. Extolling Soviet collectivization (and wholly without battle scenes) the film was a worry to the East Coast executives, who vainly tried to interest Eisenstein in a story about the early Jesuit priests who converted the Southwest Indians to Christianity. (Lasky had an originating role in a 1925 Paramount film on the theme of Native American religious conversion, *The Vanishing American*, directed by George B. Seitz.) Eisenstein replied with another historical suggestion, an adaptation of Blaise Cendrar's 1925 novel *L'Or*, chronicling the destruction of a California immigrant's fortune by the discovery of gold on his land. Waiting for Alexandrov, delayed in France while completing the short impressionist sound film *Romance sentimentale* (1930), he lectured at Columbia and Harvard, arguing at the latter that "the object of the new films is not to bring better sound effects to the audience, but to present abstract ideas ... The culture film, which makes people think, can bring a renaissance into the artistry of motion pictures" (Seton, 1952: 163).

During his stay on the East Coast, Eisenstein met Dreiser's publisher, Horace Liveright, and re-met the author himself, who entertained him in a New York speakeasy and at Iroki, the Hudson River estate he had purchased with the proceeds of *An American Tragedy*. Five years after its sale to Paramount the novel remained unfilmed, and the possibility of its adaptation was a likely spur to Eisenstein's pilgrimage to the infamous death house at Sing Sing Prison:

> I had the honour to sit in the electric chair, only, of course after I had made sure it was disconnected. A monstrous experience! But the most depressing sensation was evoked by various details near the chair. Beside it, for example, stood a spittoon. Gleaming, brightly polished, the sort you usually find beside you at the dentist's ... There was nothing fantastic about the place, no freakish lights or shadows such as people love to show in films ... It's just this primitive practicality that is so sinister. (Bergen, 1999: 193)

Sutter's Gold

The sightseeing stopped when Alexandrov arrived in June. Together the team headed west, interrupting their journey so that Eisenstein could lecture in Chicago. On June 16 they arrived in Hollywood to be reunited with Montagu and his wife, in a Coldwater Canyon villa leased by the writer for the five of them. At the studio they were allocated a two-room office and began the process of negotiating possible subjects.

Of these Montagu vastly preferred Blaise Cendrar's *L'Or (Sutter's Gold)*, based on actual events in nineteenth century California, when the agricultural empire of the Swiss settler Johann Sutter was destroyed by the discovery of gold: "On one plane, a poem of romantic irony, on another a parable of the nature of real wealth. And it actually happened" (Montagu, 1969: 101). Eisenstein, however, was fixated on an idea that had long been in gestation, dating back to his initial encounter with Bauhaus architecture on his 1926 visit to Berlin. A 1928 note for the proposed film of *Capital* mentions *The Glass House* in reference to the need to rethink frame composition, in order to represent the complexities of a mode of production distinguished by its multiplicity and contradiction: "The ideology of the unequivocal frame must be thoroughly reconsidered" (Eisenstein, 1976: 24). A satire on capitalist social isolation set in an apartment building whose walls, floors and ceilings are utterly transparent, *The Glass House* was conceived as an experiment in combining multiple actions within a single film frame. In the individualist world depicted, the building's doors remain opaque as a concession to privacy and its inhabitants ignore the visible life around them, until something causes them to change ...

Eisenstein had seen *The Crowd* (King Vidor, 1928) and in Hollywood asked Vidor about the execution of its traveling shot up the side of an office block, disclosing its clerk protagonist in an enormous open-plan office. "He would point," Montagu (1968: 102) writes

> to the system of American origin and then coming more and more into vogue, where in great concerns—banks, newspapers, counting houses, drawing offices and the like—everyone has his desk in a single huge hall, the manager and the clerk, with the only difference between them their names in gilt on a little three-sided rod resting beside the pen-tray.

Suppose, Eisenstein suggested, an event that introduces suspicion and surveillance into this milieu, transforming the inhabitants' indifferent privacy into an equally indifferent voyeurism, in which they gaze raptly at their neighbors' deaths from suicide and arson. Filmed through glass with Tisse's famous depth of focus, an individual composition could include overlapping images, complex distortions and unorthodox points of view. The combinatory force of the montage could be achieved within a single frame.

Finding a suitable narrative for this setting proved more difficult, with Paramount's writers unable to offer anything other than whimsy, despite Eisenstein's insistence that his was not a fairy tale. As for the studio managers, Schulberg's son Budd later recalled his father being warned by "a pragmatist," "it would cost us a million dollars to build that city and we couldn't use it as a standing set and write off the costs against other pictures, like our ocean liner, our castle, or our New York street" (Schulberg, 1981: 369). Montagu himself was deeply opposed to *The Glass House*, although he later conceded its possible prescience as a depiction of contemporary urban aggression. *Sutter's Gold* possessed the advantage of an actual narrative, one already offered by Cendrar. Moreover, that narrative centered on the creation of an agricultural paradise, the ecstatic fertility of flowing milk and fecund fields imagined in *The Old and the New*. After losing weeks to *The Glass House*, Eisenstein finally agreed to move on, but he would return to the tactic of combining contradictory and distorting images within a single frame.[7]

For Paramount these early weeks of Eisenstein's sojourn were not uneventful. The day after the director arrived in Hollywood, Jesse Lasky received a telegram that began:

If your Jewish clergy and scholars haven't enough courage to tell you and you yourself haven't brains to know better or enough loyalty to this land, which has given you more than you ever had in history, to prevent you importing a cut-throat red dog like Eisenstein, then let me inform you that we are behind every effort to have him deported. We want no more red propaganda in this country. (Seton, 1952: 167)

The telegram was printed in the *Motion Picture Herald* of June 28, which noted that Major Pease and his Hollywood Technical Directors Institute were also campaigning for a national ban on *All Quiet on the Western Front*. It was followed by a 24-page denunciation of "Eisenstein, Hollywood's messenger from Hell" which Pease circulated throughout the United States.

In Hollywood, according to Montagu, Pease's anti-Semitism and general ferocity marked him out as a crackpot. A studio supervisor showed them the letters and cuttings, but "No breath of disquiet or insult had ever been carried to us personally and it had made no difference to our lives" (Montagu, 1969: 121). James Goodwin interprets Paramount's silence differently, arguing that it was characteristic of the "Jewish self-rejection" (Goodwin, 2001: 100) that fuelled the assimilationist ambitions of the studio moguls. Marie Seton, Eisenstein's first and most politically sympathetic biographer, insists that Pease was no eccentric but a vocal representative of the American anti-Semitism increasing with the economic devastation of the Depression. But the association of Jews with political radicalism was anathema to Hollywood, and a publicity campaign was immediately launched to establish Eisenstein as a friend of the stars and an artist above politics.

As a part of this strategy, the studio arranged to have Eisenstein invited to speak at a banquet for members of the Academy of Motions Pictures at the Roosevelt Hotel. He did so in August, elaborating an interview he had given to the *Los Angeles Times* earlier in his visit: "[H]e is inquisitive about 'soundies'— he repeated the word, 'soundies'—as distinct from talkies, which he does not approve ... he believes that dialogue has little or no place on the screen, especially when it is used to tell what should be told in pictures" (Scheuer, 1930: B7).

At the banquet Frank Lloyd, representing the Director's Branch of the Academy, introduced Eisenstein, saying "Talkies have made us realize as never before that the whole word is not America, that the whole picture industry is not Hollywood. This is probably fortunate, as it required us to open our minds and eyes, to learn new things. We can learn from our fellow-workers abroad." Then Eisenstein, in a question and answer session with the audience, wittily set out his views on the difficulties of representing the cream separator in *The Old and the*

New with "ecstasy and excitement"; on using the associative principles of montage to edit a murder scene ("hand with knife, eye that is afraid, hand stuck out ..."); on the similar principles operating in the Japanese ideogram for sorrow ("a heart and a knife").

Predicting that the "100% dialogue" film would soon yield to an associative combination of sound and pictures, Eisenstein denounced absolute synchronization with the industry term "Mickey Mouse": "The other pictures should follow Mickey Mouse, and not Mickey Mouse the other pictures ..." Titles, Eisenstein suggested, could persist, offering comic opportunities when the title contradicted what was visually represented. Similarly he argued that "There is an enormous possibility from the moment you destruct the naturalistic correspondence of sound and pronouncing a word ... We have the same thing in Mickey Mouse (I am giving a lot of free publicity) because he has his music and finds the graphic element that corresponds to the sound." Asked whether he was "opposed to using any speech," the honored guest replied, "I am opposed to speeches made at banquets, but in pictures, elements can always be used" (August 12, 1930, Speech to Academy Banquet, Eisenstein Collection, Margaret Herrick Library, Academy of Motion Picture Arts and Sciences).

Meanwhile the group had tackled *Sutter's Gold*, beginning with a reconnaissance of its California settings, the deserted gold mines in the Sacramento valley and the wharves of the San Francisco waterfront, with Montagu taking notes and Alexandrov photographs. The three spent a week in the redwood forests, where Eisenstein studied Stuart Gilbert's commentary on the Sirens' episode in *Ulysses* in order to consider musical counterpoint. In a local museum, he had to stifle his desire to make off with its daguerreotypes of anonymous pioneers. His meditation on these images anticipates the death-in-life ascribed by Roland Barthes in *Camera Lucida* to a Civil War era photograph of a condemned prisoner, as well as the doleful figure of the convicted Clyde Griffiths: "The past, if not actual antiquity, then another world, another century, looked at me with living eyes from these tiny, opened lockets ... Young, sorrowful faces looked up from under their Confederate caps, as if expecting an imminent death in the field hospitals" (Eisenstein, 1995: 294–6).

After immersing themselves in this melancholy Americana, the group returned to Cold Water Canyon and the Stakhanovite production process that the three Russians had employed in their earlier films. Having copiously annotated his copy of the novel, Eisenstein would dictate a section of the treatment in Russian to Alexandrov, who would then transcribe it. With the aid of Paramount's translators and typists, an English text would be prepared for Montagu, who would revise it with Eisenstein. Montagu would then draft the final version, to be typed by his wife Hell, the only one who could read his handwriting. The process required immense energy (reputedly supplied by injections during *October*) and concentration, since Eisenstein would have to switch from dictating one reel to Alexandrov to correcting an earlier one with Montagu, while making supplementary sketches. For *Sutter's Gold* these were elaborate and detailed, annotated with the characters, locations and key props required for particular pages, as well as the scheduling of difficult shots. But, as ever with Eisenstein's screen writing, this was far from an orthodox script.

"A numbered script will bring as much animation to cinema as the numbers on the heels of the drowned men in the morgue," Eisenstein had declared in the 1929 preface to his screenplay for *The Old and the New*. Rather than a visual description of what the audience will see, he urged the scriptwriter to express "the purpose of the experience that the audience must undergo." The emotional tension of an incident was argued to be better conveyed in literary language than in the meticulous listing of a sequence of images. To evoke the story that will captivate the audience, the formalized shooting script was to be abandoned for what he termed "the film novella" (Eisenstein, 1988e: 134).

In practice, as the final version make clear, Eisenstein's scenario for *Sutter's Gold* was a hybrid of a descriptive "treatment" and a technical shooting script, including some lines of dialogue and instructions to FADE OUT at the end of certain scenes. The script is divided into seven reels of fourteen minutes' length. Each paragraph is confined to a scene taking place within a single time and space or a continuous sequence of scenes. Occasional titles are indicated, with some of these having considerable rhetorical force. Thus the final reel opens with the title "A MAN CAN BE FIVE YEARS OLD," followed by a smiling child, and then a second title, "AND A TOWN CAN BE FIVE YEARS OLD" (Montagu, 1969: 197), followed by a view of early San Francisco. In an ingenious attempt to incorporate written information into the action, Sutter dons a gold ring commemorating the discovery of the mineral on his land with the inscription "FIRST GOLD FOUND 1848" (198). These elements only began to hint at the eloquence of what Montagu describes as Eisenstein's prose poem, characterized by passages like the opening of reel six describing miners betting in a San Francisco saloon:

"Tra-la-la ... tra-la-la"—sings a girl and her feet dance, tripping as care-free and as vulgar as the musical refrain. A burst of male laughter, alike impertinent and gross. The men are betting on frog races.

They wager little sacks of gold. The starter stands in the middle of the room and calls the names of the gross unwinking frogs. Gambling fever, the recklessness of the gold diggers pervades the room. (191)

As this excerpt suggests, music, and musically montaged sound effects, figure far more extensively than dialogue in this treatment. The scenario opens and closes with "a song of California" (206) and Switzerland is established with church bells and mountain choruses. The multiethnic harmony of Sutter's New Helvetia is represented by an orchestra of Indians playing the Marseillaise and Sutter's favorite Swiss air. And when the old settler finally expires after winning the law suit reclaiming his land, the sounds of his life story—coyote calls, women's whispers, rolling wagon wheels and roaring mobs—climax according to the fugal form in which Joyce composed the Sirens' episode, rising "fortissimo" to a "breaking chord" (205) before lapsing into silence. As the late afternoon shadow falls over his prostrate body in an effective fade to black, an offscreen voice intones

> People die.
> Facts are covered in the dust of history.
> Legends are forgotten ...
> But songs—
> Songs remain! (205–6)

Paramount's reaction to *Sutter's Gold* was simple and speedy. First, the scenario was praised, then it was deemed too expensive. Despite the group's plea that matte painting would be used in lieu of filming expensive scenes such as the railroad rush cross-country to the gold fields, and their itemization of additional location economies in the production sketches, the costing department refused to reduce its very large estimate of three million dollars. (Six years later James Cruze was to film a version of Cendrar's novel at a cost of $2 million for Universal, where its failure caused a major financial crisis.) The department head was a close relation of Schulberg, who reversed his earlier encouragement for "a social classic like *Greed* or *Modern Times*" (Schulberg, 1981: 369) and pronounced the story too historical to interest the American audience. When Lasky arrived from the East he smoothly averted a clash with his rival by suggesting that the devastated group undertake another project. In his memoir of the episode Budd Schulberg shifts the blame for this decision from his father to the studio's financial executives, alarmed at the prospect of Marxists making a film about gold destroying an American pioneer. Montagu reckoned that Eisenstein and his collaborators were also victims of managerial factionalism, whereby the studio's number three could never back a project initiated by its number two. But it is also important to bear in mind Lasky's slight familiarity with, let alone commitment to, many of the titles he expressed in an interest in acquiring, as well as what Schulberg apparently did notice, the novel's similarity to Stroheim's *Greed*.

The latter film is not discussed in Eisenstein's collected writings, and the director may have been unaware of its close resemblance to his project. Based on Frank Norris's 1899 novel *McTeague*, *Greed* is the story of a miner who escapes the brutal life of the gold fields and becomes a dentist. When his wife wins $5000 in a lottery, she gives him a giant gilt tooth to advertise his practice, and it comes to signify their lives' decay through avarice and envy.[8] With its settings in the mining country, San Francisco and Death Valley, *Greed* anticipates *Sutter's Gold* scenically as well as thematically and the precedent is a notoriously unhappy one. The director originally shot 446 reels, of which all but 140 minutes were destroyed by MGM. The fragmentary remains earned back less than half the film's costs and Stroheim's directorial career was finished a few years later, but not before Dreiser had named him as his first choice for *An American Tragedy*.

American Reality

Dreiser's novel brings this episode full circle, for Lasky had arrived in Hollywood with his friend Horace Liveright. The publisher had suffered tremendous losses in the stock market and the theater and had become a mere employee of the company he had founded. In the hope of realizing film sales of some of the books he had published he had joined Paramount in a development role. Both men were eager to realize their investment in *An American Tragedy*, which Lasky now suggested to Eisenstein. But for the director and his collaborators, the proposal was tantamount to a notice of termination from the studio. According to Marie Seton, who discussed this period with Eisenstein four years later, they had already discovered that the novel's politics had discouraged its filming, with Griffith and Lubitsch among those who had refused it. In a 1931 letter to Dreiser, Montagu noted that Paramount had proposed the novel soon after Eisenstein's arrival in Hollywood. "We rejected the proposal for it appeared to us impossible in present social conditions of the cinema to make a true version of the book" (August 10, 1931, Dreiser Papers). And as he later observed, "It would never be permitted to foreigners, some even Russians, to make *An American Tragedy* in the way we were bound to make it ... Sooner or later, someone in authority was bound, before it reached the screen, to wake up to what was happening" (Montagu, 1969: 113–14).

In the light of this realization, Eisenstein's decision to undertake the adaptation is worth considering. Montagu's praise of the novel's "entirely convincing picture of the America of that time, its social distinctions, its ambitions, its grinding machinery" (114) suggests that their stay in the country had validated its premises, and Eisenstein had warmed to the writer during their discussions in New York and Iroki, where he had recognized the increasingly leftward movement of his political views. Moreover, although Montagu was convinced that Lasky had never read the book and probably imagined it as the personal drama of Kearney's stage adaptation, failure to accept their patron's proposal would very likely have ended the agreement with Paramount. Four months of their contracted six had already passed and it was now September. The prospect of leaving Hollywood so soon must have weighed heavily on the Russians, who were escaping privation for the first time in 13 years. Finally, as Montagu later explained to Dreiser, they were repeatedly assured by Lasky, Schulberg and other studio executives that "the uncertainty which we several times expressed, whether alterations might not be forced at some stage in the development of the story, by social interests and others, were quite groundless and unnecessary" (Montagu, letter to Theodore Dreiser, August 10, 1931, Dreiser Papers). But although this may have encouraged Eisenstein to attempt the adaptation, it did not persuade him to attempt it in the way that the studio expected.

The writing process was the same as for *Sutter's Gold* and the scenario was also co-credited to Alexandrov and Montagu, but the outcome was very different. As Montagu observes, the earlier script was "primarily *pictorial*" (118) and would have been difficult for a less visually imaginative director to employ. But the script for *An American Tragedy* included much more speech (although not, as we shall see, wholly conventionally) and was both longer and more detailed—14 reels of 21 to 39 short scenes. (Paramount had requested a twelve-reel film costing $1 million.) There are intermittent camera and editing instructions, including combined fade-outs of image and sound. Montage, both the conventional device of juxtaposing shots to compress a lengthy series of actions into a brief sequence and also Eisenstein's more radical collisions, is employed—although the discontinuities of the latter are used more sparingly. In its attempt to realize Dreiser's novel, the scenario reminded Montagu of the exercises in adaptation that Eisenstein set his students at the state film academy in Moscow: "to extract—in cinema terms—the utmost thematic essence of *another's* written creation" (119). Eisenstein's retrospective commentary on it is actually part of a polemic on training students of film direction, one whose strictures on "infrequent episodic lectures by all sorts of 'prominent' film workers" and "short little film 'studies' by the graduands" retain a contemporary relevance. His recommendation that students film excerpts from major literary works to achieve a disciplined understanding of plot construction and dramatic situation is accompanied by an insistence that their interpretation of these texts exceeds mere sloganizing to achieve "a seriously determinant ideological outlook" (Eisenstein, 1988h: 224–5). The adaptation of Dreiser's novel is offered as a case in point.

An American Tragedy, he writes, "is 99 per cent a statement of facts and one per cent attitude toward them. This epic of cosmic truth and objectivity had to be 'screwed together' into a tragedy, which was unthinkable without the direction and the emphasis provided by a particular world-view" (Eisenstein, 1988h: 228). Turning the screw of interpretation (to borrow the title of Shoshana Felman's remarkably apposite discussion of readings of Henry James' novella)[9] Eisenstein sought to clarify the true tragedy of the novel, which he describes as lying "not in the murder but in the tragic path pursued by Clyde who is driven by the social system to murder." The role of fate in the classical tragedies to which Dreiser alludes is assigned to "American reality" (Eisenstein, 1988h: 229), specifically the nation's class system, prohibition of abortion, politicized legal institutions and religious fanaticism. From the ambiguous anti-hero of Dreiser's novel, Clyde will be transformed into a wounded innocent, the victim of American injustice. The consequence is not tragedy, in which we become reconciled to the fall from eminence of an erring protagonist, but melodrama, with an adult male taking the traditionally female role.

To describe the overwhelming weight of this national reality on Clyde, and to pursue a critique of the religious dogma that destroys him, Eisenstein invokes

Engels' description of the Calvinist doctrine of predestination as "the religious expression of the fact that in the commercial world of competition success or failure does not depend upon a man's activity or cleverness, but upon circumstances uncontrollable by him" (Engels, 1968: 384). Applying this principle to the question of Clyde's culpability, he spurns Dreiser's "impartial" representation of the boating accident and elects to "sharpen the actual and formal innocence of Clyde" (Eisenstein, 1988h: 231). By formal innocence, Eisenstein refers to the role of intention in Christian doctrine and America's Christian legal system, the moral responsibility assigned to the subject's "free" will, regardless of the circumstances or the outcome. Christianity's moral equation of the wish to kill with killing itself is accused of a bizarre parody of the Hegelian dialectic, unifying the ideal and the material, thought and deed. To escape its constricting synthesis, his Clyde must not—at the crucial moment—either abet or desire Roberta's drowning.

Pursuing this critique of religion, Eisenstein followed Sergei Dinamov's deprecation of the novelist's characterization of Clyde's mother in his preface to the novel's Russian translation: "Dreiser has betrayed his usual realistic manner in his portrayal of this fanatical woman, he has idealized her, given her character hints of winning and genuine sympathy" (Eisenstein, 1988h: 233). Both men saw Clyde's mother as the agent of his destruction in her insistence that he join in the family's missionary work rather than train for employment. Moreover, the religion she espouses is that which permits Reverend McMillan to accuse Clyde of "murder in your heart" and fail to declare his innocence to the governor. To establish Mrs Griffiths' complicity with this lethal dogmatism, the director eliminates McMillan, making the mother the betrayer of her son.

Darkness and Light

Although Eisenstein's changes to Dreiser's novel incurred no criticism from the writer himself, their transformation of his narrative is discernible from the outset of the scenario. The novel opens with an allusion to the doomed citadels of classical tragedy in its description of the "tall walls of the commercial heart of an American city of perhaps 400,000 inhabitants—such walls as in time may linger as a mere fable" (*An American Tragedy*: 15). Through the summer dusk walks the Griffiths family, crossing thoroughfares thronged with traffic until, on the second page, the father halts their progress to announce a hymn and then begin his sermon. Significantly, Dreiser positions Clyde's father as the family's leading preacher, known as "Praise-the-Lord Griffiths" for his glorification of divine love and forgiveness.

Conversely, Eisenstein's scenario begins not with dusk but darkness, out of which Mrs Griffiths' voice rises in the intonations of a sermon, gradually mingled with the urban sounds of streetcars, sirens and radio music. As a montage of urban views flashes across the screen, her voice-over continues, condemning drink and sinfulness until she too begins to sing. Still, Eisenstein withholds any sight of the singer or her family until after he shows the crowd watching them pityingly. Dreiser's crowd also disapproves of exhibiting children in this manner. One says that Clyde is "outa place" (*An American Tragedy*: 19) but others are moved by "the peculiarity of such an unimportant-looking family publicly raising its collective voice against the vast skepticism and apathy of life" (*An American Tragedy*: 16) and by Mrs Griffiths' evident sincerity.

Dreiser's Clyde is twelve, and he resents the shabby spectacle presented by his family and the contemptuous smiles of passers-by. Other boys have made fun of his father and even, when he was younger, offered lewd observations about his sister Esta. At times he has responded to these insults by fighting but his main ambition is to escape. He is sorely discontented with the absence of "beauty and pleasure" in his family's impoverished endeavors (described as "philanthropic work" rather than the fiery temperance campaigning of Eisenstein's description). Yet even the unhappy Clyde of the novel is said to respect his mother, "whose force and earnestness, as well as her sweetness, appealed to him" (*An American Tragedy*: 17–18).

Eisenstein introduces his protagonist differently, as a seven-year-old shrinking from the bullying of other children. With a pathos redolent of Jackie Coogan in Chaplin's *The Kid* (1921), the forlorn boy escapes their persecution by climbing a fire escape at the back of the mission, to sit with Esta gazing at the lights of the city through a gap between tenement walls. This rewriting of Dreiser's opening to make his aspirant adolescent an intimidated child, and his mother the figure of (literal) Prohibition in her household, intensifies the oedipal dynamics of the novel as well as its critique of religion. But something more than materialist analysis is at work here, namely the antagonism to unmotherly women already evident in the director's portraits of the sadistic socialites in *Strike* and *October* and the lesbian Cossacks who guard the Winter Palace in the latter film.[10] Mrs Griffiths is another such forbidding woman, and Eisenstein's enhancement of her role in Clyde's downfall anticipates both Sternberg's and Stevens' adaptations by effectively eliminating Clyde's father. In making his mother a negative figure incorporating the paternal function of Asa Griffiths as well as the dogmatic morality of the Reverend McMillan, the director transforms the ambiguous dusk in which Dreiser opens and closes his novel into the darkness and light of his own interpretation.

A fade-out marks the passage of time between the scenario's opening and its next scene, which again begins in darkness with Mrs Griffiths' voice-over "in the cadences of a singsong sermon" (Montagu, 1969: 212). Her subject is said to be the child's transformation to manhood, possibly an allusion to St Paul's epistle to the Corinthians: "When I was a child, I spake as a child, I understood as a child, I thought as a child: but when I became a man, I put away childish things. For now we see as in a glass, darkly; but then face to face ..." (1 Cor. xiii: 11).

If so, it is fitting that at this point "the darkness dissolves" (212) to reveal Clyde at sixteen or seventeen, still sitting on the fire escape with his sister. Where the voice-over has used non-synchronized speech to summarize several pages of the novel, so contrasting off screen shouts of "Hallelujah" dramatize the conflict between the dance band chorus they listen to and the more fervent cries of the nearby congregation. The discord that Eisenstein seeks in this contrapuntal use of sound echoes the conflict within Clyde and Esta between their puritanical upbringing and the pleasures of the city.

Until the end of the first reel Clyde is speechless, his misery suggested by his abject posture and expressions, the congregation's dismal singing and—shades of Chaplin—"his little darned old suit" (215). When the hymns begin, his sister dutifully takes her place at the harmonium, but Clyde escapes—first to his bedroom and then to the street, "firmly resolved, in the direction of Life—in the direction of light and movement" (213–4). As he walks away, the congregation's drone fades and the street sounds become louder. A succession of brief vignettes then emphasizes whiteness—here in terms of glamorous white clothing—in contrast to the darkness of the slum mission. Like its direct predecessor *The Old and the New*, this scenario takes "a white tone as the leading color." Here, as in Eisenstein's celebration of collectivism, "everything connected with the theme of joy ... show(s) through as white" (Eisenstein, 1987: 393).

First, Clyde passes the window of a sporting goods store. In it pale mannequins pose for swimming, tennis and golf in clothes whose pristine whiteness proclaims the leisured wealth of their white buyers—a racial and class reference made explicit by the treatment's dig at "white society dummies" (Montagu, 1969: 214). White too is the uniform of the magically deft attendant at the soda fountain he passes, with its shining chrome and porcelain fittings. Next Clyde walks by a garage, where youths dressed in white dungarees minister to luxurious automobiles. Finally, he passes the entrance of a picture palace, whose ushers wear "uniforms of white, trimmed with gold, like those of lion tamers" (214). A "Boy Wanted" sign on a nearby door attracts his attention but the store is long closed and Clyde reluctantly returns home.

Back in his room he studies his image in a mirror, comparing it to the newspaper clippings he has collected of sport and show business stars. In imitation of their appearance, he oils and parts his hair and fashions a bow tie, smiling at his smart reflection. At this point his mother knocks at his door, saying that Esta has disappeared. When the family discovers a note announcing that she has run away with a man, Clyde finally speaks, bitterly articulating the discontent that Dreiser's character merely feels: "He says he wishes to work, but he doesn't know how to do anything because he hasn't been taught anything. He says his parents have done nothing for him, not even written to his Uncle Samuel who has a big collar factory and might have taught him to work" (218). As the reel ends, Clyde is again on the fire escape, now alone, watching the lights go out over the city.

Reel two opens with the creeping light of dawn, disclosing Clyde already at the shop with the "Boy Wanted" notice. Told that the job is filled, he sits discouraged on the shop's steps until the proprietor, noting his handsome appearance, directs him to a nearby hotel. There Clyde's looks secure him immediately employment as a bellboy and he is fitted with a uniform. This grooming continues with a montage of hands stropping razors, trimming hair and shining shoes in anticipation of the evening shift at eight, signaled by the pointing hands of the city clock. A friendly colleague explains the work to Clyde in a voice-over illustrated by bellboys opening and closing blinds and then politely standing by the door to await the expected tip. Learning that these can amount to as much as seven dollars a day, "Clyde is speechless with joy" (222). He takes his place in the parade of uniformed boys ready for duty, and imagines that he is guard at Buckingham Palace, where he "will be promoted general at least" (223).

But the true nature of this service is revealed in his first assignment, to buy a pair of pink garters for a female hotel guest on behalf of the gentleman accompanying her. He is tipped twice, first by the hotel shop where he purchases the lingerie, then by the man who sent him on his mission. His astonished elation is signaled by repeated shrieks of "Fifty cents" from "an unknown voice" (227), as an orchestra is heard playing a triumphant march in the hotel, now compared to a mighty cathedral throbbing with voices. Then a fade-out matches the darkening screen to the softening music, replaced by the mission congregation singing hymns. To the sound of "Everybody's happy," Clyde runs into his room, unclenches a fistful of silver coins and smiles into his mirror. In a 1931 issue of the experimental cinema journal *Close Up*, Harry Alan Potamkin salutes Eisenstein's rendering of this sequence, with the collision between "the cathedral anthem" and "the threadbare mission" demonstrating "the proportion of the tip to the humble delights of Clyde" (Potamkin, 1977: 192–3). As Potamkin observes, Eisenstein significantly departs here from Dreiser's narrative, in which Clyde merely feels "as if he could squeal or laugh out loud" (*An American Tragedy*: 56). Instead, the tip's importance is emphasized by externalizing Clyde's reaction and markedly amplifying it. Justifying this change, Eisenstein himself later declared to Dreiser that "the crucial moment was the first tip Clyde gets in the hotel: that is the key to the whole personal tragedy ... The boy, who in other condition [sic] might have been brought up as [a] laboring, working and creative personality" (Eisenstein, undated letter to Theodore Dreiser from Paseo de la Reforma, Mexico [1931], Theodore Dreiser Papers).

In Dreiser's novel the intimate nature of the services by which these carefully selected and costumed youths earn their tips is spelt out. The boys tell tales about the women guests with the means and inclination to pursue them and warn the appalled Clyde about certain men, "morally disarranged and socially taboo" (*An American Tragedy*: 59), who will do the same. In their spare time they become sexual consumers, initiating their fearful colleague into the delights of the local bordello. Aware of the legal pitfalls of such specificity for the novel, as well as the far greater restrictions of the Hays Office, Eisenstein pursued a different strategy in reel three, scripting a series of nearly wordless scenes in quick succession. Both the prospect of censorship and his attempt to exculpate Clyde rule out the bordello, so these vignettes are confined to the hotel. Beginning each time with the sound of the summoning bell, the scenes progress from newly weds kissing, to a married couple's indifferent acknowledgement of their anniversary, to a man and woman quarreling amidst the detritus of a drunken party, to a woman guest suggestively beckoning to a handsome bellboy with bejeweled fingers. Finally three bells summon three boys to a sobbing woman being evicted from her room after her companion has walked out on her—a fate anticipating that of Clyde's sister Esta. When he returns to the mission after a night out with the other boys, his distraught mother informs him that Esta has been abandoned "in a terrible plight" (233) by the man she ran away with. Throughout this sequence, the sparse dialogue provides a minimum of material for the censor's scissors, while enabling the rapid demonstration of the doomed sexual relations of these representative Americans.

After a sequence detailing the accident in which the boys strike a child with a borrowed car and Clyde runs from the scene, reel four opens with him encountering his uncle in Chicago. Incorporating a title into the dramatic action once again, Eisenstein identifies Samuel Griffiths with his company's electric sign—a shining neon collar exuding rays of light above his own illuminated signature. A downward pan reveals Griffiths standing beneath the sign, outside the discreet residential hotel where Clyde is now working. The nephew soon meets his uncle and is offered a chance to "be somebody" (238). At the Griffiths factory, Clyde is directed to his cousin Gilbert, whose resemblance to him confounds both men. The resentful heir brusquely assigns him to the shrinking room, in whose basement precincts Clyde sweats over the boiling kettles. As James Goodwin (1993: 128) points out, the fade to these hellish chambers from the Griffiths mansion admired by the passing Clyde sharply etches the novel's class oppositions, while clearly indicating the labor on which the family's fortunes are founded.

Finally invited to the mansion for dinner, the Griffiths' poor relation is snubbed by Gilbert and bewildered by their silverware. Then Sondra Finchley arrives with Gilbert's sister. Dreiser's Sondra is a smartly dressed flapper in a tailored suit and a little leather hat who leads a toy bull terrier. Eisenstein's resumes the scenario's thematic motif of white glamour in the pose of an art deco figurine: "Her white dress, the orchids on her shoulder, the straining wolfhounds make her appear as a being from another world" (244).

Dreiser's Clyde takes months to describe Sondra as "like an angel almost" (*An American Tragedy*: 336), but Eisenstein's immediately sees her as a saint ascending to the heavens. The light that haloed the Griffiths collar sign now emanates from this young woman, and her body is suffused by whirling white clouds. In this evocation of female desirability, the director could be accused of parodying the cream separator scene from *The Old and the New* whose "ecstatic" rendition he described at the Academy banquet. As the peasants watch the Young Communist Vasia turn the separator's handle with ever-increasing speed, each cut becomes shorter and its tonality alternates between the brightness of intensifying hope and the darkness of increasing suspicion. The churn spins, emitting rays of light refracted by mirror splinters pasted on the revolving disk of its mechanism. Then, at just the right moment, a cut to the separator's spigot reveals a swelling drop at its tip. The peasants stare in enlarging close-ups as the swollen meniscus trembles and then breaks off. A spray of milk hits the empty pail, and the cream bursts through the separator: "By now, through editing, the spurts and spray pierce through the stream of enthusiastic close-ups with a cascade of snow-white streams of milk, a silvery fountain of unchecked spurts, a fireworks display of unceasing splashes" (Eisenstein, 1987: 53). As for Sondra, in Clyde's ecstatic apprehension she too is "like a firework bursting in the darkness ... And her figure is covered in mist, growing thicker every moment, and whirling upwards in its movement. She is hidden in white clouds, and these clouds expand" (244).

But unlike that of the peasant co-operators, Clyde's ecstasy collapses into detumescence. In an ironic matching shot the clouds that surround Sondra become the steam of the shrinking room, where the literally liquefied youth groans in the heat. Seen in this state by his passing uncle, he is transferred to another department to forestall family embarrassment. Again, the description of Clyde's new duties—supervising the women in the collar stamping department—is delivered in voice-over by Gilbert. As he admonishes his cousin to set a moral example by eschewing relationships with the factory's female employees, the scene shifts to "twenty-five pairs of eyes flirtatiously centre[d] on one spot," and the reverse shot reveals Clyde, "elegantly dressed and severe" (247).

Reel five opens in springtime, with pigeons cooing at the factory windows as a roomful of young women workers stamp "mountains of snow-white collars" (247). When one of them shyly approaches Clyde to confess a mistake, he is forced to notice Roberta Alden. The two lonely workers are then shown separately, gazing out of their bedroom windows at the spring moon. Back in the factory they exchange glances, which later become smiles. As the early summer's light plays on the whitewashed walls of the factory, it is synchronized with the rhythmic beating of the machines. Then the noise softens to the sound of singing couples as the light dances on the surface of a lake where Clyde is rowing. At the lakeside he meets and woos Roberta, kissing her amidst the rushes at sunset. The frightened girl reproaches him, but Clyde smiles "as he smiled that day when he earned his first money, and heard that grand music, that majestic—swelling—hymn in the hotel. And the echo of that music rises in the tune of a dance hall distant on the other side of the lake" (253).

Winter arrives with reel six, and Clyde and Roberta are equally chilly in their public encounters. Unable to court openly, the couple shivers in side streets while Clyde urges Roberta to invite him in. When she insists that it wouldn't be right, a tense pause between them is interrupted by the beseeching bark of a small dog. Finally Clyde stalks off as the Eisensteinian analogy is driven home by the dog's wail. The despairing Roberta remains in the street as a door opens and an inquisitive woman shoos the animal away.

When Roberta eventually relents and allows Clyde entry into her dingy lodgings the two embrace passionately to a reprise of "that majestic music that Clyde hears in the happiest moments of his life" (254). And again the heavenly heights of this happiness are represented by a celestial vision, as the apartment's ceiling and walls open to the skies. Promising to never, never abandon his sweetheart, Clyde proudly departs the next day, only to be hailed by a voice from a luxurious automobile. Mistaking him for his cousin Gilbert, Sondra Finchley apologizes and offers Clyde a lift and then an invitation to a local society dance. The two survey each other with admiration until the chauffeur stops at Clyde's street, where the youth stands savoring Sondra's pronunciation of "Mr Griffiths."

Reel seven commences with a repetition of the bellboys' grooming routine, as disembodied hands button a formal waistcoat and knot a black tie. This time, however, the hands are Roberta's, primping Clyde for an evening at the Griffiths. But when Clyde consults his invitation in the street outside, a lamp illuminates an accompanying note from Sondra, inviting him to a dinner dance at another address. There he is ignored by the well-dressed throng, compared in the scenario to the "society dummies" modeling clothes in shop windows. Only when Sondra arrives in a characteristically "dazzling white dress" (264) is Clyde taken up, as she conspires with her friends to spite Gilbert. Suddenly the youth is the object of female attention, with a succession of young women dancing and flirting with him. As the jazz dies away, Roberta is seen in the factory rest room, where gossip is rife about Clyde's appearances in the local paper's society pages. The rueful woman glances at his note in her hand, apologizing for having to dine yet again with his uncle. The scene ends with the dance music resuming, faster and louder in "a poem of the days that follow" (266), a rapidly paced montage of tender glances, gorgeous evening wear, elegant settings and increasingly bright light as Clyde and Sondra dance together.

One such evening ends with a disheveled Clyde calling belatedly on Roberta. Accused of weeks of neglect, he claims family obligations until she tearfully shows him the society pages. When she mentions "Miss Finchley" he angrily seizes her by the shoulders, only to be so moved by her tender expression that he kisses her passionately instead. As he imagines Sondra's embrace, the lights go out in Roberta's room and the gleeful laughter of a little child is heard in the distance. This particular encounter and the child's cry at its end are Eisenstein's additions, with the acoustic effect employed to intimate the disastrous consequence of this vicarious coupling, Roberta's pregnancy. It will be heard in subsequent scenes, as the scenario attempts to avoid the censorable consequences of presenting this difficult subject in dialogue.

A fade-out marks the passage of time as the action shifts to the factory, where the harsh lighting intensifies the anxiety on Roberta's face. Failing to catch Clyde's eye, she tosses him a note insisting that they meet that day. He nods his agreement, but spends the evening at Christmas party with Sondra, dancing reels to the suggestive sound of a children's tune. Afterwards Sondra invites Clyde into the sumptuous precincts of her family's immense kitchen for a nightcap. There, regarding the young woman "as a faithful believer would look at a holy relic" (270), Clyde kisses her while the logs in the hearth shoot a fireworks of sparks. As he walks through the snow to Roberta later, he hums his familiar hymn of happiness. But the mood changes abruptly when the frightened young woman reminds him of his promise to help her in the event of "a misfortune" (271) and lifts her hands to her midriff. Again the scene ends with a child's laughter, now with a pronounced tone of mockery.

In what surely cannot be coincidence, Eisenstein's reflections on filming the cream separator scene in *The Old and the New* move from its description of the ecstasy represented by the spurting white liquid to a "digression" on "moments of intense 'shock'." His example of the latter state is taken from a novel whose adaptation he assigned to his student directors, *Anna Karenina*—namely, the scene in which Anna's lover, Vronsky, learns of her pregnancy. In Eisenstein's account of the scene, the distraught young officer suffers such a shock that his powers of association are undone. He "stares senselessly at the dial of his watch, incapable of connecting the outlined position of the hands with any idea of what time it is" (Eisenstein, 1987: 55–6). This notable vignette is not the director's only meditation on the unwanted consequence of ecstatic experience or the difficulties of its representation within censorious regimes. His essay "Montage and Architecture" returns to the theme of extramarital pregnancy in its commentary on the coats of arms that decorate the plinths of the papal throne in St Peter's.

Designed by Bernini in honor of Pope Urban VIII, these eight heraldic shields display three bees, symbol of the Barberini family to which the pope belonged. Above each shield is the life-sized head of a woman, below it that of a satyr. But these apparently conventional decorations exhibit a number of unusual features. Starting with the left-hand front plinth, the expression on the female face changes from contentment to terror before returning to tranquility at the eighth shield. Moreover, the shields themselves change shape, bulging outwards from the second one and subsiding at the sixth. At their base the lineaments that form the mask of the satyr also undergo a notable transformation across the sequence. The sixth shield offers a key to this mystery, replacing the woman's head with a different, albeit equally traditional figure, the winged head of a child. As scholars have divined, the sequence is a narrative of childbirth, in which the woman's face registers the fear, pain and eventual relief of labor, graphically represented below the swelling belly of the shield by the satyr's outline, which takes on the identifiable shape of the external female genitals.

Eisenstein's contribution to this scholarship is an amused refutation of its sentimental interpretation as an allegory of Holy Mother Church. Instead he cites popular tradition to recall the legend that a nephew of the pope, later to become a cardinal, impregnated a sister of one of Bernini's pupils. When the artist sought papal approval for a marriage to save the situation, the outraged Urban scolded him for presuming that his nephew could possibly marry the sister of a stonemason. But if Urban condoned the sexual transgressions of his own notorious family, he was less lenient with those of others. In 1642 he issued a papal decree banning "all images that are obscene, lascivious and immodest" (Eisenstein, 1991a: 78) from every Christian house—an act of *ex cathedra* censorship wholly in keeping with another in the year after the papal throne was built, the enforced recantation of Galileo for espousing the teachings of Copernicus. The director's commentary on this episode is a lesson in how montage can elude such restrictions, because its meaning only emerges in sequential juxtaposition. In his scenario for *An American Tragedy* the infant heard on the soundtrack is the director's *putto*, another cherubic figure that takes on an increasingly legible significance.

Trying to Escape

Reel eight opens with a proliferation of these infant images in the window of a drug store. Cardboard children advertise milk and sweets, observed by real children peering in from the street. Over its glass doors, an electric sign illuminates the figures of "a naked little boy and his sympathetic father" (Montagu, 1969: 272). Next to it stands Clyde, who turns away when he sees that the store's attendant is female. Entering another drug store he hears the treble of a children's song through its radio loudspeaker. Filmed through the store's window, he makes embarrassed gestures of inquiry as the volume of the voices increases. When the druggist shakes his head, Clyde exits to the sound of laughing children. On the street he passes more children and a record shop playing a child's recitation of love for its parents, the sunshine and the forest. This sound continues over a scene of Clyde in another drug store, again viewed from the street as the proprietor gestures angrily. As the night draws in, illuminated advertisements featuring enormous images of children loom at Clyde from out of the darkness. Taking refuge in an alley, he discovers another, less reputable-looking, drug store, and this time he emerges with a small package.

When this remedy fails to work, Clyde is forced to make more inquiries in a dialogue scene with a salesman at a men's wear shop he frequents. Claiming to ask on behalf of a factory worker "very much worried over the condition of his wife" (276), he and the salesman begin to whisper as Clyde writes down an address. Eisenstein then continues his oblique treatment of this situation by again keeping the spectator outside Roberta's window, from where she's heard saying that she won't go alone. As Clyde attempts to calm her, the cries of a sick child are heard from one of the upper floors of her lodging house. The scene then shifts to inside Roberta's room, where the miserable woman slowly declares that she will let Clyde go and make her own way in the world. But what, she asks, if the doctor is unwilling? For a final time, their conversation is punctuated by the child's cries, "a monotonous, low wail" (278).

The sequence in which Roberta visits the doctor continues this strategy of alternating the spectator's viewpoint from within and without the room in which a dramatic scene takes place. Her initial discussion is filmed inside his consulting room, and then from outside in the street where Clyde nervously paces. When the scene shifts back to the doctor's room, his refusal to undertake "such an operation" (279) on medical, legal and ethical grounds is met with Roberta's anguished declaration that she is unmarried and desperate. At that moment a car passes outside, and the terrified Clyde cowers in the bushes. As Roberta emerges into the street, her expression reveals the doctor's refusal, but Clyde remains in hiding from passing cars and pedestrians. When he finally catches up with the stricken woman, she again offers to let him go, but not immediately: "I can't be alone with a child on my hands, and no husband" (280). A new spring moon rises over the factory as Clyde—in what the scenario describes as both cowardice and genuine pity—nods his agreement.

Reels nine and ten include the episodes most extensively commented upon by Eisenstein, and following him, his critics—those in which Clyde contemplates and then attempts to carry out Roberta's drowning. Again the scenario sharply contrasts poverty and wealth, this time in two rural settings. Reel nine mines the film melodrama's Victorian mise-en-scene by opening, in a shot characteristic of the scenario's general strategy, with Roberta seen through the open window of her family's decaying farm house. A broken-down cart in a filthy yard confirms their destitution. After telling her mother that she's planning to marry, Roberta looks sorrowfully through the window as she writes a letter to Clyde. Its praise of the pastoral beauty around her approximates the contradiction between the written title and the image that Eisenstein had recommended at the Academy banquet, but here the effect is pathetic rather than comic. The letter hopefully asserts that *"you will come for me"* (282) but again the sentiment is contradicted by Roberta's sorrowful expression.

This scene of writing is not in the novel, which includes instead the finished text of a much longer letter from Roberta begging Clyde to arrive by the date he has promised. The details of the impoverished farm are taken from a later episode, when Clyde happens upon it after getting lost with Sondra and her friends on a motor trip. There the description of the Alden farm is rendered in the adjectival phrases of the free indirect style typically used to evoke Clyde's subjective impressions: "For what a house, to be sure! So lonely and bare, even in this bright, spring weather! The decayed and sagging roof. The broken chimney to the north ... The unkempt path from the road below, which slowly he ascended!" (*An American Tragedy*: 463).

To these images Eisenstein adds not only Roberta's presence, but other details that indicate the Victorian text he is invoking, Tennyson's poem "Mariana." Like Roberta, Mariana awaits a deliverer who "cometh not" to rescue her from rural decay:

> The rusted nail fell from the knots
> That held the pear to the gable-wall.
> The broken sheds look'd sad and strange;
> Unlifted was the clinking latch;
> Weeded and worn the ancient thatch
> Upon the lonely moated grange. (Buckley, 1958: 18)

In Mariana's lonely exile, "the blue fly sung in the pane" (Buckley, 1958: 19); in Eisenstein's description of Roberta's, "Along the dirty glass of the window, buzzing, crawl flies trying to escape into freedom" (Montagu, 1969: 282). The misery of her circumstances is intensified by scenic juxtaposition after her mother summons her to the local post office to take a telephone call from Clyde. As Roberta's plaintive appeals break off, a cut discloses her caller emerging in tennis whites from a telephone booth on the verandah of a resort restaurant. Then, at Sondra's invitation, Clyde jumps into her waiting sports car.

The drive with Sondra inaugurates the scenario's second major montage of luxury and romance, this time in "a pictorial symphony that matches with a symphony of music, laughter and the natural sounds" (283). Where its predecessor centered on the winter round of Christmas dances, this sequence unrolls like a holiday brochure illustrated with images of summer sports—swimming, shooting, golf and tennis. The tennis scenes—as in the novel—accentuate the word "love" when the score is called. The sequence ends with Clyde emerging from another automobile ride to seek directions at the Alden farm. The vision of poverty that appalls him there brackets his summer idyll and with it another letter from Roberta, which he opens back in his Lycurgus lodgings. Its last lines threaten to expose him unless he contacts her immediately. As he wearily pulls the letter towards him, he discloses the newspaper lying beneath it, with the headline:

ACCIDENTAL DOUBLE TRAGEDY AT LAKE PASS
UPTURNED CANOE AND FLOATING HATS REVEAL
PROBABLE LOSS OF TWO LIVES. (285)

Here Eisenstein sought a very different method of psychological representation from Dreiser's internal debates or the pseudo-classicism of Eugene O'Neill's stage soliloquies (which would soon receive their cinematic treatment in the 1932 MGM production of *Strange Interlude*, with multiple images of talking heads surrounding that of the silent hero). In his reflections on his scenario Eisenstein asks "What is the syntax of inner language, as distinct from external? What quiverings of inner words accompany the corresponding visual image? What contradicts what?" (Eisenstein, 1988h: 236). The Sirens episode of *Ulysses* offered one example, with its theme of vocal seduction and its opening overture of incoherent words and onomatopoeic expressions: "Bronze by gold heard the hoofirons, steelyringing. Imperthnthn thnthnthn" (Joyce, 1993: 244).

Yet even *Ulysses*, the director argues, is constricted by the limitations of literature, whereas the sound film can offer the combination—synchronized or not—of images and sound; representational and abstract sound effects; syntactic statements combined with a blank screen; sequences of just nouns or just verbs; interjections synchronized with visual figures; visual figures in complete silence; a polyphony of sounds or images or both. And some or all of these could be "interpolated into the external course of action, then interpolating elements of the external action into themselves." To represent Clyde's thoughts, Eisenstein drew up lists of such montaged combinations, arguing that the form was itself "a reconstruction of the laws of the thought process" (Eisenstein, 1988h: 236).

Eisenstein's memoirs only mention the German director F. W. Murnau in passing, as the director of his beloved Yvette Guilbert in *Faust* (1926) and as a friend of Garbo in Hollywood, but the drowning attempt in his *Sunrise* (1927) bears a strong resemblance to that in Dreiser's novel. *Sunrise* is based on Hermann Sudermann's novella *Die Reise nach Tilsit* (*The Excursion to Tilsit*) but it also features a humble protagonist seduced away from a country woman by a beautiful sophisticate. Urged by her to drown his wife, the protagonist invites her to ride with him across the lake. Reaching a remote spot, he rises to carry out his plot. Staring menacingly at his quailing wife, he moves toward her, until her prayer for mercy and the ring of church bells stop him. Eventually at the city the couple is reconciled, falling in love once more. But on the return journey, a storm upsets their boat and the wife is apparently drowned.

A "pre-talkie," Fox's first feature with a recorded score but no synchronous dialogue, *Sunrise* employs a number of experimental devices which may have influenced Eisenstein. Wooed away from his cottage supper to a moonlit tryst with his lover, the protagonist is urged to sell his farm and move with her to the city. When he mentions his wife, she replies "Couldn't she get [the title pauses] drowned?" (In an innovation that may have influenced Sternberg's adaptation, the title's letters begins to soften and sink downward, dissolving into a shot of the husband throwing his wife overboard.) "Then overturn the boat," the temptress continues. "It will look like an accident." As she urges him to "Leave all this behind ... Come to the City," the lakeside rushes dissolve to the neon lights of an urban thoroughfare, huge boulevards, spotlit skyscrapers. A jazz band is super-imposed over a dance floor, and then over the ecstatically dancing figure of his lover. Returning home later the man lies in bed, his eyes wide in thought as the lake waters slowly dissolve over him until he is covered by their misty depths at dawn. On waking a series of superimposed images of his lover embracing him returns the scene to his fantasies, and he invites his wife to a journey across the lake. As she hurries to pack, the man presses his fists to his temples, his thoughts again revealed by a dissolve to him heaving his wife to her death.

Patrick Kearney's little-regarded stage play is also not cited by Eisenstein, but it too seems to offer him a precedent for the temptation scene. In the play Clyde's landlady brings him the newspaper and mentions the accident. Later, after Roberta telephones her threat to tell his uncle about their relationship, he returns to the paper, reading it by the sole lamp in his darkened room. Then he leans back and closes his eyes, whereupon a mask appears out of the darkness and a voice speaks: "What if ... Roberta and you ... were in a canoe ... and had an accident like that ... Roberta cannot swim."

Clyde then argues with the masked voice as though it were speaking from inside him, exclaiming "why am I thinking this way?" As the plot takes form, Kearney has him rise "as though thrown into action by the horror and compulsion of the thought," strike his head and fall onto his bed sobbing. After a moment he leans on his elbow, "his face in the light now frenzied, almost insane." As the voice continues to advocate "the way of the lake" (Act III, Scene 1, Kearney, 1926) the scene is interrupted by the landlady's knock at the door.

Eisenstein's scene starts like Kearney's, with Clyde sitting wearily in the dark until he hears a whisper, "And what if Roberta and you—" Then, in the dark corner of his room, he imagines he sees an upturned boat. Jumping up, he turns on the light and rereads the article, until the whispered voice rises to insist "KILL! KILL!" As Clyde becomes increasingly distracted, the scene departs from cinematic illusionism altogether, "distorting the real union between things and sounds" (Montagu, 1969: 286).[11] Before a series of back projections of the street, the lake, the factory machines, Roberta's farm and Sondra's summer residence, he moves without logic or synchronization, dashing about and falling to the ground. The soundtrack is seized with a similar incoherence, segueing from city noises to the whistling of the wind to the roar of the factory, and finally to the low whisper of "Kill! Kill!" as an unemotional voiceover reads: *"Fifteen years ago a similar accident occurred, but the body of the man was never found."* Then, just as suddenly, "Clyde jumps out of his nightmare" (286–7) and runs to a telephone booth, where trembling he rings Roberta and arranges their wedding journey.

Although it has apparent debts to the temptation scenes written by Dreiser and Kearney, as well as Murnau's use of superimpositions, Eisenstein's scenario more thoroughly objectifies Clyde's distraction, representing his hallucinatory perceptions as visual and aural realities, without the reasoned debate in Dreiser's and Kearney's versions. His version could be said to exculpate Clyde further, as the victim of a psychotic breakdown caused by the overwhelming conflicts of the circumstances projected behind him—conflicts that are vividly presented to the spectator. Posing Clyde against these back projections is an attempt to realize the combinatory effect of montage within a single frame that Eisenstein sought in *The Glass House*. As he had argued about the Japanese combination of two ideographic characters into a third, different concept, "The degree of incongruity determines the intensity of the impression" (Eisenstein, 1988f: 165). The spatial depth of the scene, with Clyde in the foreground and the various projected settings in the background, suggests both psychological interiority (the rushing succession of images in his mind) and social exteriority (the circumstances that have lead to this terrible temptation), a stereoscopy of subject and object with which Eisenstein sought to create the third dimension of his dialectical montage.

Warring Voices

Reel ten begins at the railway station where, pretending to be strangers, Roberta and Clyde arrive separately and enter different carriages. Each surreptitiously watches the other, Roberta with pride and admiration, Clyde with shame and dislike. The novel intermittently resorts to a stream of consciousness narration to represent his anxious impressions of the journey in a series of imagist parentheses:

(Those five birds winging toward that patch of trees over there—below that hill.) *(An American Tragedy:* 514)

(The long, sad sounding whistle of this train. Damn. He was getting nervous already.) *(An American Tragedy:* 516)

Roberta's thoughts meanwhile—hoping that Clyde still cares "for her a little—just a little" *(An American Tragedy:* 517)—are conventionally described. Eisenstein, however, employs audio-visual montage in this scene to very different effect. As the wheels of the train take up their characteristic rhythm, Roberta hears the strains of the wedding march and smiles in the sun. But Clyde sits in a dark corner, listening to "the rhythm of death," that of the wheels repeating "Kill—Kill—" (Montagu, 1969: 289). The sounds intensify until the train's whistle signals their arrival at a town near the lake. As Keith Cohen (1977: 243) has persuasively argued, this acoustical conflict prepares the spectator for Eisenstein's alterations to the scene that follows, in which the two warring voice "remain equally powerful right up to the end."

Later, as Clyde rows across the lake, the two voices return, one urging him to kill Roberta in pursuit of "Sondra and society," the other opposing this out of "weakness and his fears ... his sadness for Roberta and his shame" (293). Each voice dominates in turn, resounding while they picnic and he photographs his increasingly cheerful companion. As Clyde's face registers this conflict, it is given expression by the long call of a water bird. The internal argument reaches a crescendo, with his mother's remembered "Baby—Baby" heard in counterpoint to Sondra's seductive "Baby boy" (294). The thought of Sondra powerfully intensifies the command to kill but it is ultimately overwhelmed by the sight of Roberta, her face glowing with hope. As "Don't Kill" audibly wins out, Clyde realizes that Sondra is lost to him and breaks down in despair. Eyes closed, he sits immobile until Roberta anxiously crawls forward to take his hand, still clutching the camera. His revulsed withdrawal brings it across her face, cutting her lip and knocking her against the stern. As he moves towards her in apology, the frightened woman tries to rise, loses her balance and the boat overturns. The bird's cry sounds a second time as first Roberta rises to the surface and then Clyde, his face distorted by fear. Misunderstanding his move to help her, she thrashes in terror and goes under again. Clyde prepares to dive after her but then hesitates as she fails to surface. A third cry from the bird marks the passage of time, with a wide shot revealing the calm surface of the lake and Clyde swimming to shore. At the water's edge he trembles and shrinks into himself, as the scenario has shown him doing when bullied in childhood. Then the voice returns, declaring Roberta's death an accident granting him life, liberty and Sondra.

Reel ten ends with Clyde changing into the dry suit left onshore in his valise and hurrying away from the lake in the darkness. Reel eleven opens in the sunlight as Clyde, dressed once again in white, sits with Sondra on the deck of a motorboat. Imagining that his gloom is money worries, she tries to cheer him with an offer of cash. Around the oblivious couple, Sondra's friends swim and race their boats, until one alarms Clyde by reading out a newspaper story of a couple drowning in Big Bittern. That night at their campsite, Sondra promises Clyde that she will marry him, and the two embrace passionately for what he fears will be the last time. After seeing Sondra to her tent, he walks exhausted into the trees and falls asleep. There—in another sentimentalization of the novel, in which Clyde is apprehended trying to escape the police—this babe in the wood is awakened and arrested by the deputy sheriff.

In shortening Dreiser's immense book, Eisenstein chose to omit much of Clyde's lengthy trial, concentrating instead on the party politics that structure its conduct and outcome. The District Attorney is running for judge, and he needs the support of the Aldens' farming community. To oppose him Samuel Griffiths is advised to appoint two local lawyers of the rival party but not, as Eisenstein observes, of a different class: "For one side, as for the other, Clyde is merely a means" (Eisenstein, 1988h: 232). Sondra's father is otherwise occupied, pulling strings to keep his family's name out of the proceedings. A bravura Eisenstein invention in reel twelve shows him dialing the telephone at night. Elsewhere in the dark a ring is heard and a lamp turned on. Then a succession of telephones ring and lights go on as his request is passed across the city, with each house becoming larger and more luxurious. The final house is revealed to be the grandest and from it the promise of anonymity is issued.

Throughout the preparations for Clyde's trial Eisenstein intensifies Dreiser's demonstration of how both the prosecution and the defense falsify the evidence and his testimony. When the post-mortem examination reveals that the cuts on Roberta's face could not have been fatal, a detective remains behind for a scene of fetishistic menace. Pulling the sheet from the dead woman's face in apparent admiration of her beauty, he fingers one of her curls. Then he severs it with a knife and tucks it away, to later attach it to Clyde's camera, recovered from the lake. Leaving the morgue the detective symbolically extinguishes the light. Later Clyde's lawyers try to delay the trial until after the elections by exhuming the victim in an ostensible search for additional evidence. (In the novel there is a genuine forensic purpose for this exercise—in Eisenstein's scenario it is pure prevarication.) The exhumation scene itself is another of Eisenstein's inventions, one of the few for which his production sketches still exist (see Figure 2.1). Its echoes of a scene in *Hamlet* are underlined by two references to the play in his notations. Shakespeare's tragedy, with its vacillating hero and his drowned lover, offers many precedents for Dreiser's, and Eisenstein seizes on the scene in which Ophelia is brought to the churchyard for burial. This, however, is not the only

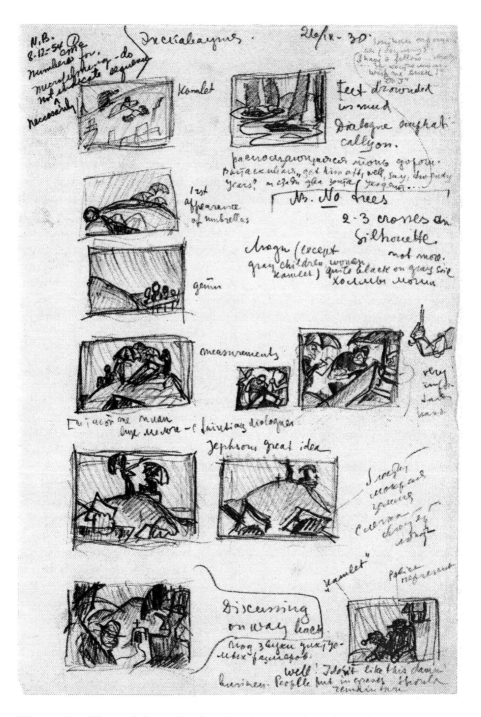

Figure 2.1 Eisenstein's production sketches for the exhumation scene of *An American Tragedy*, 1930. © Photo SCALA, Florence. The Museum of Modern Art, New York, 2007.

parallel his scenario invokes. For in it he stages a conversation between Clyde's lawyers that takes place elsewhere in the novel, the one in which they concoct the story he offers in his defense.

Conspiring under umbrellas as Roberta's grave is uncovered in the rain, one tells the other that their safest course is to claim that Clyde had never contemplated murder but had merely taken her to the lake to persuade her to give him up. There, however, he became moved by her plight, and eventually offered to marry if she still wished it. In her elation, Roberta rose and accidentally upset the boat. As Eisenstein later wrote, "it is with this outright lie, that is so near the truth and at the same time so far from it, that they try in this false fashion to whitewash the accused and save him" (Eisenstein, 1988h: 233). The apposite lines from *Hamlet* are those in which the hero contemplates a skull thrown up by the gravediggers: "There's another. Why might not that be the skull of a lawyer? Where be his quiddits now, his quillets, his cases, his tenures, and his tricks?" (Act V, Scene 1, 106–8).

The irony of Shakespeare's scene is that the legal brain whose contrivances once enabled the acquisition of land titles has itself become dust, "his fine pate full of fine dirt" (116). The irony in Eisenstein's scenario is that the same contrivances will provoke the jury to condemn Clyde. In his destruction by the "machine of bourgeois justice," the director argues, the fate of a single individual "is tragically expanded and generalized into a real general 'American tragedy,' a typical story of a young American at the beginning of the 20th century" (Eisenstein, 1988h: 232).

But if Clyde is the victim of the American legal system, the scenario also represents him as a victim of its press. The newspapers heaping scandal on the Griffiths name are literally heaped on chairs and carpets in the family mansion, and the District Attorney intensifies this notoriety, and his own fame, by reading Roberta's letters aloud to reporters. A cut replaces his office with the Alden farm, where the same reporters interview and photograph her mother. Another cut discloses Clyde's mother, singing with her congregation while photographers approach. As she lifts her hands heavenward, she is caught in their magnesium flares and reporters surround her. Defending her son, she describes his religious upbringing and unwisely shows them a photograph of the family preaching on the streets. The next scene reveals a printing press emitting thousands of copies of this image on the pages of newspapers. Reel thirteen opens with the sound of newsboys hawking these papers and a pamphlet of Roberta's letters to the crowd outside the courthouse as Clyde's trial begins.

Determined not to make a courtroom drama, Eisenstein contracts the novel's 100-page trial into a single reel. As the case against Clyde is presented by the District Attorney, the latter's image yields to his voice over a series of brief illustrative scenes, each preceded by the witness describing it. In rapid sequence the druggists, the doctor, the bus conductor and the proprietor of the lake hotel are pictured prior to the moment they recall. These flashbacks are not literal repetitions of the action hitherto, but re-presentations of it in what the scenario describes as "a different lighting, a different composition" and "In the movements and in the actions ... a different Clyde" (Montagu, 1969: 322). Then, to the objections of the defense, the prosecutor begins to read aloud Roberta's pathetic letters to Clyde. When the defense accuses him of courting electoral support, the Judge narrowly averts a brawl before permitting him to continue. By the time the District Attorney finishes reading the sun has set and Roberta's mother has collapsed under the strain. As the prosecution rests the screen goes dark.

A fade in reveals snow falling outside the courtroom, and a ghostly light within it. The pale defendant takes the witness stand and eventually describes how his love for Roberta waned in favor of the beautiful "Miss X." When he agrees that he was bewitched by her charms, the young women in the gallery sigh in romantic fascination. At his attorney's prompting Clyde stammers out his defense—that at the lake he was moved by pity to forgo his love and marry Roberta. A further snowfall ices over the courtroom windows in an effective fade to white. Then he is disclosed swearing before God that he never struck Roberta Alden or threw her in the lake. Asked by his lawyer if her drowning was "unpremeditated and undesigned" (326), he dishonestly agrees. But cross-examined by the District Attorney, he quails at his accusations of deceit and loses the support of the watching gallery. Over his shrinking figure a voice is heard, praying that the Lord help her son. The scene changes to the mission, where Clyde's mother kneels proclaiming the power of faith.

That power is abruptly disproved as the District Attorney concludes his case. Although the boat is not brought into the courtroom, the crowd roars at the revelation of Clyde's failure to ask its hire charge and the evidence of the hair planted in his camera. To cries of "Hang him" the jury retires. While they deliberate their verdict, the judge, the prosecution and the defense also retire—to the same local restaurant, a succinct summation of their shared class interests. In the jury room the sole member who persists in voting not guilty is discovered to be a friend of one of Clyde's lawyers. Threatened with a boycott of his hardware store, he nervously reverses his decision. When the jurymen somberly emerge to pronounce their verdict, the voices in the courtroom become faint and those outside louder. As the hurrahs of the crowd ring out, Clyde dictates a telegram: "Mother, I have been found guilty. Come. Clyde" (333).

The film's final reel begins in darkness as Clyde's mother descends from a train at night. For Eisenstein, who later wrote of the horrors of the gigantic railway yards at Smolensk during the civil war and after, when he was billeted in a sidetracked boxcar, the image of the night train had a haunting significance:

> How many times during my hours of wandering along the tracks have the night monsters of trains sneaked up on me so treacherously, alongside me, scarcely clanking, out of the darkness and back into the darkness! ... This image of a night train has wandered from film to film, becoming a symbol of fate. In *An American Tragedy*, this image is first the inertia of crime, then the course of the soulless automation of justice and law ... (Eisenstein, 1983: 198)

Down an unlit street Mrs Griffiths walks to the prison. Then the screen goes completely black until a cell is disclosed where she sits holding her son's head in hands that the scenario describes as "huge." As Clyde sobbingly protests that he didn't do it, the scene fades to black. The next begins with a locomotive driving forward into the camera, with its wheels beating out "Death—death—death" (Montagu, 1969: 334). Inside the train Clyde is handcuffed to a guard. Stopping at a station, the train is met by a crowd of young people who bring flowers and photograph the prisoner—now the romantic hero of a tabloid tragedy.

Told by his lawyers that the Griffiths will not fund an appeal, Clyde's mother resolves to raise money in a public campaign but is refused church premises by several denominations. As her son languishes on death row, a banner advertising "A Mother's Appeal for her Son" is erected over images of the scantily clad performers at a burlesque house. In Dreiser's novel, Mrs Griffiths is given a platform by "a Jew who controlled the principal moving picture theatre of Utica—a sinful theatre" (*An American Tragedy*: 823)—words underlined by Eisenstein in his copy of the novel. But unlike the novel, with its copious references to the cinema, Eisenstein's scenario includes only one, the picture palace whose white-uniformed ushers dazzle the young Clyde in Reel 1. Mindful of the social anxieties about the film industry that were fuelling the growing forces of censorship at the time, and the anti-Semitism often linked to them, Eisenstein tactfully eliminates its role in the tragedy. In particular, his scenario foregoes the irony of this evangelical Christian's resort to a place of sinful entertainment run by a Jew (difficult to represent without invoking the stereotypes then being directed at Eisenstein and his employers) in favor of the broader irony of a puritanical woman performing on the stage of a strip show. The venue selected offers a further opportunity to criticize the sexual hypocrisy that contributes to this tragedy when the burlesque performers in "their sparkles and feathers" (Montagu, 1969: 337) prove highly susceptible to this ample woman's maternal sincerity. Weeping at they watch from backstage, they emerge to offer her money.

The scene shifts to Clyde's cell, where he is roused from his cot by the delivery of a letter. Like that in the novel it is brief and typewritten, but the scenario clarifies its origins by showing it signed "Sondra." Where its unsigned predecessor cruelly signals the end of Clyde's hopes, fainting with the last "remaining gleam of dusk in the west" (*An American Tragedy*: 848), the letter in the scenario represents the sole light in his imprisonment. In a moment that will have a significant influence on Stevens' adaptation of the story, Clyde looks out at the sun after reading it and declares "To live—how good it is" (Montagu, 1969: 338). When his mother appears to comfort him with the news of her appointment with the Governor, he becomes a child once more, laying his head in her capacious lap. As she promises that the Lord will deliver her innocent boy, he confides that although he didn't kill Roberta, he "'did—think of it, mummy' ... And the mother's caress slows, her fingers have become stiff and her face set" (338). Challenged by the Governor to proclaim Clyde's innocence, she hesitates and delivers him to his death.

The execution scene begins in darkness with the sound of an iron shutter opening on the window of the death cell where, just as Eisenstein had seen in Sing Sing, a "clean brass cuspidor" sits next to the leather-strapped chair. In the condemned cell Clyde and his mother sing psalms together until he breaks off to plead "I want to live!" (340)—a refrain that echoes across the sunlit courtyard of the prison. A subsequent shot through the cell window reveals Mrs Griffiths singing alone. Then the light and the sounds of this spring day are blotted out in a final montage that represents Clyde's discovery of the "soulless automation" of the prison system. In the novel's description, "It was iron. It moved automatically like a machine without the aid or the hearts of men" (*An American Tragedy*: 866). In Eisenstein's scenario the bars and gates and shutters of this ruthless machine slide across the screen, effectively wiping it to "blackness and quiet." And then "A sharp crackle and the sharp light of an electric contact— and again quiet—again blackness" (341).

The last scene of the scenario parallels the coda of the novel, which returns to an urban setting and repeats its opening sentence, "Dusk, of a summer night." Eisenstein's coda also opens with a city scene in gray, so uncharacteristic of the scenario's pronounced blacks and whites. But this is revealed to be not dusk but smoke, a chilling reminder of the effect of electrocution on human flesh. As the camera descends from the city's chimneys to the streets, it approaches a small group singing to the accompaniment of a harmonium. Clyde's sister is now a sickly adult, his father is frail and his mother's hair has gone white. With the group is Esta's seven-year-old son, the same age as Clyde when the scenario opened. Together they sing "Everybody's Happy" as the scene fades out.

Interpretation and Indeterminacy

The scenario of *An American Tragedy* was submitted in early October with a letter acknowledging its two-reel overrun of the length commissioned. A promise to reduce it was offered, pending "the benefit of notes and advice from":

1. The West Coast Magnates.
2. The East Coast Magnates.
3. Theodore Dreiser.
4. The Hays Organization. (Seton, 1952: 183)

Despite the defiant tone of this missive, Paramount's first reaction to the scenario was extremely enthusiastic. Schulberg pronounced it the best the studio had ever received and Lasky urged the group to follow him on his imminent trip to the studio's East Coast headquarters in order to inspect the New York State settings of the novel. But en route Eisenstein wrote his mother that, although the scenario had been much praised, there remained "many questions in connection with the 'propaganda' theme, particularly now when even my name, as always, is being knocked about by the committee of Fish" (Seton, 1952: 184).

The head of an early precursor to the House of Representatives' Committee on UnAmerican Activities, the New York congressman Hamilton Fish was one of several legislators who had received a telegram from Major Pease demanding Eisenstein's deportation. On October 8 and 9, his congressional committee held hearings in Los Angeles on Communist subversion, with the support of the arch-conservative Better America Federation, the Los Angeles police and the Hays Office. As friendly witnesses testified to the predominantly Russian Jewish origins of American Communists, the Hays Office offered to compel Eisenstein to appear before the Committee. The hearings were adjourned before the Office could test its mettle, but its West Coast representative Fred W. Beetson promised its members that "We have all the machinery necessary to suppress Communistic propaganda in *An American Tragedy*" (Seton, 1952: 185). By October 13, the *Los Angeles Times* columnist Harry Carr was complaining that "Paramount might have found other directors without bringing over from Russia one who had made propaganda pictures for the Russian government. Some of them sound like a revolutionary war whoop" (Carr, 1930: A1).

Meanwhile the young executive who had so praised *Potemkin* when he worked at MGM sent a memo to his Paramount boss Schulberg inquiring if it was too late to stop Eisenstein's film. The scenario, he argued, was far too effective, "positively torturing ... [L]et's not put more money than we have into any one picture for years into a subject that will appeal to our vanity through the critical acclaim that must necessarily attach to its production, but that cannot possibly offer anything but a most miserable two hours to millions of happy-minded young Americans ... David O. Selznick" (October 8, 1930; Behlmer, 1972, 26–7). A Selznick memo of a month later complaining to Schulberg that their Friday Executive Meetings were casually agreeing to options worth hundreds of thousands of dollars indicates the financial recklessness that worried him. By 1930, the studio's write-offs amounted to $390,000, almost eight times the 1927 figure (Schatz, 1996: 78). It was a year of record profits but these could not withstand the devastating effects of the Depression for long.[12] Eisenstein himself later attacked the Hollywood "debauchery of unaccounted volume, large staffs and useless expenditures" to which his group's small payment of $30,000 had contributed. And yet, as he sadly observed, "this squalor of ideas, thought and thriftlessness is served by the world's most perfect technical apparatus" (Eisenstein, 1933: 104–5). The advanced sound registering systems and perfected microphones he longed for were not to be employed by his group. When they arrived in New York, Lasky showed them a pile of letters denouncing Paramount for treason and regretfully terminated their agreement.

Although Lasky always maintained that Paramount's decision was forced by these complaints, Montagu wrote in the 1960s that it was more likely prompted by a combination of this red-baiting, Hollywood's mistrust of foreigners and intellectuals, the group's inexperience and factionalism within the studio. Looking back at the affair, Eisenstein characterized the mogul and his allies as "the old romantic pioneers of the movie industry," forced out (as early as 1931 in Lasky's case) by "the dry bureaucrats—creatures of Wall Street without initiative, avoiding anything that is not absolutely certain beforehand of bringing in sure returns" (Eisenstein, 1933: 102). But despite his acknowledgement of these factors, Eisenstein still believed that the crucial issue in adapting *An American Tragedy* was the question of Clyde Griffiths' culpability. This he knew was no small matter to the Paramount bosses, convinced that a guilty hero would be shunned at the box office. But if he were not guilty the problems would be even greater for the studio, caught in the double bind that had stymied the novel's filming for years.

In March 1930 the Production Code drafted by the Hays Office was formally promulgated by the Motion Picture Producers and Distributors of America. Among its strictures was a clause stipulating that "The courts of the land should not be presented as unjust" (The Motion Picture Production Code of 1930, www.artsreformation.com/a001/hays-code.html, p. 8). Writing on the largely unregarded history of the trial movie, Carol Clover argues that the judgment of Hollywood's citizen juries in this period was effectively aligned with that of its citizen audiences, making such injustice impossible. In the famous observation of *Cahiers du Cinema's* editors on *Young Mr Lincoln* (John Ford, 1939), it is "America itself which constitutes the Jury, and who cannot be wrong, so that the truth cannot fail to manifest itself by the end of the proceedings" (*Cahiers du Cinema*, 1970, cited in Clover, 2000: 257). Yet in Dreiser's novel the jury is manifestly harsh, rushing to its unanimous verdict of first-degree murder via the intimidation of the sole hold-out typical of such narratives. Eisenstein's scenario intensifies this injustice by making the jury literally wrong: Clyde is seen trying to rescue Roberta. Whatever his initial intentions, he commits neither murder nor manslaughter. Like the drowned Roberta, he is presented in Eisenstein's adaptation as the traduced victim of a melodrama rather than the erring hero of a tragedy. Although the Production Code permitted the representation of a single (presumptively anomalous) trial's injustice, the generalizing force of both the novel and the scenario, not least in its nationalizing title, extends this to "the court system of the country." Thus, when the group emphatically declared Clyde innocent to Schulberg, he warned them that this would present "a monstrous challenge to American society" (Eisenstein, 1988h: 228).

In his argument for the subversive power of Eisenstein's adaptation, Keith Cohen maintains that it goes even further, transforming Clyde's ambition from a constitutional trait to an ideological construction. Where Dreiser nationalizes Clyde's already existing aspirations by situating them within the American Dream, Eisenstein attributes them to "a system based on cutthroat competition and the maximization of profits" (Cohen, 1977: 250). Capitalism is found guilty of murder. By contrast, Lawrence Hussman suggests that Eisenstein's own description of his scenario undermines this verdict. Despite the director's assertion of Clyde's innocence, he repeatedly uses the term "murder" when describing his actions, three times in the following sentence: "We shall only touch upon the central point of the external plot aspect of the tragedy—the *murder* itself, although the tragedy lies, of course, not in the *murder*, but in the tragic path pursued by Clyde who is driven by the social system to *murder*" (Eisenstein, 1988h: 229; emphasis added.)

If murder will out even in Eisenstein's adaptation, it may be because Dreiser's "epic of cosmic truth and objectivity" effectively thwarts being "screwed together" (Eisenstein, 1988h: 228) into a melodrama of wounded innocence. Hussman attributes this to the novelist's own engagement with the ambiguities of the Gillette-Brown case, which, he argues, overwhelmed the determinist convictions with which Dreiser approached it. But Cohen's own discussion of the novel's prose style, its intermittent shifts from a causative subject-verb-object syntax to the fragmented use of participial and prepositional phrases, suggests a further explanation. These asyntactical passages not only serve to heighten narrative tension and to represent mental processes, they also give reign to an indeterminacy that both incites and resists interpretation. Eisenstein's collected writings cite the psychologist Williams James rather than his brother Henry, but he was familiar enough with the American novelist's predecessor Edgar Allan Poe to commend his observation that "in fictitious literature, we should aim so as to arrange the incidents that we shall not be able to determine of any one of them whether it depends on any other or upholds it" (Eisenstein, 1991b: 207). Had he read James' ghost story *The Turn of the Screw*, with its preface confessing the writer's design "to catch those not easily caught" with its "tone of tragic, yet of exquisite, mystification" (James, 1986: 38–9), he might have questioned his own ability to exonerate the accused in a case whose unresolved causation is one of its most compelling features.

One final illustration of this irresolution is arguably provided in Eisenstein's discussion of the montage lists he drew up to represent Clyde's train of thought. Far from suggesting a rigidly determinist materialism, these lists—with their synchronized and non-synchronized sound and "sound images," their fragments of speech and "zigzags of aimless figures" (Eisenstein, 1988h: 235)—are recommended by the director to his students as a "practical embodiment of the unforeseen particular concrete instance of expressiveness" (Eisenstein, 1988h: 236). Writing in *History: The Last Things Before the Last*, Siegfried Kracauer seizes on these sketches as powerful representations of the unforeseen contingency of human experience, the indeterminate multiplicity he seeks to retain in historical narrative:

> Eisenstein's objective in preparing these lists was quite obviously to sensitize the audience to the infinity of factors involved in Clyde's ultimate decision. But in suggesting (and thus aesthetically presenting) infinity, the sequence demonstrates something very important ... There are actions and emergent situations which so

stubbornly resist a breakdown into repeatable elements or a satisfactory explanation from preceding or simultaneous circumstances that they had better be treated as irreducible entities. (Kracauer, 1995: 29)[13]

That Eisenstein's Marxist rewriting of Dreiser's determinist novel can support Kracauer's particularist historiography is not the final irony in this sequence of adaptations. If the stark blacks and whites of his scenario contrast with his own ambiguous discussion of its strategies, both they, and that ambiguity, will persist in Hollywood's American tragedies.

Notes

1. See Nowell-Smith, G. (1991), "Eisenstein on Montage," in M. Glenny and R. Taylor (eds), *S. M. Eisenstein, Selected Works, Volume II, Toward a Theory of Montage*, London: British Film Institute, p. xiv.
2. See Goodwin, J. (2001), "Eisenstein: Lessons with Hollywood," in A. la Valley and B. Scherr (eds), *Eisenstein at 100: A Reconsideration*, New Brunswick NJ: Rutgers University Press, p. 94.
3. In Hollywood, Samuel Goldwyn, an admirer of *The Battleship Potemkin*, would delight Montagu and Eisenstein by asking the director "to do something of the same kind, but rather cheaper, for Ronald Colman." See Montagu, I. (1969), *With Eisenstein in Hollywood*, New York: International Publishers, p. 122.
4. Later still, Warner Brothers would briefly consider filming the book, and in 1935 Joyce would pronounce Charles Laughton "too Aryan" for Bloom and suggest George Arliss, who had played Disraeli. See Ellmann, R. (1982), *James Joyce*, New York: Oxford University Press, p. 654.
5. See Bulgakowa, O. (2001), "The Evolving Eisenstein," in A. la Valley and B. P. Scherr (eds), New Brunswick NJ: Rutgers University Press, p. 43 and, for Eisenstein's own comments on synecdoche, see Eisenstein, S. (1996), "Speeches to the All-Union Creative Conference of Soviet Filmworkers," R. Taylor (ed.), *S.M. Eisenstein: Selected Works, Volume III, Writings 1934–1947*, London: British Film Institute, pp. 30–1.
6. See Goodwin, J. (1993), *Eisenstein, Cinema and History*, Urbana: University of Illinois Press, p. 205: "Certainly after *Old and New* he was far more willing to center films on exemplary individuals. John Sutter, Clyde Griffiths, Dessalines, Stepok in *Bezhin Meadow*, and Maxim in *MMM* all typify social forces of their epoch."
7. See J. Leyda and Z. Voynow (1982), *Eisenstein at Work*, New York: Pantheons Books, Museum of Modern Art, pp. 43–5; and Goodwin, J. (1993), *Eisenstein, Cinema and History*, Urbana: University of Illinois Press, pp. 122–3.
8. As Jonathan Rosenbaum has stated in a review of Rick Schmidlin's 1999 video reconstruction of the film for Turner Classic Movies, *Greed* "has to be

the most negative depiction of what money can do to people that exists in movies," yet it has been largely neglected by Marxist critics. See "Fables of the Reconstruction," www.chicagoreader.com/movies/archives/1999/1199/991126.htm.

9. See Felman, S. (1977), "Turning the Screw of Interpretation," *Yale French Studies*, number 55–56, pp. 94–207. Note, however, that Jay Leyda's translation of "screw together" is the more mundane "assembled" in Eisenstein, S. (1997), *Film Form*, New York: Harvest, p. 96.

10. See R. Taylor (2002), *October*, London: British Film Institute: 62–3.

11. Although neither Eisenstein nor Montagu mention it, there is a precedent for this use of sound in Hitchcock's *Blackmail* (1929), to which Montagu (1969: 108)—who edited Hitchcock's 1926 *The Lodger*—briefly alludes. In it a young woman, having stabbed a man who attempted to rape her, comes to the family table the next day. As a customer discusses the murder in the shop next door, the word "knife" is repeated louder and louder until, when the distraught girl's father asks for the breadknife, she nearly throws it at him.

12. As Montagu pointed out to Dreiser in a letter the following year, the group were told that the "suddenly accelerated economic depression of America made it impossible to produce the story on the million dollar scale contemplated in the scenario according to our original instructions" (Ivor Montagu to Theodore Dreiser, 10 August 1931, Dreiser Papers).

13. Kracauer (1995: 59) argues that the camera itself has an "affinity for the indeterminate," surrounding its ostensible subjects with "a fringe of indistinct multiple meanings."

CHAPTER 3

A Courtroom Drama

What richness of images, which never become their own goal; what richness of exquisite faces, which represent an American world ... and yet the criticism is razor-sharp, the rejection of a world is accomplished through representation alone.

Herbert Ihering, "An American Tragedy"

In November 1930, Josef von Sternberg finished shooting *Dishonored* (1931) with Marlene Dietrich. The star then departed to Germany for the Christmas holidays and the European release of *Morocco* (1930). The five-month interval before her return at the end of April created a gap in the director's schedule that Paramount chief Adolph Zukor seized upon. "He told me," Sternberg recalled in his autobiography, "that the company had a dormant investment of half a million dollars in *An American Tragedy*, and pleaded with me to undertake to salvage this by making an inexpensive version of it" (Sternberg, 1966: 46). Zukor was exaggerating. As we have seen, Dreiser and Liveright had been paid $90,000 for the rights to his novel and Eisenstein's group had received $30,000 in total for their six months development work. Paramount's entire write-off for unused screenplays in 1930, although considerable, totaled only $390,000. But *An American Tragedy* was a wasting asset five years after its publication, even if the Boston obscenity trial had renewed its notoriety. At David Selznick's suggestion Samuel Hoffenstein, a former drama critic and an acquaintance of Dreiser, was commissioned in December to write a screen adaptation for Sternberg to direct.

Paramount's investment increased on January 2 when, after several months of bargaining, Dreiser sold the sound production rights to his novel for an additional $55,000. Advised by the Dramatists Guild that the studio had only purchased the rights to a silent version in 1926, the writer argued that he had made every attempt to facilitate production. He blamed Paramount's delay on the pressure applied by religious organizations to the Motion Picture Producers and Distributors of America. The highly restrictive Production Code adopted by the MPPDA in 1930 had been co-written by the Reverend Daniel A. Lord, a Jesuit priest, and as Richard Lingeman (1990: 322) points out, Dreiser had been outspoken in his criticism of the Catholic contribution to American censorship.[1]

The Association had been pressed to oppose the filming of Dreiser's novel, increasingly since Eisenstein's involvement had become known. Before his treatment was even completed, Alice Ames Winter, its conduit to conservative women's organizations such as the Daughters of the American Revolution, had warned Jason Joy, head of its Studio Relations Committee: "The book is as Arbuckle was[—]a symbol of everything objectionable" (Jason Joy, resume of conversation with Alice Ames Winter, February 6, 1931, An American Tragedy file, Production Code Administration Archive, Margaret Herrick Library, Academy of Motion Picture Arts and Sciences, Los Angeles—hereafter AAT file, PCA Archive). To assuage Dreiser's anxieties, Paramount offered a contractual undertaking that it would "use its best endeavors to accept such advice, suggestions and criticism that the Seller may make in so far as it may, in the judgment of the Purchaser, consistently do so" (Swanberg, 1965: 369).

Whether Hoffenstein wrote the script of *An American Tragedy* with Sternberg or simply carried out his instructions is not clear but the first draft was signed by both and submitted on January 30. (The director later described the film as "written with the help of Samuel Hoffenstein" (Sternberg, 1966: 258) but it was credited exclusively to the writer.) This "Yellow Script" is not available to consult but the subsequent "First White Script" of February 12 reveals that the entire first book of Dreiser's novel had been omitted. Kearney's stage drama, of which Dreiser approved, also opens its first act in Samuel Griffiths' Lycurgus,[2] but a prologue shows Clyde's family singing hymns on a city street and being derided as religious fanatics. When the young boy becomes absorbed in the music emerging from an ornate hotel, his mother reproaches his susceptibility to temptation. Throughout the play Clyde is presented sympathetically, with several lines elaborating his impoverished background and deep love for Sondra. But Kearney's drama had been ruled out as a source for Paramount in its second contract with Dreiser, which stipulated that the property purchased was his novel and not the stage play in which Liveright, as its producer, retained additional rights. In any case, Sternberg's interpretation was neither Kearney's, nor Eisenstein's (whose treatment he claimed never to have read) nor Dreiser's. The "sociological elements" of his novel, he later argued, "were far from being responsible for the dramatic accident with which Dreiser had concerned himself" (Sternberg, 1966: 46) and so had been eliminated.

On February 2, Selznick sent a memorandum to B. P. Schulberg describing his disappointment with the Yellow Script, particularly the first half leading up to Clyde's trial. "Seeing the thing in actual script form" renewed the skepticism Selznick had previously expressed about filming the novel at all:

It is so depressing and so pointlessly futile a task, that I wonder whether anybody will get anything out of it when it is all over, except a sour taste ... Because of the glamour surrounding the literary triumph of the book, and the general importance of the subject, maybe its violation of all our accepted standards, and all the knowledge of public taste born of our experience may go for naught. But I am damned if I think so. (unpublished portion of February 2, 1931 memo from David O. Selznick to B. P. Schulberg, courtesy of Rudy Behlmer)

Moreover, he argued, Sternberg was the wrong director for the story: "I don't think he has the basic honesty of approach this subject absolutely requires, that he has the sympathy, the tolerance, the understanding that the story cries for. Joe's series of triumphs have all been those of good theater, in each case dealing with completely fake people in wholly fake situations" (continuation of February 2, 1931 memo from Selznick to Schulberg; Behlmer, 1972: 28). If Sternberg's anti-realist inclinations were ill-suited to Dreiser's narrative, Selznick deemed them disastrous for its protagonist: "Apart from the lack of knowing his early life, which alone makes subsequent developments understandable, he is for the rest of the story a thoroughly complete cad, liar and murderer, without a single redeeming trait; and without even extenuating early years or other circumstances" (continuation of unpublished memo from Selznick to Schulberg, February 2, 1931). A week later, Paramount executive Albert Persoff sent a memo concurring with Selznick's condemnation of the draft, although he blamed its fidelity to Dreiser's story for the negative portrayal of Clyde: "When the court room is cleared after the jury brings in a verdict of guilty, the crowd outside cheers the decision. In my opinion, the audiences that see this picture will be in a position corresponding to that of the court room spectators and there is no reason to assume that their reaction will be different" (February 10, 1931; David O. Selznick files, Harry Ransom Humanities Research Center, University of Texas at Austin).

Meanwhile, Lamar Trotti of the MPPDA's East Coast office listed the script's "danger spots" (February 4, 1931; AAT File, PCA Archive) in a report to its president, Will Hays. These comprised Clyde's attempt to seduce Roberta; his visit to her room and the fadeout suggesting his success; her pregnancy and their talk about having "tried" everything; the district attorney's political calculations; the discussion of abortion at the trial; and the influence of the mob and the intimidating jurors on Clyde's conviction. Hays' recommendations were to tone down the story's more "salacious" elements and present Clyde's fate as a moral lesson for the nation's youth, "a picturization of a terrible possibility for any boy … It is a chance for a real contribution by this picture to our social problems in America" (letter from Will Hays to Jason S. Joy, February 9, 1931; AAT File, PCA Archive). These two reactions to the script's initial draft underline the different problems it presented to Paramount and the MPPDA. While the former worried about its unhappy ending and unsympathetic protagonist, the latter was primarily concerned about the sexual and judicial elements of the narrative.

On February 9, Hoffenstein telegraphed Dreiser's office from Hollywood to say that he was bringing the script to New York. Dreiser, however, had left on the February 1 for a Caribbean cruise. Told that he might not return until March 1, Paramount sent a warning dated February 13 that production would commence on February 23 unless the studio heard from him by the February 20. On February 15, the *Los Angeles Times* quoted Lasky's announcement that sound technology would enable Paramount to film the "tragic aspects of American life depicted" in the novel with "dramatic power" according to "accepted community standards" (1931: 21). On February 16 Dreiser, contacted in Florida by his publisher, wired Hoffenstein, asking him to wait until his return to New York on February 27. In reply, the screenwriter claimed that it was too late to confer since production was about to start but he assured Dreiser that his novel had "been carefully and sympathetically followed" (telegram February 17, 1931, Dreiser Papers). Dreiser sent back a furious demand that Paramount honor its agreement to send him the screenplay and insisted that he meet him in New Orleans. Arriving there on February 26, Hoffenstein was given a letter written by the novelist after reading the script:

> To me, it is nothing less than an insult to the book—its scope, actions, emotions and psychology. Under the circumstances, and to avoid saying personally how deeply I feel this, I am leaving New Orleans without seeing you ... If, at any time, the studio should permit the construction of a script representative of the book and will seriously agree to work along the lines I know to be most valuable for this purpose, I will be glad to cooperate, and at once, but not before. (letter from Theodore Dreiser to Samuel Hoffenstein, February 26, 1931, in Elias, 1959: 509–10)

Dreiser's objections to the screenplay were not the only ones Paramount was contending with. On February 18, Jason Joy of the MPPDA assured Will Hays that both Schulberg and Sternberg "now sense the worries that you have been carrying these many years, involved in this particular story." In the White Script the word "seduction" had been deleted, the suggestion of pregnancy minimized and the dialogue about abortion reconsidered. "While these are important," Joy observed, "the major gratification came when it seemed apparent that plans to produce the picture as broad entertainment were discarded in favor of the development of a social problem" (AAT File, PCA Archive). A few days later his colleague Lamar Trotti wrote Hays with further suggestions. Here, instead of material restricted by the Production Code, he addressed the screenplay's narrative: "Briefly, my idea is to shift the emphasis of the story from the perfectly obvious and outworn topic of a boy who seduces a girl, gets her in trouble, murders her, and is electrocuted for it, to the more dramatic mother-son story every incident of which the book contains and which we have overlooked."

At a stroke, Trotti suggested, his revisions would assuage public objections, satisfy Dreiser and create "a far more dramatic story with a broader public appeal, even more dramatic and appealing, in my opinion, than such mother stories as Stella Dallas" (February 24, 1931, AAT File, PCA Archive). Trotti's proposal to transform the screenplay into a maternal melodrama was radical, even by the standards of the MPPDA. The ten-page treatment he sent with his letter restores much of Book 1, including the Griffiths family's preaching, Esta's pregnancy and desertion and Clyde's mother's reaction to his arrest. Dreiser's coda is also restored, with Mrs Griffith showing a greater kindliness to Esta's child at the film's conclusion. In these respects the MPPDA executive urged *fidelity* to the novel in order to make the moral points eliminated by Sternberg. But time was running out. On March 2 Lasky wrote Hays that footage limitations and the novel's complex narrative made most of Trotti's suggestions impractical, although Schulberg had agreed to develop the mother-son story "consistent with the treatment worked out by Hoffenstein and Dreiser himself." A "provision in our contract," he noted, "made it necessary for us to submit our treatment to him ... Hoffenstein is returning to Hollywood today, and Von Sternberg starts shooting his first scenes today" (letter from Jesse L. Lasky to Will Hays, March 2, 1931, AAT File, PCA Archive).

That final admission suggests the limited extent to which Paramount planned to accommodate Dreiser's suggestions, a point that the author took up on his return from holiday. His distrust was fortified by a March 3 article in the *New York Times* quoting Sternberg pronouncing his writing "antiquated" (Elias, 1959: 511) and the same paper's review of *Dishonored* panning the director's screenplay: "like most motion picture directors who turn their own literary aspirations into film form he gives more attention to the cinematic qualities of his incidents than to the reflection or portrayal of ordinary human emotions" (Hall, 1931a: 31). In a rapid exchange of correspondence with Lasky, Dreiser complained of the script's rush to the courtroom and its neglect of the electoral contest surrounding the trial and the events in the death house afterward. He concluded with a four-page letter questioning the producer's sincerity in consulting him at such short notice before proceeding with the scheduled filming. Rumors had reached Dreiser of Paramount sidetracking another production starring Sternberg's leads in order to speed up *An American Tragedy,* and he knew that the Eisenstein treatment had been much more favorably received by the studio's executives than Sternberg's screenplay. "Worse," he noted, Paramount's version would inevitably "give the impression to the millions of people throughout the world who will see this picture, that the novel on which it is based is nothing short of a cheap, tawdry, tabloid confession story which entirely lacks the scope, emotion, action and psychology of the book involved. Here is an inequitable infringement of a vested property." The threat of legal action was clear, but Dreiser also offered an alternative—that he travel to Hollywood to work on the film in order to "repeat the artistic and financial success which it has been both as a novel and a play" (March 17, 1931, in Elias, 1959: 521–2).

Lasky relented and Dreiser flew to Hollywood, accompanied by his producer friend Hy Kraft, known to Lasky through his previous work at Paramount's Long Island studio. There the author wrangled with Sternberg over the screenplay's fidelity to his novel. To Dreiser's consternation, the director was able to cite the pages from which several scenes derived, since his adaptation was one of contraction rather than substitution. "This I admitted," Sternberg later wrote,

"and told him that the footage and the budget were, as he might know, prede-
termined by the organization, not by me, though the choice of what was to be
filmed rested with me" (Sternberg, 1966: 259). In order to restore key elements
in the first book and conclusion of the novel, Dreiser and Kraft set to work
writing additional scenes for the film. By the end of March they had drafted
twelve new ones, including Clyde singing with his family on a city street, confessing his ambitions to his mother, soda clerking in the drug store, mixing highballs for a wild hotel party, his involvement in the road accident that kills the
child, his labors in his uncle's shrinking room and his final walk to the execution
chamber, fading into his family again singing "Onward Christian Soldiers". In
addition, they offered several suggestions to make Clyde's romance with Roberta
more youthful and idyllic and to dramatize his later preparations to drown her,
rather than relying on his testimony at the trial. One notable example suggests
the influence of Eisenstein, whose treatment Dreiser had read and praised, in its
recommendation of optical effects to represent Clyde's fantasies of the crime and
its punishment:

> After Clyde comes out of the telephone booth and buys a newspaper, he goes to
> the Lycurgus house, gets a folder and takes them [sic] to his room to study. He
> bolts the door, sits down and opens the folder (map). As he looks it over there is
> a faint suggestion of water, a boat, woods. They disappear. He looks straight out
> into space ... He looks at the map again. As he looks at it, right through the closed
> door comes a gigantic detective with a pair of handcuffs. He stands looking at
> Clyde. Startled, Clyde jumps to his feet. ("Mr Dreiser's Suggestions, An
> American Tragedy", March 28, 1931, Dreiser Papers)

On March 31, Dreiser discussed these ideas with Schulberg, whose letter
summarizing them praised the introductory scenes but pronounced those of the
drowning and the death house debatable "from a picture point of view."
Nonetheless, the producer agreed to convey his proposals to Sternberg, then
shooting at Lake Arrowhead, to avoid a return to the location later. However, he
concluded that the director should be allowed to complete the production as
planned and then show an edited version to Dreiser, "at which time you can look
at it with us and we can then determine together what need there is for amplifi-
cation and what room there is for the same" (B. P. Schulberg to Theodore
Dreiser, April 1, 1931, Dreiser Papers). A few days later Dreiser left Hollywood
in disgust.

On April 25 he wrote to eighteen leading figures in the fields of literature and
the arts—including novelist Fannie Hurst, drama critic George Jean Nathan,
publisher Harrison Smith and literary editor Carl Van Doren—setting out his
quarrel with the studio. Outlining their contractual agreement, his "ideographic
plan" for the novel and Sternberg's emphasis on Book 2, Dreiser denounced
Paramount's storyline as that of "a more or less over-sexed and worthless boy
who, finding himself in a world in which his sensual desire might be indulged

fairly easily, concerns himself rather lightly with several girls and finally destroys one in his efforts to further his success with another, more wealthy and more beautiful." Such a treatment, he argued, belittled not only the novel but its author. To test this view, he invited his addressees to view the film with him at an advance screening in New York and consider whether it "sufficiently carries out the ideology of the book as to hold me free from any personal or artistic harm before the world" (letter from Theodore Dreiser to Harrison Smith, April 25, 1931, in Elias, 1959: 526–30).

While Dreiser prepared to test his objections to Paramount's contraction of his novel, the MPPDA was conferring with Schulberg on the sexual details of the assembled scenes. On April 26, Jason Joy wrote asking him to shorten Clyde and Sondra's kiss in a canoe and to cut Clyde and Roberta's "passionate half-reclining positions" in her bedroom. The dialogue about abortion was now deemed "thoroughly justified under the Code," but Joy asked if it could be eliminated nonetheless. Noting that any reference to the subject might encourage its inclusion in other films currently being prepared for production, causing the Association "a great deal of trouble with its equivalent economic waste," he appealed to Schulberg's "large and generous interest in the industry as a whole" (AAT File, PCA Archive). In May the MPPDA reiterated this request, along with the elimination of an introductory title clearly designed to propitiate Dreiser and flag the artistic prestige of the production: "Crimes of passion have given substance to many great novels, but none has told the story of an ill-starred love with such sympathy, such justice, such tremendous detail and terrific power as 'An American Tragedy'" (John V. Wilson, resume of conversation with BP Schulberg, May 25, 1931, AAT File, PCA Archive).

When Alice Ames Winter opposed this promotion of a novel loathed by conservative women's groups, Paramount agreed to omit the title, opening the film with a public-spirited dedication "to the army of men and women all over the world who have tried to make life better for youth". But the reference in the trial scene to abortion methods remained, covered by the defense attorney's line "And none of them did any good, did they?" which, Schulberg pointed out, Father Lord himself had approved (telegram from John V. Wilson to Will Hays, May 25, 1931, AAT File, PCA Archive).

The questions of sexual representation that preoccupied the MPPDA were minor compared to those of structure and characterization that still worried the studio. When Dreiser wrote Lasky to protest rumors of an opening prior to his promised preview, the Paramount boss replied that the film's editing was taking longer than planned "due to careful consideration having been given to the changes and additions suggested by you" (May 27, 1931, Dreiser Papers). His colleagues may have been indifferent to Dreiser's suggestions but they had come to a similar opinion of Sternberg's first assembly. On May 29 Selznick wrote to Schulberg that a new opening sequence was necessary to understand Clyde and that the scenes with his mother should be reshot with a different actress. Schulberg followed on with a letter to Lasky suggesting an extensive opening title lamenting US crime statistics and asking "What is wrong with America? What is wrong with American youth?" To give the film a "spiritual lift" at its end, he proposed filming new dialogue using "another player without accent" as Mrs Griffith, declaring "They may not understand you on earth but there is one above who will understand and redeem you" (June 2, 1931, Dreiser Papers).

While Paramount reviewed the initial assembly of the film, Dreiser and his lawyers prepared their case. The Dramatists Guild was asked for a resolution of support and a number of writers approached for possible precedents. From Florida the adventure writer Rex Beach observed:

> I have had stories mangled, plots emasculated, titles changed, and suffered all the shocks and surprises conceivable in viewing pictures made from my stories but I have never felt that I would gain anything by protesting. I'd be glad to see Mr Dreiser carry his case through and have the courts determine just how far a producer can go. It would be a great help to every author. (letter to Alan S. Hays, May 21, 1931, Dreiser Papers)

In mid-June Lasky permitted Dreiser and Kraft to view the first assembly, followed by his jury of experts. However, the producer stipulated, "we will not participate in any discussion with them, because as I have pointed out to you before, we fear that their views might be confusing rather than helpful" (letter from Lasky to Dreiser, June 10, 1931, Dreiser Papers). In the event, Dreiser's panel came to the same view of the picture as the studio's executives had. Although one juror, magazine editor Ray Long, wrote that the author need not be ashamed of it, most condemned it in remarkably similar terms. A. A. Brill diagnosed Phillips Holmes' Clyde as "shut-in, unemotional, catatonic" (Swanberg, 1965: 376)—far less sympathetic than the novel's protagonist. Worse, the literary critic Burton Rascoe declared that "even as an ordinary movie it is doomed to be a terrific box-office failure as it stands now. For a popular audience it is deficient in precisely that emotional content which made the novel so great a success" (letter to Dreiser, June 16, 1931, Dreiser Papers).

Property Rights and Personal Rights

Dreiser's path and Paramount's then diverged. The studio commissioned additional scenes for the film's opening and ending from S. K. Lauren, a Broadway writer who would subsequently work with Jules Furthman on Sternberg's *Blonde Venus* (1932), but Dreiser's were not filmed. Meanwhile, the novelist's lawyers wrote to Paramount, setting out the history of the dispute and the negative reactions of Dreiser's jurors in an open letter circulated as a pamphlet. In an epigrammatic reading of Sternberg's adaptation, the letter declares "the murder motive (not plot) of the book is not the murder plot (not motive) of the film"

(Arthur Garfield Hays and Arthur Carter Hume to Paramount Publix Corporation, June 26, 1931, Dreiser Papers). It concludes with the claims that the studio had violated their contract with Dreiser, misrepresented his novel and ignored his comments about the film. Lasky replied on June 30, retailing the difficulties of contacting Dreiser in Florida and his broken appointment with Hoffenstein in New Orleans. The film had cost Paramount an estimated $538,000—this was made up of $135,000 plus an additional $3,000 for the extra scenes to Dreiser, $15,000 to Liveright and the remainder for the production itself. (Zukor's complaint that Paramount had spent half a million on *An American Tragedy* had come true, albeit six months after it was made to Sternberg.) Lasky reported that the introductory titles suggested by Schulberg had not been adopted, but Lauren's additional scenes had been filmed. He offered to screen these for Dreiser in New York. Complaining of the writer's indifference to "censorship problems or attacks on American institutions" during the discussions in California, he concluded with the announcement that the company would open the film in July (letter from Jesse L. Lasky to Arthur Garfield Hays and Arthur Carter Hume, June 30, 1931, Dreiser Papers).

With the stage set for litigation, Dreiser's lead attorney, the veteran anti-censorship lawyer Arthur Garfield Hays, warned that he would lose: "It is the old question of a contest between property rights and personal rights ... money invested will weigh much heavier than the author's right to have his work properly presented." But even a losing suit would constitute a claim for such rights, while warning the public about the misrepresentation of the novel, so Garfield promised "a damn good fight" (letter from Arthur Garfield Hays to Theodore Dreiser, July 3, 1931, Dreiser Papers). He and his colleagues searched for legal precedents to Dreiser's action, discovering a promising New York District Court judgment in the 1922 case of *Curwood v. Affiliated Distributors*. The young writer James Oliver Curwood claimed that a story he had sold Affiliated had been converted into an unrecognizable picture said to be based on his work. The court found that "while scenery, action, and characters may be added to an original story, and even supplant subordinate portions thereof, there is an obligation upon the elaborator to retain and give appropriate expression to the theme, thought, and main action of that which was originally written" (quoted in a letter from Arthur Garfield Hays to Dreiser, July 17, 1931, Dreiser Papers). Armed with this precedent, Dreiser's lawyers obtained an injunction compelling Paramount to defend its distribution of the picture.

The studio's contract lawyers replied with depositions portraying Dreiser as a difficult ideologue whose cooperation was at best erratic. Henry Herzbrun recalled the novelist denouncing Sternberg's *The Blue Angel* as a "terrible picture" during the negotiations for the sound rights but praising the selection of Hoffenstein. In Hollywood Dreiser had viewed Sternberg's rushes and complained that Clyde did not "sweat enough" under cross-examination. When the director warned that some of his suggestions would be censorable, Dreiser had "denounced censors, as well as religious and patriotic institutions." Echoing

Herzbrun, Paramount attorney William T. Powers claimed that in their Hollywood discussions Sternberg had displayed a greater knowledge of Dreiser's novel than the writer. In vain the director had attempted to convince Dreiser that the film's audience should "draw its own conclusions as to the responsibility of society and religion for Clyde." Powers also detailed the scenes added by Lauren, but never viewed by the writer, arguing that they complied "substantially with almost all of Mr Dreiser's suggestions" (Henry Herzbrun and William T. Powers, Depositions to the Supreme Court of the State of New York, July 18–21, 1931, Dreiser Papers).

But at the hearing on July 22 Paramount's trial attorney, Humphrey J. Lynch, offered a remarkable new argument—that Dreiser's novel constituted "cold blooded plagiarism" (Swanberg, 1965: 377) of the press coverage of the Gillette case and the published edition of Grace Brown's letters. Lynch drove the point home by citing a similar claim by the novelist Sinclair Lewis, who had accused Dreiser of lifting passages from his wife Dorothy Thompson's articles about a Moscow visit in his own memoir of his travels there. The accusation made the writer so volubly angry that he had to be admonished by the judge. He had indeed employed some of Thompson's descriptions of Moscow social life as descriptive padding in *Dreiser Looks at Russia*, but his own conclusions about Soviet society were very different and she had not pursued legal action. As for *An American Tragedy*, its debts to the New York *World's* reports of the Gillette trial and Grace Brown's letters are demonstrable, both in regard to specific phrases and the adoption of the newspaper's selection of the highlights of the case. But as Dreiser's lawyers replied, "this immediately arouses the query as to why the defendant did not make a picture out of People v. Gillette, without paying a large amount of money to Dreiser for the motion picture rights of his novel." In their summation, the only two issues before the court were whether the purchaser of the motion picture rights to a novel could "produce a picture which fails to carry out the intent, purpose and psychology of the novel and omits a large part of the story" and whether Paramount's film had done so. Nevertheless, the plaintiff's case closed with a broader indictment—not of Lasky, Sternberg or the studio, but of popular American cinema:

> Every picture represents a wish fulfillment. Every hero is one's self. Ordinarily at marriage, life is ended in an aura of success; or if perchance life continues, all is serene unless one or the other does "wrong." ... Virtue brings her own, as well as other, rewards. Vice leads to the gutter and suicide ... Wars are crusades fought for righteous, idealistic and selfless causes, where the enemy is always cruel, and therefore gets licked. The immigrant welcomed to America, the place of sure opportunity, loves this land of justice and liberty. People and actions are good or bad. Life is a success or a failure. There are no tones, no shades or shadows. And the moral effect is said to be certain. There is no portrayal of reality, yet it is thought that these lies will affect life. They do. (Memorandum on Behalf of Plaintiff, Supreme Court of the State of New York, County of Westchester,

Theodore Dreiser, Plaintiff, against Paramount Publix Corporation, Defendant, undated, Dreiser Papers)

As Justice Graham Witschief contemplated his ruling, a telegram arrived to the court from Major Frank Pease, now representing the "National Film Improvement Committee of American Defenders (The Blue Shirts)." In it Pease warned that the case was "just a typical Hollywood publicity scheme ... Paramount and Dreiser are equally guilty [,] Dreiser for writing it [,] Paramount for filming it[. F]or this is the film which red Eisenstein [,] Moscows [sic] cinema propagandist in chief was imported by that socially irresponsible disloyal producer Lasky to direct" (telegram from Major Frank Pease to Hon Graham Witschief, July 23, 1931, Dreiser Papers). Rabid though his accusations were, Pease did not underestimate the press coverage of the dispute. His suspicion that it was a publicity stunt was echoed elsewhere, notably in the *Port Chester, N.Y. News*, which ran an editorial headlined "Brains on the Auction Block" on July 23, concluding that if the whole affair was a promotional gambit, "we hold no ill will. The courtroom scene in White Plains between former Supreme Court Justice Lynch and Arthur Garfield Hays was almost as good as the murder trial scene in the book itself and deserves front-page display."

On August 1 Justice Witschief issued his ruling. The studio, he argued, had only promised to accept the plaintiff's suggestions when it judged that it could "consistently do so." It had made "greater than reasonable effort" to confer with Dreiser, including adopting several of his written suggestions. As for the film's fidelity to Dreiser's determinist view of Clyde's tragedy:

> The difficulty in picturing such a viewpoint of the book is apparent. That view depends upon the frame of mind of the individual, upon his outlook upon life, and whether a fatalist or a believer in the power of the individual to overcome weaknesses of character, to rise above his environment, to subdue his physical desires, and to be the master of his body, rather than be mastered by it.

Whether Witschief meant by this that the novel was open to the differing interpretations he had received from the author and the film-makers, or that the very question of determinism was difficult to represent or perceive visually—to "picture", to "view," he did not make clear. Critical opinion on the relation of the picture to the book had been submitted by both sides, but he concluded that "the producer must give consideration to the fact that the great majority of the people, composing the audience before which the picture will be presented, will be more interested that justice prevail over wrongdoing than that inevitability of Clyde's end clearly appear" (memorandum from J. Witschief, Supreme Court of the State of New York, County of Westchester, Theodore Dreiser, Plaintiff, against Paramount Publix Corporation, Defendant, August 1, 1931, AAT File, PCA Archive). The injunction was refused and Dreiser ordered to pay $10 costs. A few days later *An American Tragedy* was released by Paramount.

A Fine Face

An American Tragedy opens with the sound of a jazz band and the first titles, superimposed on the surface of water, through which the rocky bottom can be seen. Notable among those credited is the cinematographer Lee Garmes, who had filmed *Morocco* and *Dishonored* for Sternberg and who would go on to film *The Shanghai Express* (1932). Each change in the five title frames is signaled by the dropping of a pebble or two into the water, rippling the surface and the title lettering in a manner resembling the "drowning" title in *Sunrise*. The consequent disturbance renders the water opaque, obscuring the dissolve into the subsequent title. A fade to black concludes the sequence, fading up to the film's dedication "to the army of men and women all over the world who have tried to make life better for youth." The dedication is also superimposed on water but here, as in subsequent titles, its surface is dappled with light.

A second title, superimposed on the same brightly lit water, reads "Our story begins in Kansas City, in the lobby of the Green-Davison Hotel—" and then dissolves into a wide shot of the hotel lobby, where two expensively dressed women are checking in. Behind them stands Clyde Griffiths (Phillips Holmes) in a row of smartly uniformed bellboys. Summoned to show the guests to their room, Clyde picks up their luggage and precedes them across the marble columned lobby into the elevator. The camera follows from behind the two women as they observe the slender blonde youth in his closely tailored suit. As Clyde takes their suitcases into the hotel bedroom, the daughter watches, provocatively standing in the doorway to make him brush past her on his exit. After offering him a very generous tip, she explains to her protesting mother, "I rather like his looks ... Didn't you notice what a fine face he has? I wonder how a boy of his type comes to be doing this type of work?" Outside the door Clyde is discovered eavesdropping on the compliment by the chambermaid. Reminding him of their date that evening, she is irritated when Clyde attempts to call it off: "Don't kid yourself, Number 7. You ain't got a chance with a classy dame like that, or anybody like her." Clyde replies that he won't be a bellboy all his life.

A dissolve from the maid's proprietary grasp of Clyde's shoulder to a matching shot of a closely dancing couple changes the scene to a cheap road house, through which the camera moves past a drunken Clyde clinging to the chambermaid. Another dissolve reveals their group in a speeding car, hurrying through the rain-swept night. To the scream of a bystander, the car strikes a child, turns a corner and crashes into a building. Clyde emerges with the other passengers, halts for a moment in confusion and then runs from the scene to the Star of Hope mission, identified by its sign offering "Food and Lodging for the Needy." At the mission, Mrs Griffiths (the Irish-accented Lucille LaVerne, not replaced despite Schulberg's suggestions) is first seen standing amidst a group of elderly destitutes. Hearing Clyde enter his room, she finds him packing hurriedly to leave town. A mid-shot clarifies the image of the Madonna and Child on the wall behind them, as Clyde's mother also clasps him by the shoulders and asks why he didn't stay to ascertain the condition of the child. When Clyde protests that he would have been abandoned to prosecution for a crime he didn't commit, she asks why he'd gone out "with girls and boys like that?" "I didn't want to go out with them tonight," he replies bitterly, "but they're the only friends I've got." Disregarding his mother's entreaties to go to the police, Clyde leaves, brusquely kissing her goodbye. The scene ends with her praying in the foreground with the Madonna and Child behind:

God, Thou knowest how I love my boy. I've done all I could to guide his steps to Thee, but I've been weak and helpless. We've always been so terribly poor. We've never been able to give him the happiness, the simple joys and pleasures that should come to every young boy. All his life long, his young eyes have seen only misery and evil. Even the very strongest among us will stray from Thy path without happiness or contentment. Bestow some of Thy manifold blessings upon him, so that the light may flow into his troubled spirit, that he may be led aright. Oh God, watch over my boy all the days of his life and keep him!

A dissolve superimposes the figure of Clyde's mother over a freight train, where Clyde is discovered hiding beneath a carriage. A further dissolve reveals him being upbraided for not washing dishes faster in a restaurant kitchen. A third shows him caught up in a raid on a pool hall, where again he hesitates in confusion before escaping through a window. Throughout these scenes Clyde is speechless, but in the next he lies to the hotel manager interviewing him and claims to have come from San Francisco. Hired, he is told by another bellboy of a new guest by the name of Griffiths hailing from Lycurgus. A fade to black marks the interval before Clyde's arrival in the city, and a title describes his rise from an apprenticeship in the shrinking room of his uncle's factory to foreman of the stamping department.

These scenes are the ones added to the film's opening by S. K. Lauren and not viewed by Dreiser prior to the court hearing. In Paramount's defense, studio attorney William T. Powers argued that they substantially complied with Dreiser's suggestions in presenting Clyde's early home life and unhappiness in the mission. Although Dreiser's proposed scenes of Clyde working in the drug store and being tipped for mixing highballs in the hotel were not filmed, the scenes with the wealthy mother and her daughter were claimed to be suitable alternatives. The automobile accident was added and also Clyde telling his mother of his intended flight. Where Dreiser suggested that Clyde's father write him a letter of introduction to his rich uncle, a detail not in the novel, Lauren substituted the scenes of Clyde riding the rails and washing dishes, both of which are in it.

If these additions to the picture (dated June 22, 1931, Paramount Script Collection, Margaret Herrick Library, Academy of Motion Pictures Arts and Sciences, hereafter Paramount Script Collection) suggest a greater fidelity to the novel than Dreiser had anticipated, the style in which Clyde is filmed also accords with its reversal of gender conventions. Throughout the opening Clyde is presented as an object of erotic spectatorship and appropriation by the young hotel guest and the chambermaid. He is coded as feminine by his close-fitting clothing, slender frame, delicate features and illuminated fair hair, as well as by being filmed from behind.[3] Dramatically, Clyde is excluded from an authoritative look in each scene, continually caught (eavesdropping, under the freight car, washing the dishes too slowly) or hesitating in crises. He is physically grasped by his mother and the chambermaid, and lolls against the latter when drunk. Moreover, she addresses him by his bellboy designation "Number 7," echoing the instrumental codename given to Dietrich's spy, "X27," in Sternberg's previous film, *Dishonored*. Finally, in the religious iconography so conspicuous in his bedroom, he is the Holy Mother's fatherless child. But unlike Dreiser's protagonist, Holmes' Clyde is not appealing in his femininity. He shrinks from the hotel guest's flirtation, responding only to her large tip. He tries to break his date with the chambermaid and gets drunk when he can't. He hardly listens to his mother's pleading, and only kisses her goodbye as an afterthought. If the added scenes suggest his unhappiness and suffering before he reaches Lycurgus, they do little to soften an apparently cold and calculating character.

After the title announcing Clyde's promotion from the shrinking room to the stamping department, he is revealed in the noisy factory, again with his back to the spectator, leaning on the railing of a staircase. As an attractive woman worker passes by, she surveys him frankly before climbing the stairs. He looks back at her before turning away dourly to the factory floor, where scores of women stamp sizes on piles of collars. As he passes by to examine their work, they look up at him with evident curiosity. Finally, the bored young man reaches his desk at the end of the hall (a set dressed with actual machinery operated by experienced factory workers, as Paramount's publicity stressed at the time).[4] As Clyde watches his charges, a close-up of two young women's shapely calves underlines his sexual interest. At this point Roberta Alden (Sylvia Sidney) enters the factory with another male supervisor, descending the staircase and walking through the hall. As they approach Clyde, he is again seen from behind, perched on his desk looking out the window. Then he starts and turns around to be introduced to Roberta as a prospective employee. As he takes the name and address of the shy young women, she tells him that she's from a farm upstate but will rent lodgings in Lycurgus. In reply he smilingly discloses that he also lives in the town "alone" and then offers to show her how the work is done. The scene ends with Clyde escorting Roberta to the women's cloakroom, from where she anxiously gazes back at him as he furtively glances at her and then looks away, his eyes darting in thought.

Another watery title announces "Sunday evening at Samuel Griffiths." There Clyde's cousin Gilbert asks his father petulantly whether Clyde's invitation to dinner will make him think that the family will "take him up socially." A butler announces Clyde's entry past an ornate staircase into the drawing room, where he is introduced to his aunt and cousin Myra. After Gilbert rudely excuses

himself to go out, Clyde tells his aunt that his parents run "a kind of mission."
"Oh," she replies with disdain, "I see." A cut to a town street shows Clyde loi-
tering in front of a department store. Its windows display women's wear—negli-
gees, bathing suits and ball gowns, clothing whose emphasis on bodily display
confirms his own voyeurism while anticipating "the white society dummies," to
use Eisenstein's phrase (Montagu, 1969: 214), later in the film. Here Clyde
encounters Roberta out walking with a women friend and bids her good evening.
The smiling young woman introduces him to her friend and then continues
walking, insisting that they shouldn't look back. But as Clyde watches her
retreating figure, she eventually returns his gaze.[5]

A title declares "Springtime" as the sparkling water dissolves into a sunlit lake
where Clyde, clad in white flannels, is canoeing beneath a canopy of spring
foliage. (Garmes' use of vegetation to screen or shadow the characters is a key
device in the film, and it will be adopted by George Stevens 20 years later.)
Along the bank walks Roberta, carrying flowers she's gathered. Clyde greets her
and invites her into the canoe, where she confesses that she can't swim. Later,
as they walk along the bank, he looks around anxiously until Roberta says
"Maybe I oughtn't to be seen with you." But, after a cut to a close-up of the
now-seated couple, he proposes that they should ignore the factory rule forbidding foremen from socializing with the female workforce. Again, Clyde is filmed
from behind as he suddenly kisses the wide-eyed woman. Roberta's shocked
reaction dominates the shot, which concludes with a dissolve to a wider shot of
the two sitting apart, yet again with Clyde's back to the camera and Roberta
facing it. After lighting a cigarette he turns toward her in profile, declaring that
"there's something about a day like this that makes me want to love somebody."

"Any girl would do, I suppose," Roberta observes skeptically.

"Sure, if she were half as sweet as you are," he replies.

When the hesitant woman points out that she's just a factory hand and he's
the owner's nephew, meeting "lovely girls with money and education," he offers
further compliments, prompting her to remark on how different he seems at
work, always so cross and anxious. Here a cut to the reverse angle shows Clyde
full face, smiling and relaxed for the first time in the film. But as the scene ends
he suggest that they use code in the factory: "If I feel I have to say something
like I love you, I'll just walk by and say you're pretty slow, Miss Alden."

A title announcing "Late Autumn" moves the action from the sunlit park to
a street at evening, down which the couple silently proceeds until Clyde petulantly asks where they'll meet on cold winter nights. Densely shadowed by the
lamplit branches of the bare trees, they quarrel about whether he can come to
Roberta's room. When Clyde turns away angrily, Roberta runs after him,
begging him not to go. The next day he brandishes a yardstick as he coldly
inspects the stamping room—until she slips him a note when he passes her workbench. He reads it behind the staircase, almost wholly obscured from view. As
Roberta watches anxiously, a close-up reveals Clyde looking up at her in
triumph, his lips slowly puckering into a furtive kiss. Her joyful smile in return

dissolves over the two surreptitiously entering her lodging house. In her darkened room she asks him to promise that he'll never leave her, and he swears to "Bert" that he never will, drawing her into the embrace shortened by the MPPDA.

If You Only Knew

A fade to black marks an interval, fading up to Clyde walking past a smart automobile on a city street, where he is hailed by Sondra Finchley (Frances Dee). As he doffs his hat in surprise, she apologizes that she thought he was someone else. But Clyde greets her by name, explaining that he's seen her pictures in the newspaper society columns. The flattered Sondra puts her hands on her hips and begins to vamp, asking Clyde if he's going to see his girl. When he replies that he hasn't got a girlfriend, she offers him a lift in her chauffeur driven car. A quick dissolve to an invitation card for a society dance reveals Sondra's signature. Another shows Clyde pirouetting at his mirror in a dinner jacket, practicing "How do you do, Miss Finchley?" and then more slowly, "May I call you Sondra?" His illuminated figure is contrasted with a dissolve to Roberta in her dressing gown, gazing through the ice-covered windows of her darkened room (Figure 3.1). A quick cut shows Clyde meeting smartly dressed guests at the dance until Sondra enters. When she asks if he's enjoying it, he looks avidly around the room and declares that he wouldn't miss it for the world. A cut back to Roberta shows the despondent woman taking to her bed, dissolved over Clyde and Sondra, discovered by a tracking shot in a tête-à-tête behind a large floral display. "You don't know how I love all this," Clyde declares, "this music, this kind of life." When Sondra complains that he's left her out, he insists that he hasn't stopped thinking of her since they met. "You are nice when you're intense like that," she flirts, and gives him a gardenia from her corsage.

After a fade to black Clyde is seen at his factory desk, absently smelling the flower as he gazes away from the workers toward the window. Roberta watches from her workbench and then, dressed in a capacious cardigan, walks wearily toward him. As two other women look on knowingly, she approaches their unseeing supervisor and drops a note at his desk. It reads: "Clyde, I'm writing this only because you've been avoiding me for weeks, and I can't get even a word with you alone. I must see you tonight—sure. Bert."

A dissolve to her room shows them together, as Roberta protests "I don't see any way out of this unless you marry me"—eliminating the White Script's references to abortion, "We may be able to do something yet" and "Oh, we've tried everything." Here the staccato tempo of previous scenes slows as Roberta and Clyde have it out, with her sitting on the bed and him standing above in his overcoat. He protests that he can't afford to marry and risk losing his job and she that he's more concerned about his new society friends. Refusing to "be left this way," Roberta rises to insist that Clyde help her—even if wishes to leave her after

Figure 3.1 A despondent Roberta (Sylvia Sidney) in *An American Tragedy*, Paramount 1931 (Kobal Collection).

she's "out of this." When Clyde urges her to return home to her parents, where he'll send money, she answers bitterly, "So you want me to go off all by myself, just so you can stay here and get along and marry someone else, that Finchley girl maybe. Well, I won't do it. It's not fair." After Clyde finally promises to marry her, he moves quickly to the door, stopping only to agree to write, just as he earlier did when leaving his mother. But as Roberta begins to weap, he moves back to her and gingerly strokes her hair. At this she clasps him, tearfully asking why his feelings have changed. He looks away, standing with his back to the camera as the scene fades to black.

A title announces "Vacation time," its watery background dissolving into a lakeside resort in summer, where Clyde is greeting Sondra: "You don't know how glad I am to see you again," he exclaims, using the same phrase as at the party. Together the white-clad duo jump into her motorboat and speed away. The scene dissolves into the two, elegantly clad in jodhpurs and boots, riding horses in a sun-dappled forest. There Sondra warns Clyde that they'll need to be careful with her disapproving mother until she comes of age in the autumn. Clyde urges her to elope with him immediately, but Sondra insists that it's too soon. Plaintively he gazes into the distance and says "If I could just tell you everything. If you only knew ..." But Sondra closes the conversation, insisting that they must return before they're missed. The two kiss passionately, with Clyde turning his back to the camera once again.

"Back to reality—after two days of dreams" the next title declares, its shining waters fading to Clyde in a crowd of workers leaving the factory. Passing by a newspaper vendor shouting "Double tragedy at lake," he enters a drugstore phone booth to ring Roberta and claim that he must postpone their wedding for a few more days. Buying a paper afterwards, he reads of the discovery of "an unidentified girl's body" and the disappearance of her companion. Its description of "an upturned canoe and two hats found floating" in the lake dissolves into the imagined scene proposed by Dreiser as Clyde, shadowed by his fedora, looks up from the page and darts his eyes in thought. He is then seen through the fronds of a palm in the Lycurgus House hotel lobby furtively collecting two travel brochures. After a dissolve to Clyde studying a map in his room, a longer dissolve overlaps the map with a dock on a lake where he is rowing with Roberta.

Stowing his oars to light a cigarette, Clyde is questioned by Roberta about his use of aliases in their hotel registration and whether he really intends to marry her at all. When he reacts angrily, she tries to calm him by suggesting lunch. After picnicking on the shore, he fixes his camera to its tripod and takes her picture. Then, scanning the lake, he suggests taking a few more on the water. As Roberta walks to the boat, Clyde packs their things in his suitcase, revealing a second straw hat among its contents. At the water's edge Roberta embraces him and declares her love but Clyde detaches her arms and helps her into the boat.

Out on the lake he drifts before taking up the camera, only to pause and stare menacingly at Roberta in close-up. When the alarmed woman asks what's wrong, he continues to stare—his eyes shadowed by the brim of his hat. Then, in a flat, almost expressionless, voice, Clyde explains "It's nothing now. I'm alright. Just leave me alone. I brought you up here to drown you, but I'm not going to do it now. Just stay where you are. I'll marry you—I'll go through with it. Just leave me alone." As the anguished Roberta reaches out to him, he pulls away, shouting "Stay where you are! Don't come near me! Leave me alone!" A cut to a longer shot shows him rising to his feet as she clasps him, warning "Look out! You'll upset the boat!"[6] A distant shot reveals the dinghy turning over and two figures coming to the surface. Clyde is seen first in close-up, swimming away. At Roberta's appeal for help, also in close-up, he takes a brief stroke towards her but then changes direction as she struggles to stay afloat. The desperate woman surfaces a third time, but Clyde continues to swim away. Then a long shot of the lake discloses the upturned boat with a straw hat floating beside it. The sound of its rippling waters is that which has been heard throughout the film under its titles.

A lengthy dissolve overlaps the lake with the drowsy figure of the coroner, as though he is dreaming of the accident. Finally woken by the repeated ring of his telephone, he relays its report to a note-taking assistant: "... straw hat without any lining ... letter found in the pocket of her coat. Addressed to whom? Mrs Titus Alden ... Still dragging for the man's body ..." After a fade to black, a close-up of headlines about the mysterious drowning dissolves to Clyde, seen from behind once more reading the newspaper in question. Guiltily, he turns toward the camera and looks around (Figure 3.2). After still another black-marked interval, District Attorney Orville Mason (Irving Pichel) is shown into the old-fashioned Alden parlor, where he asks Titus about his daughter. When Mrs Alden joins them, he reveals the drowning and she faints as the scene fades to black.[7]

Another headline, superimposed over a printing press, announces "ALDEN COMPANION MAY BE ARRESTED TODAY" dissolving to Mason and an assistant discovering the dried gardenia and two bundles of letters, from Roberta and Sondra, in Clyde's room. Mason instantly deduces a motive for murder, and in the next scene he instructs the sheriff's posse to arrest Clyde. The image of these suited middle-aged men dissolves to a idyllic party of white-clad youths, singing in harmony as they paddle their canoes, and then to Clyde and Sondra, further out on the sunlit lake. As they drift toward the others, Clyde bends down to receive Sondra's kiss. Then two shots ring out and the singing stops. Claiming he wants some cigarettes, Clyde jumps onto the dock and pauses to kiss Sondra, once quickly and then again. A close-up displays her perplexity.

Figure 3.2 Clyde (Phillips Holmes) learns of the discovery of Roberta's body in *An American Tragedy*, Paramount 1931 (Kobal Collection).

Another dissolve reveals Clyde, now wearing a tweed traveling suit as he hurries anxiously through the woods, straight into the waiting deputies. Questioned by Mason, he denies all knowledge about the tripod and the letters found in his room. But when the district attorney threatens to return him to Sondra's campsite for further questioning, the horrified youth admits his presence at the lake, arguing that the boat upset after his hat blew off. Clyde is taken away and Mason goes to collect his effects at the camp, where he informs the incredulous Sondra of Clyde's arrest for the drowning of Roberta Alden. Sixty minutes into *An American Tragedy*, Clyde, who has so often turned away from the camera and the film's other characters, must face his accusers. The courtroom drama begins.

A Full House

At the Griffiths mansion, Clyde's aunt and cousin Gilbert read the voluminous newspaper coverage of the case as his uncle declares that he will finance a defense "to the limits of the law—but no more than that … If the boy's guilty he'll take the consequences." A cut to a high-angled shot shows the defendant being bundled through a howling mob into the county jail. The sound of a harmonium then accompanies a dissolve to a placard asking "How Long Since You Have Written Home to Mother?" and a tracking shot through the Star of Hope Mission ends at Clyde's own mother, also anxiously reading a newspaper. A group of pressmen enter and question her aggressively, with a photographer in the foreground taking a series of pictures to loud bangs from his noticeably cruciform flash. Cornered on the mission staircase, Mrs Griffiths eventually admits that Clyde's eastern relations don't want her to attend his trial. Asked if she took him preaching as a child, she replies that she is to blame for any wrong he has committed. A cut from the newspaper photographer to the Finchley home reveals Sondra's exasperated father plotting to keep her letters out of the trial. To her pleas that he help Clyde, Mr Finchley protests that he'll be lucky if he can help her.

After a fade to black, the image of a telegraph key and then a newspaper appears, announcing that Clyde's defense team, Belknap and Jephson, are the "foremost opponents" of the district attorney. The headlines dissolve into a medium shot of the two lawyers standing above Clyde explaining that they've "invented this other story about a change of heart." The silent defendant is told that they accept his sworn insistence that, whatever his initial provocation, he did not intend to strike Roberta at the end: "You're not guilty." Another image of a printing press then dissolves into a headline forecasting "capacity crowds" at the trial and a further dissolve discloses them in the courtroom, sitting on theatrically raked seats rising high above the floor of the court. Outside, vendors hawk peanuts, popcorn and pamphlets of Roberta's letters to the crowd, and a woman denounces Clyde as he is brought into the court. He is led through the clamor to his seat, where he observes to his lawyer, "Quite a full house, eh?" The printing presses emit their products, now headed "NATION WATCHES GRIFFITHS TRIAL."

As District Attorney Mason sets out the prosecution's case in the film's only long speech, Clyde—now seen in repeated middle close-ups—rests his chin on his hand. Watched by the enormous press gallery, Mason pays tribute to Roberta, pointing out that the dutiful young woman had gone to Lycurgus "in order that by working with her own hands, she could help her family"—and a close-up shows the elderly Aldens. As Clyde continues to stare over his closed hand, Mason's stentorian tones rise to defend her consent to premarital sex: "And so loving him, in the end she gave him all that any woman can give the man she loves. Friends, this has happened millions of times in this world of ours; it will happen millions and millions of times in the days to come. It is not new and it will never be old."

The District Attorney's oratory sustains its melodramatic tenor, portraying Roberta as a "little factory girl in [her] pathetically shabby room … good enough to betray but not good enough to marry" and a cut again shows her grizzled parents. As Mason describes Roberta informing Clyde of her pregnancy, his hand leaves his face. When his attraction to Sondra's beauty and wealth is excoriated, he begins to frown. But by the time Mason claims that he struck Roberta with his camera, his expression has again glazed over, until his attorney murmurs "Don't worry, we'll get you off with 20 years at the worst."

A dissolve to another headline announces the opening of Clyde's defense. The frock-coated Belknap (Emmett Corrigan) leads by baldly describing his client as "a mental as well as a moral coward" but not the "crime-soaked produce of the darkest vomiting of hell, as the District Attorney would have you believe." Clyde's failure to report Roberta's drowning is attributed to his fear of distressing his "wealthy relatives" and "Miss X, the brightest star in the brightest constellation of all his dreams." After an address to the jury whose (largely unheard) length is signaled by a dissolve to the court clock, Clyde is called to testify, and the camera tilts upwards to show the rows of spectators murmuring in anticipation. Standing at the right of the frame, Clyde is sworn in. Then, in a notable violation of the 180-degree rule, he is pictured at its left, sitting in the witness stand with his back to the camera.

As his second attorney, Jephson (Charles B. Middleton) questions him, the clock shows the passing of several hours. A cut returns to Clyde, now facing the camera with a church spire silhouetted in the large window behind him. As he declares that he ran away from the fatal accident in Kansas City because he was afraid he might be arrested, a track past the stern-faced male jurors reveals their evident disapproval. When Jephson repeats Belknap's description of Clyde's "mental and moral cowardice," the District Attorney's objection to his interpretation is sustained. Then Clyde is taken through his itinerant labors before arriving in Chicago, and a dissolve to two pages removed from a calendar indicates the length of his testimony.

Continuing it, Clyde explains that his genuine love for Roberta, and hers for him, led to what Jephson describes as an "evil relationship." The lawyer's questioning then switches to "Miss X." Had Clyde already been "intimate" with Roberta before meeting her? What were Clyde's plans for his future with Roberta before he met Miss X? At this point a close-up shows him swallowing and slowly admitting "I never had any real plan to do anything." Denying that he had ever promised marriage "in so many words," he squirms as he explains that he had hoped to "help her out of" her pregnancy before parting.

This brings the interrogation to the abortion references that so troubled the MPPDA. Although the Release Dialogue Script indicates that these had been cut, the UCLA print of the film retains:

Jephson: You went to that druggist who testified here?
Clyde: Yes, sir.
Jephson: Did you go to that young haberdasher who testified here as he said?
Clyde: Yes, sir.
Jephson: Did he give you the name of any particular doctor?
Clyde: Yes, sir.
Jephson: And did you send Miss Alden to that doctor?
Clyde: Yes, sir.

Jephson sums up this testimony by asking Clyde, "After she got into trouble and you couldn't help her, then what?"—a line whose confirmation of the inefficacy of the methods described may have propitiated Father Lord. But Jephson's leading of Clyde in this way provokes the District Attorney to protest. When Jephson replies that it is Mason who has coached his witnesses, the two square up for a fight. As the spectators stand to watch and the Judge gavels loudly for order, Clyde looks on in horror.

After the attorneys are made to apologize the case continues, but Jephson's increasingly histrionic questioning maintains the volume. Asked if he plotted to drown Roberta in order to marry Miss X, Clyde—now leaning forward with his hands on his knees—insists that he did not. Clasping his hands in a prayerful gesture that accords with the steeple behind him, he explains that he intended to tell Roberta that he loved another girl but that if she still insisted he would quit his job and marry her. A cut to Mason shows him muttering "Of all the bunk ..." The boat's upsetting is ascribed to Roberta's happy movement toward Clyde when he agreed to marry her. Describing how he tried to catch her as she stumbled, he stands up, his own voice now nearly as loud as Jephson's: "The next thing I knew the boat was overturned and we were in the water." As he did on his first night with Roberta, he swears repeatedly to his good intentions, rising once more to his feet.

With Clyde's clearly rehearsed interrogation concluded, the exhausted Jephson sits down, his efforts rewarded by a pat and a glass of water from his partner. But Clyde is again disconcerted when Mason begins his cross-examination by having the boat brought into the courtroom. Despite his attorney's objections, he is ordered to sit in it with a young woman clerk and go through the accident. As the calendar is torn to reveal the fateful date of Friday the thirteenth, Clyde remains in the boat, now describing his and Roberta's relative positions when they first rose to the surface. A long shot reveals the massed ranks of spectators as he admits that Roberta was only a few feet away from him and the boat. With the District Attorney standing above him on one side, and his own on the other, Clyde protests that he was too dazed and fearful to go to Roberta's aid. When a spectator shouts his condemnation from the gallery, he experiences the judicial power bearing down on the defendant. Hauled from his seat he is marched to the judge who has him arrested for contempt and sets the bail at a thousand dollars.

The calendar sheds another page but Clyde is still being cross-examined. Standing at first behind him, Mason asks about his expenditures on his trip with Roberta. When the meticulous defendant mistakes the boat's hourly rental charge, the District Attorney thunders that he had no intention of returning it. A cut to the defense team shows them concluding that he is guilty after all. Finally Mason exposes Clyde's argument that he hadn't chosen to visit Big Bittern until he and Roberta were already traveling by revealing the travel brochures he had collected earlier in Lycurgus. As these are passed to the jury for examination, a tracking shot surveys the twelve men, whose bald heads and old fashioned tailoring so markedly contrast with Clyde's youthful appearance. A cut returns to Clyde in middle close-up, his eyes looking around wildly in fear.

A fade to black and then up to a ticker tape machine dissolves to its message: "GRIFFITH JURY STILL OUT ... VERDICT OF GUILTY EXPECTED." This expectation is confirmed in a cut to the jurors. When one argues that he doesn't believe that Clyde's lawyers would let him lie and that he dislikes Mason's politics, he and the juror who supports his right to disagree are summarily told they will be run out of town. They immediately cave in, assenting to a unanimous verdict of first-degree murder. (In a brief moment of subversive comedy, the second juror then protests to the others, "He had a right to his opinion. He changed his mind, didn't he?") The crowd files into the gallery as Clyde is brought handcuffed into the court. In medium shot he rises to hear the verdict and in long shot he listens to his attorney's request to defer sentencing. Then he is preceded out of the court by the rushing reporters. A dissolve to his waiting mother reveals that she too has been employed by a newspaper in order to fund support for Clyde, now abandoned by his uncle. In mid-close-up she clasps her son and demands the truth. Again with his back to the camera, he replies that he is not guilty and she embraces him with relief, thanking God for not making her doubt her child. Another printing press then spews out its contents, a front page featuring Mrs Griffiths' photograph and announcing her presence as a reporter at Clyde's sentencing. The image dissolves to her in the courtroom as the judge enters. Offered a final statement, Clyde emphatically

declares his innocence, to his mother's joy. As the judge begins his pronounce-
ment, the convicted youth turns toward the gallery, sees her and smiles. Then
he turns back again as she watches him serenely accept a sentence of execution.

The First White Script concluded immediately after the trial with Mrs
Griffiths joyfully proclaiming to a journalist, "You heard my boy say he was
innocent" and the journalist replying, "Sure I did! It will be all right, Mother.
Don't you worry. You know, this thing could have happened to any one of us"
(First White Script, February 12, 1931, Paramount Script Collection). In the
completed film, that scene is replaced by one written by Lauren, in which a dissolve takes Mrs Griffiths to the dark corridor of death row. There she finds
Clyde in his cell. They embrace through the bars and he laments that he has
done nothing in his life but make her miserable. When she declares her intention of proving his innocence, he suddenly replies, "But I'm not ... really."
Then, holding her in a very close shot, Clyde lowers his eyes to say, "I didn't kill
Roberta, but when she fell in the water I could have saved her ... I swam away,
because in my heart I wanted her to die." Looking more directly at his shocked
mother, he exclaims "I don't know how I could have done this thing!" and
throws himself on his cot. But Mrs Griffiths insists that it's not his fault: "We
brought you up among ugly, evil surroundings, and while we were trying to save
the souls of others, we were letting you go astray." Clyde listens in his dark cell,
a light illuminating his fair hair and anguished countenance. Then, rising to his
mother, he asks "Are they really going to ...?" She urges him to face his punishment bravely, promising that "somehow, somewhere, you'll be given the right
start." As Clyde embraces her once more, he turns away from the camera for the
final time.

To Photograph a Thought

The US reviews of *An American Tragedy* were, at best, mixed. *The New York
Time's* Mordaunt Hall praised the "emphatically stirring" trial scenes, but criticized the omission of the beginning and end of Dreiser's novel. Holmes's performance prior to the trail was described as "flabby," conveying little of Clyde's
enthusiasm for either Roberta or Sondra. Ironically, in the light of Eisenstein
and Dreiser's rejected temptation scenes, Hall observed: "Mr Von Sternberg had
a wonderful opportunity to make the most of sound and photography in the
scenes in which Griffiths thinks up the idea of drowning Roberta, but he contents himself with presenting them in a somewhat stereotyped pictorial fashion,
frequently turning to presses pouring out newspapers in order to emphasize his
action" (Hall, 1931b).

In Germany, by contrast, the film was a critical success.[8] After seeing a
preview in October 1931, Herbert Ihering hailed it as "a masterpiece":

A young man's hollowness and frivolousness ... In the hotel, in the simple apartment, in society, on the water, on the street—what richness of images, which never

become their own goal; what richness of exquisite faces, which represent an American world ... and yet the criticism is razor-sharp, the rejection of a world is accomplished through representation alone. (Ihering, in Baxter, 1980: 26)

Where German critics like Ihering praised *An American Tragedy* as a characteristic Sternberg work in its ability "to make art enjoyable and yet critically reject the world presented by it" (Ihering, 1980: 26), subsequent commentaries have largely regarded it as an ellipsis in his 1930s output, if they discuss it at all. Staccato in tempo, sparse in mise en scene and static in composition compared to his Dietrich films, its relative deficiencies are exemplified by the even-then clichéd tearing of calendar pages to signify the length of the trial, particularly when compared with Professor Rath scorching another calendar to cool Lola's curling iron in *The Blue Angel*. Yet Dreiser's themes of poverty and its determination were addressed by Sternberg (albeit from very different convictions) in his earliest feature, *The Salvation Hunters* (1925), which concludes with a title proclaiming "It is not conditions, nor is it environment—our faith controls our lives." And the key visual devices of *An American Tragedy* would not only be developed in the director's more celebrated films, in the aquatic title sequence of *Blonde Venus* (1932) for example, but would also influence George Stevens' adaptation of the novel twenty years later.

Beginning with the opening titles, the transparent water, whose surface is rippled by the dropped pebbles, and its association with the use of the dissolve does much more than anticipate Roberta's drowning, as Harry Potamkin complained. John Baxter's reading of this imagery as representing the "pale liquidity" (Baxter, 1971: 88) of the characters' motivations suggests that Sternberg's film also shares an interest in the stream of consciousness that Dreiser and Eisenstein sought to represent. If the transparent depths of the water provide a patent figure for psychological interiority and the "flow" of cognition, the widening ripples caused by the pebbles offer an equally legible suggestion of the continuing consequences of such thought. By manipulating this imagery to show the rapid alternation of limpidity and obscurity in a body of water, the film eloquently establishes not the transparency of Clyde's motives, but their opacity—to himself as well as others. The young suitor who repeatedly prefaces his declarations to Sondra with "If you only knew ..." ends the film exclaiming "I don't know how I could have done this thing!" The answer, as Eisenstein complained, is the crucial issue for both Christian morality and American jurisprudence. The culpable connection of intention and act that he ridiculed in the face of the powerful determinations of wealth and social hierarchy comes to the fore in Sternberg's adaptation, whose multiple overlapping dissolves are often narratively consequential as well as temporarily sequential.

To be sure, the dissolve—at its simplest, a fade-out overlapped with a fade-in—was most often used by Sternberg in *An American Tragedy* for its conventional purpose, to advance the story and in so doing, as David Bordwell points out, to "soften spatial, graphic and even temporal discontinuities" (Bordwell,

1988: 47). By the time of its production, dissolves between shots taken with synchronous sound no longer required a re-recording of sound after the edit, which had hitherto intensified distortion on the combined sound track. This permitted Sternberg to employ dissolves in order "to make small adjustments to the rhythm within a shot or to juxtapose two shots that he had not originally planned to use in that way" (Salt, 1980: 110), facilitating his idiosyncratic use of the device to "graphically superimpose two discrete story actions" (Bordwell, 1988: 78). Such a superimposition occurs early in *An American Tragedy*, when after Clyde's mother prays that God watch over him, her image is visible over the freight train on which he is traveling, effectively representing her "watching over" Clyde. But if such a dissolve can represent maternal concern, it can also represent malevolent plotting, most notably when Clyde's scrutiny of the map collected at the Lycurgus House dissolves into the lake where he is boating with Roberta. Although the latter functions as a simple continuity device (identifying the lake with the site seen on the map via its sequential juxtaposition), it also conveys something more sinister—the efficacy of his intent, the consequentiality of his murderous fantasies. ("Our aim has been to photograph a Thought," a title announces in *The Salvation Hunters*.) As a linking device such dissolves can—like the literary free indirect—operate both objectively and subjectively, furthering the narrative while revealing the thoughts of a character. This possibility is illustrated in a characteristic Sternberg dissolve between two discrete story actions, the dissolve from Roberta lying in her room to Clyde and Sondra flirting at the party. Here the effect is both that of objective contrast (the dark silence of the factory girl's lodgings versus the bright gaiety of the dinner dance) and of subjective fantasy (Roberta imagining Clyde enjoying himself in Lycurgus society, thoughts that she will bitterly express later in the film).

Finally, Sternberg's constant use of dissolves in this tragedy gives it the fluency of fatalism, a doomed inevitability as scene glides into scene. This sense of inevitability is arguably heightened by the extraordinary plethora of titles and textual inserts (notes, newspaper headlines, calendars, telegrams, etc.) used to tell the story. Mordaunt Hall was not exaggerating when he described such devices as already hackneyed in 1931. The over-the-shoulder shot of Clyde reading about Roberta's drowning in the newspaper was a recognized storytelling technique as early as 1911.[9] The conspicuous resort to these devices (greatly exceeding their use elsewhere in the director's early sound films) may be attributed to the narrative demands of Dreiser's immense novel, as well as its own attention to the mass media's role in Clyde's formation and prosecution. But in his extremely helpful discussion of his lawsuit, Thomas Strychacz offers a further interpretation of the novel's appropriation of such documents that also sheds light on Sternberg's adaptation.[10]

Reviewing Paramount's claim that Dreiser's use of newspaper reports and Grace Brown's letters constituted "cold-blooded plagiarism" (Swanberg, 1965: 377), as well as the critical discussion of his often clichéd style, Strychacz traces the book's extensive telling and retelling of its tale, most obvious in the trial's lengthy reconstruction in Book Three of the narrative of Clyde's life in Books One and Two. Moreover, what Roberta condemns as Clyde's duplicitous "storying" (*An American Tragedy*: 390) is both his default reaction to the questions asked by her, his mother, his uncle, Sondra, the District Attorney etc. and also his method of self-fashioning. Clyde is not alone in attempting to create a plausible account of his life. Both the defense and the prosecution invent narratives of Roberta's drowning, and afterwards Reverend McMillan formulates his own—lethal—interpretation of the case. As we have seen, the American newspapers have a considerable role in this life writing, climaxing with a journalist at the trial helping Mrs Griffiths "arrange her impressions in the form in which he assumed her Denver paper might like them" (*An American Tragedy*: 810). The repetitiousness of these accounts far exceeds the replication of passages from the New York *World's* coverage of the 1906 case or Brown's letters. As Strychacz notes, the novel's final chapter quotes extensively from its own opening one. If the readers who remembered the Gillette-Brown case would have regarded Clyde's conviction and execution as a foregone conclusion, they are not alone.

As an adaptation of Dreiser's novel, Sternberg's film is yet another retelling. And however limited in length and expenditure, it too repeats the novel's use of repetition. After we have seen the car hitting the child, Clyde tells his mother about it. After we have watched his travels to Lycurgus, his lawyer describes them in court. After we have witnessed Roberta's drowning, the coroner repeats the police report to his assistant and the District Attorney offers his damning reconstruction to the jury. Clyde describes it three times, offering different explanations of his innocence to the deputies and the court and finally his confession of guilt to his mother. Moreover, the film replicates Dreiser's replication of the newspaper accounts of the 1906 trial with its own repeated use of news vendors, printing presses and headlines. These last anticipate events to come by literal prediction ("VERDICT OF GUILTY EXPECTED") and visual prefiguration (the front page photograph of Clyde's mother dissolving to her sitting in court). As in the novel, they underline the inevitability of Clyde's fate. Combined with the plethora of titles in the early part of the film, these texts also serve as a blatant reminder of the film's prestigious literary source, itself invoked as further evidence of a tragedy foretold.[11] In this regard, Bernice Klimans' complaint that the newspaper presses are "tired" and the titles "redundant" (Klimans 1977: 264) misses the point, which is the preordination suggested by that very redundancy.

In Sternberg's adaptation, Clyde is both a cause and a victim of the film's events, looking into the future through the map, but failing to see destiny coming up behind him time and time again. The director's desire to downplay the "sociological" determinants of his fate would construe him as the erring protagonist of tragedy rather than the wounded innocent of melodrama, as would his self-questioning at the film's end. Nevertheless, the rejection of the American world remarked by Ihering necessarily dilutes moral responsibility. However unsympathetic we find Clyde, the rich hotel guests, the hit and run driver, his uncle's snobbish family, the narcissistic Sondra, the rapacious pressmen, the grandstanding DA, the dishonest defense lawyers and the bullying jurors appear no less so. Given Roberta's fornication and Mrs Griffiths' confession to Clyde's neglect at the film's end, no one is entirely innocent. If the ambitious youth is part of this oppressive milieu, "Number 7" in an identical line of bellboys when we first glimpse him, this only serves to spread the blame. Seen so often at a distance, or from behind, this *homme fatale* is rarely given Dietrich's mysterious close-ups, yet like her his "identity is enigmatic and shifting", his "control over" his "life alternately absolute and partial" (Baxter, 1993: 115).

Had Lauren's additional scenes not been added, Clyde would have been even more enigmatic—confessing neither his plot to Roberta in the boat nor his abandonment of her to his mother in the prison. Without his despondent final confession, our last glimpse of him would have been his serene acceptance of the sentence he had pronounced unfair. In their different ways, the studio's desire for a sympathetic hero, the MPPDA's pressure for a clear moral lesson and Dreiser's wish to retain the opening and closing of his novel undermined Sternberg's characterization, producing incoherence rather than ambiguity. But neither the director's initial assembly nor the final film bears out the condemnation of Hollywood cinema pronounced by Dreiser's lawyers in his suit against Paramount: "People and actions are good or bad. Life is a success or failure. There are no tones, no shades or shadows." The gliding dissolves and chiaroscuro lighting of Sternberg's film offered neither moral certainty nor a profitable return to Paramount, but they would be seen again in Hollywood's next *American Tragedy*.

Notes

1. This account will contest Lea Jacobs' claim in her important article on the film (Jacobs, L. (1995), "An American Tragedy: A Comparison of Film and Literary Censorship," *Quarterly Review of Film and Video*, 15(4), pp. 87–98) that Dreiser was unaware of the influence of the MPPDA on Paramount. He was not only warned by Liveright about Hays in 1925—he was warned again in Hollywood in March 1931. But although he deplored the censorship of the MPPDA he was even more concerned about the changes in his story initiated by the studio. As the documentation of the production shows, Paramount and the MPPDA often had different concerns about the filming of the novel.

2. Sternberg's adaptation retained Dreiser's name, apparently chosen in reference to the Athenian orator who established an official edition of the tragedies of Aeschylus, Euripides and Sophocles in 330 BC.

3. A 1929 interview of Phillips Holmes supports this feminine persona with the actor's proclamation that he played the leading lady in college productions at Princeton: "Somebody had to be the girl, so I was always 'it'"—

"Son Follows Own Career," *Los Angeles Times*, October 27, 1929.

4. See Baxter, P. (1993), *Just Watch! Sternberg, Paramount and America*, London: British Film Institute, p. 186.

5. Sylvia Sidney was much praised for her performance in this film and Dreiser himself was delighted when she was cast in the title role of *Jennie Gerhardt* in 1933. Her contemporary impact was memorably recorded by B. P. Schulberg's son Budd: "The film had an ambivalent fascination for me: How many sons have an opportunity to stare at their father's mistress on the screen of a darkened movie palace? Watching Sylvia Sidney crinkle her face in a provocative smile, first sexually aroused, then socially rejected, watching her pout, suffer, plead ... I could understand her attraction for Father. Clara Bow had been cute and saucy, but Sylvia had a sensuous Jewish quality that reached out to me and troubled me. In that vast audience held under her spell, I knew that I was the only one involved in personal drama with her," Schulberg, B. (1981), *Moving Pictures: Memories of a Hollywood Prince*, New York: Stein & Day, p. 393.

6. As Lea Jacobs points out, none of Clyde's dialogue here is included in the First White Script (Jacobs, L. (1995), "An American Tragedy: A Comparison of Film and Literary Censorship," *Quarterly Review of Film and Video*, 15(4), p. 93). It was inserted later, presumably to exculpate him.

7. The First White Script's dialogue about the District Attorney's political motives in prosecuting this case has been removed. See Jacobs, L. (1995), "An American Tragedy: A Comparison of Film and Literary Censorship," *Quarterly Review of Film and Video*, 15(4), p. 92. However, brief references to the politics surrounding the trial survive in newspaper headlines and the jury scene.

8. See Thomas J. Saunders (1994), *Hollywood in Berlin*, Berkeley, University of California, p. 238.

9. See Thompson, K. (1988) "The Formation of the Classical Narrative", in D. Bordwell, J. Staiger and K. Thompson, *The Classical Hollywood Cinema*, London: Routledge, p. 189.

10. Thomas Strychacz (1993), *Modernism, Mass Culture, and Professionalism*, Cambridge, Cambridge University Press, pp. 84–116.

11. The extensive incorporation of this literary material is ironic in the light of Sternberg's later admission that he would have appeared as a witness for Dreiser in his suit against Paramount: "Literature cannot be transferred to the screen without a loss to its values; the visual elements completely revalue the written word" (Sternberg: 1966, 259).

CHAPTER 4

A Place on the Screen

I took Mr Eastman, from the Eastman-Kodak, and called him George.

George Stevens in an interview with Robert Hughes, 1967

In 1921, the year before Dreiser left Hollywood, sixteen-year-old George Stevens arrived there with his parents, itinerant actors seeking work. Stevens had been a child actor and stage manager in his family's touring company, but his photographic talents soon secured him other employment. The Hal Roach Studios hired him as an assistant cameraman and he later filmed dozens of comedies for Laurel and Hardy, Harry Langdon and the "Our Gang" ensemble. In 1932 Stevens moved briefly to Universal and then to RKO and eventual success as an accomplished director of comedies, melodramas, musicals, and adventure pictures, notably *Alice Adams* (1935), *Swing Time* (1936), *Gunga Din* (1939), *Woman of the Year* (1942) and *The More the Merrier* (1943).

Many of the themes and stylistic characteristics of this generic fare anticipate his post-war productions, with his penultimate prewar film, *The Talk of the Town* (1942) an extended excursus on the American legal system, conducted as a romantic triangle in which a law professor and a fugitive labor organizer contend for the affections of a school teacher while debating the question of class justice. Nevertheless, Stevens would later claim that both his personal views and his filmmaking were transformed by his service as head of the Army Signal Corps' Special Motion Picture Unit. Between 1943 and 1945 he directed filming in Tunisia and then in Europe with an unusual company of creative personnel, including the novelists William Saroyan and Irwin Shaw (co-writer of *The Talk of the Town*) and two of his most important future collaborators, the Hollywood cameraman William Mellor and the young Anglo-American documentarist Ivan Moffat. Their footage and accompanying commentary scripts were sent back to the likes of Carol Reed, John Huston, William Wyler and Frank Capra for the production of documentaries and newsreels. Offered greater mobility than combat photographers attached to specific military units, the group filmed the Normandy invasion, the liberation of Paris, the Battle of the Bulge and the opening of the concentration camp at Dachau. Mostly they shot on 35 mm black and white but Stevens also kept a personal record on 16 mm Kodachrome that would figure significantly in a later history of the cinema.

The 1994 compilation of this color footage (*George Stevens: D-Day to Berlin*) includes images from Dachau of the massive piles of dead and the skeletal bodies of the dying, agony on a scale that Stevens later described as "unbelievable," like "one of Dante's infernal visions" (Kirschner, 2004: 18–19). One incident in this hell particularly troubled the director, and it is telling for the examination of guilt and complicity in his later work. To several interviewers he recalled a moment when, grabbed by a begging prisoner covered with lice, he felt revulsion rather than pity. As he later described this scene in the documentary *George Stevens: A Filmmaker's Journey* (George Stevens Jr., 1984), "I feel the Nazi in myself. I abhor his man, and I want him to keep his hands off me. And the reason I want him to keep his hands off me is because I see myself capable of arrogance and brutality to keep him off me. That's a fierce thing, to discover within yourself that which you despise the most in others."[1] A sense of shocked complicity also infused Stevens' recollections of the beating of the camp's officers by their US military interrogators and the angry reproaches of their victims. Horrified by the events he had witnessed, he remained in Germany after the war, preparing concentration camp footage for two documentaries presented as evidence in the Nuremberg War Crimes trials, *Nazi Concentration Camps* (1945) and *The Nazi Plan* (1945), the latter directed by him with commentary by Budd Schulberg, the son of Paramount producer B. P. Schulberg.

At the end of 1945 Stevens came back to Hollywood, where several studios bid for his services. Reluctant to return to work immediately, and determined to choose less upbeat entertainment, he joined Capra, Wyler and producer Sam Briskin in an independent company, Liberty Films, contracted to supply nine features to RKO. But the company's only independently produced film was to be Capra's *It's a Wonderful Life* (1946), which could not recoup its profits in time to finance subsequent productions. By April 1947, against Stevens' wishes, Liberty was sold to Paramount. As compensation he became both a shareholder and a contract director there. To settle Paramount's obligation to RKO, he was immediately loaned back to the studio to direct *I Remember Mama* (1948), based on Kathryn Forbes' nostalgic novel of a Norwegian immigrant family's life in San Francisco at the turn of the century. Raised in nearby Oakland during this period, and an adept maker of "women's pictures," Stevens executed this project with his characteristic meticulousness, requesting rewrites from the set and shooting so much coverage that the budget soared, reducing his own salary. The sentimental success that resulted was not the "serious" film that Stevens was determined to make but neither was it his last study of a strong mother or the aspirations of the poor.

Committed to delivering five films by 1952, Stevens had several proposals rejected by Paramount, including a film about the war to be adapted from Irwin Shaw's novel *The Young Lions* or Norman Mailer's *The Naked and the Dead*. "I thought that since I knew at least something of the local color of war, somebody would ask me to direct a war picture," he later recalled. "I sat around waiting—and that was a big mistake" (Boyle, 2004: 14). But there was one possible compensation in joining the studio. Stevens had first read *An American Tragedy* in the 1920s, and he knew that Paramount retained the rights to the novel. Rereading it in a 1948 edition, he underlined and annotated passages including those describing the protagonist's desire for "something different, better, more beautiful" (*An American Tragedy*: 18) and his "straight, well-cut nose, high white forehead, wavy, glossy, black hair, eyes that were black and rather melancholy at times" (*An American Tragedy*: 27). He also ordered books and clippings about Dreiser, who had died three years earlier after joining the Communist Party in his old age. In December of 1948 Stevens suggested a new film of *An American Tragedy* in a memo to studio production chief Henry Ginsberg. Ginsberg's reply raised the rather implausible problem of copyright conflict with the Kearney play, which had, after all, preceded Paramount's first adaptation. Convinced that such considerations were negligible, Stevens continued preliminary work on the novel. When, in January, permission to make it was again withheld, Stevens replied with a letter (George Stevens to Henry Ginsburg, January 22, 1949, George Stevens Collection, A Place in the Sun, Margaret Herrick Library, Academy of Motion Picture Arts and Sciences, Los Angeles, hereafter GSC, APS), listing those of his suggestions that were rejected by the studio, among them a production of *Madame Butterfly* to star Jennifer Jones, adaptations of Shaw's *The Young Lions* and of *An American Tragedy*. The greatness of the latter, he argued, had not been "explored at all" in the Sternberg version and "could make a male star." Noting that Ginsburg had already agreed that Montgomery Clift would be "particularly suitable" for the leading role, Stevens protested that the studio's delays in greenlighting any of his proposals would make it impossible for him to meet his contractual commitments.

At a crisis meeting with studio chiefs in March, Stevens asked their opinion of Arthur Miller's new play, *Death of a Salesman*. When they responded enthusiastically, he argued that Dreiser's novel offered the same values that made the play so popular and could be filmed "at a cost of a million two or three using one famous name only." In response to one executive's claim that the title *An American Tragedy* (by then identified with a dead Communist, a dated novel and a failed early "talkie") would jeopardize the success of any new adaptation, Stevens insisted that he would not be making a period piece: "he wanted it to be in the highest sense a representation of contemporary life" (Inter-office Communication from Ivan Moffat to George Stevens, re: March 8, 1949 meeting, GSC, APS). Still refused permission, the exasperated director—like Dreiser before him—turned to the law, engaging an attorney to sue Paramount for effective breach of his employee's contract and his rights as a shareholder. Faced with actions on two fronts, Paramount quickly relented. By April 4 a memo from Stevens records that Clift's services had been secured for the production.

That same memo also noted that screenwriter Michael Wilson had been signed to work on the story, and in an April 29 telegram to Clift, Stevens wired that Wilson was writing the screenplay and was "happy to hear of your pleased interest in this regard." "Mike is good," the telegram continues. "The drama becomes quite new to us as it unfolds in terms of 1950" (GSC, APS). On the following day, the director sent another telegram to screenwriter Joel Sayre reporting "About American T. I have been working on it for about three months with Mike Wilson who has been with us at Liberty ... Opposition to this terrific throughout the organization here and generally in Hollywood" (April 30, 1949, GSC, APS).

Officially, Michael Wilson's participation in the adaptation of *An American Tragedy* for the screen began on March 24, 1949, according to a studio memo stipulating a first draft treatment by August 1 of that year and a second by September 24. A Liberty contract writer who had written episodes of *Hopalong Cassidy* before becoming a communications officer in the Marines during the war, Wilson had never worked with Stevens. But his uncredited polish of *It's a Wonderful Life* had impressed Frank Capra enough to commission an adaptation of Jessamyn West's 1945 *Friendly Persuasion*. Capra had hoped to make this portrait of a Quaker family in the Civil War his second film for Liberty, but the reactionary mood that gave the Republicans control of Congress in 1946 and fueled the House Committee on Un-American Activities' investigations of Hollywood in 1947 would postpone its production for several years. After completing a script dramatizing its youthful hero's decision to become a stretcher bearer rather than engage in combat, Wilson turned to Dreiser's novel with the leftwing convictions that had led him in 1938 to join the Communist Party, an affiliation of which Stevens was aware.[2] The precise extent of Wilson's contribution to the final film, how it changed and why, have been the subject of extensive speculation.

In an interview shortly before his death, Ivan Moffat claimed that employing Wilson followed by another screenwriter was his idea. The son of an American photographer and the great-grandson of the British actor-manager Sir Herbert Beerbohm Tree, Moffat had been educated at Dartington Hall and the London School of Economics. He then wrote scripts for British propaganda pictures before joining Stevens' unit. After his service in the Army Signals Corps, Moffat had joined Stevens at Liberty, working first on *I Remember Mama*. He became the director's factotum, contributing to treatments, scripts and production decisions. As he later recalled, "I thought we should take a very unusual step and have in advance two writers following each other." Wilson was chosen for his sympathy with Dreiser's novel and its politics, but another writer was deemed necessary to realize the wealthy characters' milieu, "for dialogue, for the more frivolous aspects of life" (Moss, 2004: 155). That writer was Harry Brown, a poet, playwright and novelist, whose 1945 story of a platoon left leaderless at the Salerno landing, *A Walk in the Sun*, had been successfully adapted by Robert Rossen for filming by Lewis Milestone in 1946.

A Modern Story

The first treatment submitted by Michael Wilson is dated April 27, 1949. Headed *Theodore Dreiser's An American Tragedy* and retaining the novel's key character and place names, it opens in an unemployment office in Chicago, where Clyde describes his background in an interview with a social worker:

> Clyde had been drafted just as the war ended; consequently he was one of the last to be discharged, and returned to find the best job opportunities already taken by veterans who preceded him. Pre-war work experience? Throughout his youth, Clyde had helped his widowed mother run a skidrow mission in downtown Chicago—hardly a recommendation for entry into the business world. Anything else? What's he done the past two years? Worked as a bellboy in a big Chicago hotel—till he was fired.

The treatment continues with a description of Clyde's career aspirations, "like a success story straight out of the slick magazines ..." After meeting his rich uncle he hitchhikes to his factory town, where he's told that "If you spit out the window in Lycurgus, the chances are you'll spit on Griffiths property." His first encounter with the glamorous Sondra Finchley reveals "a lovely, vivacious girl of twenty" whose "surface gaiety" overlays "an unarticulated dissatisfaction with the frivolous society doings that fill her days." Roberta, the factory worker who becomes Clyde's lover, is also "very pretty indeed—but when she is despondent she can look like something the cat dragged in." In a parenthesis Wilson notes his wish to make Roberta "less dependant and pitiful" than in the novel, with "a certain capability, an outgoing warmth, great need for love without being a clinging vine." Not only are both female characters projected more positively than in the novel but so is Clyde's uncle, who praises his nephew to Sondra's father and recommends him as a good match for his daughter.

The climactic scene on the lake in which Clyde contemplates murdering Roberta is set out at length in this first treatment. As he rows she dreamily wishes on a star, prattling about their future life together, "unaware of the torment she is causing Clyde—for in every picture that Roberta paints, Clyde substitutes the image of his lost Sondra." Instead of Dreiser's conflicting inner voices commanding him to kill! and not kill!, Clyde's dejection makes Roberta suddenly realize: "Clyde—you wished I was dead. Didn't you, Clyde? And Clyde suddenly sitting up, gripping the camera between his hands, trembling, with almost a sob of denial—No, it isn't true! He doesn't want her to die! He swears he doesn't!"

As Roberta rises to comfort him, Clyde shrinks back and the boat begins to rock. Reaching up to steady her with his camera still in his hand, he accidentally strikes her in the face, upsetting the vessel. He swims towards the terrified woman, but she pulls them both under. When he rises again choking, he whirls around and calls her name. Only when there is no answer does the "exhausted, gasping" Clyde swim to shore.

At the treatment's conclusion Sondra, "kept practically incommunicado" at a resort by her parents during Clyde's trial, hears on the radio that he is to be executed. Her farewell visit to him in the death house "casts a light on the dark shadows in his life, leaves him with a certain tranquility of spirit." Here Wilson makes another radical departure from the novel, where Sondra abandons Clyde on his arrest, with her unsigned letter of goodbye destroying his last hopes. And finally, again unlike Dreiser, he gives Clyde a vivid epiphany with the sun streaming down on his walk to the execution chamber: "And quietly, his voice filled with wonder: It's so bright" (GSC, APS).

A second version of this early treatment, dated May 9, experiments with new names for the central characters. Clyde is called Glen Hackley and his uncle Marcus owns the Hackley Mills shirt factory. Clyde's factory lover is named Rosemary Adams and their first encounter outside work takes place at the Springfield Community Park public pool. Sondra is now Beatrice Forbes. Most importantly, the treatment is retitled *A Modern Story*.

Throughout their collaboration Wilson and Stevens disagreed about how faithful their film should be to the novel, with Stevens arguing that the postwar United States was a far less stratified society than that of Dreiser's setting.

> The scene that he'd reported so carefully was a crueler scene by far than existed today as far as the social structure was concerned. People didn't have a chance. A girl got $5 a week if she worked in a store, and a young man got $11, and he worked at that until he got to be thirty-five, and he got $15. And the war came along, and a young man had a chance. (George Stevens interviewed by Robert Hughes, February–March 1967, unpublished MS, GSC)

And to Eduardo Escorel (unpublished interview, June 1969, GSC) he maintained that the wartime Army was for many poor GIs "a means of mixing, mingling, being a part of ... The entrance to the other world of class was quite simple at that time: reasonable charm, good demeanor and average intelligence, and that bridge could be jumped."

Moffat, who had himself briefly been a member of the Communist Party, was more inclined toward the novel's politics and aesthetics, but he too criticized Wilson's early characterizations. In his May script notes, he argues that Clyde should exhibit a "tremendous, pent-up zest for life" for which the audience "will forgive ... much that is morally condemned" (May 9, GSC, APS). When Sondra and Clyde dance together alone, Moffat saw them "in a sort of motionless ecstasy. Sondra is dreamy and at peace, but Clyde still is tense, set, passionate." Their scene together after the drowning, when Clyde "is clutching the last and great symbol of a life he knows is doomed" should be "the moment when the audience gets its reward—the reward it must be given in full" (May 17, GSC, APS). To update the story, Moffat suggests that Sondra laughingly interpret the police car pursuing Clyde as a speed patrol, and he urges Stevens to commission a jazz score for the film. The director claimed not to have read Eisenstein's adaptation until after he completed his own, but Moffat's 10 May note echoes the Russian's description of Clyde leaving the mission "firmly resolved, in the direction of Life—in the direction of light and movement" (Montagu, 1969: 213–14):

> This will be a picture about Life and its determined pursuit. And Clyde, although he is, on the surface, shy, has acquired from his past a strong taste for the vivid aspects of life, and a strong sense of denial for all the dead things in his own past— the old and decrepit men in the fusty, tomb-like mission with its old religion and faded books. Upon all this Clyde turns his back when he leaves for his uncle's factory, away from decay and towards the bright future, the place in the sun ... (GSC, APS)

By May 23, Wilson submitted another treatment, which introduces Clyde hitchhiking in a "white T-shirt and a pair of jeans" as a Cadillac sweeps past. Determined to seize his chance at his uncle's shirt factory, he thumbs a ride to his mother's mission and asks her "Is it wrong to want to live? To belong in the world? To want a little happiness?" Taking him in her arms to apologize for the poverty and humiliation of his childhood, she warns him "that he is now entering a different world—a world of temptations and bright promises, a world where men have enthroned the Almighty Dollar over God almighty—and Clyde shouldn't let it break his heart if not all doors are open to him." Later, when Clyde's efficiency plan is turned down at the factory, another worker tells him to "forget the Horatio Alger stuff" and accept his lowly status there. At a local car lot, Clyde longingly sits in a Cadillac, but buys a jalopy. Invited to his uncle's Christmas party, he is excluded by Sondra (now a Vassar girl) and her friends' Ivy League banter. Taking refuge alone in the billiard room, he proves a "terrible pool player." When he's discovered there by Sondra, she jokes "I see your mother kept you out of the pool halls." Eventually his uncle enters and insists that Clyde telephone his Christmas greetings home to the mission, as Sondra looks on.

In this longer treatment, Dreiser's interior monologues are attempted, with a voice over the lake scene exhorting "Now! Do it now! It is so easy ... just a little blow with the oar, to stun her ..." Although Roberta drowns accidentally when the boat capsizes, Wilson adheres to the novel in this version by having Clyde's defense propose a fictive explanation—that the despondent woman had decided to end her life. Retained from the previous treatment are Sondra's last visit to Clyde and the dazzling brilliance of the sun as he walks to his execution, but its final shot pulls back from the prison to the highway. There another young man is seen hitchhiking—"hopeful, eager, lusty with life" (GSC, APS)—repeating the novel's ironic return after Clyde's execution to his missionary family, still preaching on the streets.

Throughout the summer of 1949 Wilson submitted preliminary drafts, all of them titled *A Modern Story*. But, as ever, he was not working alone. Stevens' annotations to the 1948 edition of the novel include the underlining of a passage in which a friend of Gilbert's ridicules his claim "that there was some social importance to making and distributing collars, giving polish and manner to people who wouldn't otherwise have them" (*An American Tragedy*: 352). In the margin he has written "bathing suits." The transformation of Dreiser's collar factory to one making women's swimwear had a number of advantages. It introduced water sports—and the danger of drowning—immediately into the story; and it shifted attention from male vanity to female glamor, particularly the maternal curves of hip and breast emphasized by the one-piece suits of the period.[3] Like Sternberg, Moffat sought out an actual garment works, the Jantzen[4] swimsuit manufacturers in Portland, Oregon. In a June 15 memo to Stevens he wrote: "On the walls of the work-rooms were hanging posters which glorified in color the faces and bodies of the beautiful girls who were going to wear the bathing-suits being mass-produced by the tired, blowsy and listless-eyed women and girls who fed cloth through the sewing-machines and cut material with long shears."

The layout of the factory offered a vivid representation of the economic distance between the "listless-eyed women" sitting at their machines and the "beautiful girls" on the walls above them. In his memo, Moffat described Clyde mediating between these two levels, "perhaps aroused by the same erotic expectations of the men who whistle at the idea of a bathing-suit factory—[he] would indeed scan most carefully and most indulgently the ranks of the live women who worked below the pictures" (GSC, APS).

Soon afterwards, the figure of the bathing beauty became the key visual motif of the draft screenplays. On September 1, Harry Brown submitted a preliminary draft opening with the protagonist hitchhiking at the outskirts of his uncle's town. As a woman and two men hurl past him in a Cadillac, he sees "a huge billboard on which is a gaily colored picture of a curvilinear girl floating on a lake. Beneath her is the slogan ... IT'S BETTER THAN FLOATING ON AIR" (GSC). Referencing this aquatic theme, and the Shakespearean precedent that had led Eisenstein to reference *Hamlet* in his treatment, Brown's draft seals the female victim's fate by siting a print of Millais's pre-Raphaelite painting of the drowned Ophelia in Clyde's boarding house.

Michael Wilson turned in a complete preliminary screenplay in early August, and Brown followed with his in September. As the lead writer, Wilson was first to register several major changes in the conception of the central characters. By the end of July, his drafts reveal names changes for the central protagonists. Roberta becomes Alberta and then Alice Smith. The evolution of her given name from Roberta ("Bert") to Alberta to Alice ("Al") Smith (and later to Alice Tripp) is clearly governed by the wish to retain a masculine nickname like that of the real-life drowning victim Grace ("Billy") Brown while adding the implication of a social impediment. Sondra Finchley becomes Angela Douglas (later Angela Vickers), echoing Clyde's declaration to Sondra in the novel that he had once seen her in a local flower parade looking "beautiful, like an angel almost" (*An American Tragedy*: 336) and its intensification in Kearney's play, where

Clyde tells Sondra "From the first time I ever saw you ... you were like a beautiful angel to me ... a beautiful angel that I couldn't ever touch ... couldn't even look at" (Patrick Kearney, *An American Tragedy*, II-I-17, undated manuscript, GSC, APS). Most importantly, Clyde Griffiths becomes George Eastman.

In her memoirs Shelley Winters recalls being puzzled on learning that George Stevens had named his protagonist after himself. The director would admit to changing a name that evokes a founding father of the American cinema to one that combines his own with that of another pioneer of the medium. The possibility of the director's identification with his character is central to Marilyn Moss's biographical interpretation of the film, which she reads as a reflection of the tragic awareness of moral ambiguity he developed during the war. Comparing Stevens' impoverished childhood and demanding father with Dreiser's own, she also argues that the director, like George Eastman, idealized the female nurturance portrayed in *I Remember Mama* and the character of Angela Vickers. But, although Stevens often said that Clyde Griffiths' story could happen to anybody (the claim for universality made by the reporter at the end of Sternberg's First White Script and in Paramount's publicity for his film) and although he seemed to endorse his protagonist's romantic choice, his own account of his renaming differs from that of Moss.

Interviewed by Robert Hughes, Stevens discussed Dreiser calling his tragic youth Clyde Griffiths in alliterative allusion to Chester Gillette. The sense of realism lent by the fictional name's resemblance to its referent seems to have been one motive for his own choice, with the cinematic implications of the name Griffith(s) another: "I took Mr Eastman, from the Eastman-Kodak, and called him George. And so everybody knows that an Eastman isn't necessarily a fictional character" (February–March 1967, GSC). Significantly, the director compares his selection of this real-life brand name to the one finally chosen for Angela, Vickers. Unlike the fictional manufacturing firms of Dreiser's novel—whose products are Griffiths shirt collars and Finchley vacuum cleaners—these are actual names from Stevens' wartime experience, with Eastman-Kodak supplying his 16 mm color film and Vickers building British bombers. (The latter name preserves the lethal reference of an earlier script's patronym for Angela, Douglas, since Douglas Aircraft developed the United States Army Air Corps' standard bomber.) But the choice of "George Eastman" for Stevens' protagonist clearly goes further than this. Like Chester Gillette, the industrialist George Eastman was a resident of upstate New York, where his Rochester factory perfected the first transparent roll film, whose flexibility made Edison's motion picture camera possible. In 1909, Eastman developed safety acetate film to replace combustible nitrate stock and in 1912 the company introduced 22-mm film configured in three linear rows of pictures with perforations between them. By the early 1920s the company was developing color film, bringing out its 16-mm Kodachrome in 1938. In the light of these innovations (of which Stevens, who had worked as a cameraman across much of this period, was well aware) the name "Eastman" cannot fail to signify the cinema.

In other significant changes, Wilson turns a contemporary expression into a witty premonition when Alberta/Alice reminds her democratic supervisor that "If you're an Eastman, you're not in the same boat with anybody." And indeed George is sufficiently changed in this later version to play pool well at his uncle's party, eliciting Angela's flirtatious greeting, "I see you had a misspent youth." Later in this erotically charged scene, when the embarrassed George is persuaded by his uncle to telephone his "Mama" at her mission, the daring Angela "leans down and says roguishly into the phone: Hello Mama." Afterwards she asks George: "Did you promise to be a good boy?"

Throughout Wilson's revisions, the protagonist's back story, the entire first book of Dreiser's novel, was pared away. His preliminary screenplay takes the hitchhiking George directly to his uncle's factory, with his mother (now named Hannah Eastman) and her mission unseen until he telephones her at Christmas. George doesn't discuss his past at any length until, in a highly declamatory speech after the drowning, he confesses to Angela's father:

I was raised in a skidrow mission. I grew up with poverty and failure. That's why I came to hate poverty and fear failure more than anything in the world. I left home to do something about it. I worked at several jobs that didn't last—the best of which was being a bellhop. I was just another punk kid—with no talent, no education, no nothing. I used to look at those magazine ads—the kind that showed a big flashy car with a girl at the wheel—and she's waving at a guy, her sweetheart. I always wanted to get ahead and be that guy.

Later in this screenplay, Hannah Eastman visits George in prison, first with a minister to tell him that her petition to the governor has failed, and then to help him write a final declaration of faith. In both scenes the question of George's culpability is discussed at some length, with the minister pronouncing the condemnation "In your heart was murder, then" from the novel. But in Wilson's script the minister comes to this conclusion after the petition to the governor has failed, obviating the ironic responsibility for his execution that Dreiser ascribes to religion. And although this draft has George repeat his defense of trying "to get ahead" (Michael Wilson, first preliminary green screenplay, *A Modern Story*, August 5, 1949, GSC, APS), the question of his guilt or innocence remains unresolved.

Having read this script, Moffat complained to Stevens that its omission of the protagonist's past prevents the spectator from knowing what he "was up against" (Ivan Moffat, script note, August 7, 1949, GSC, APS). In a twenty-page script note dated August 10, he argues for greater representation of the early influences on his character, and for the use of a subjective voice to dramatize the reasoning that leads him to the lake. Moffat had championed the retention of this device throughout the preliminary writing stage of the film, arguing in a June 14 memo to Stevens that it was one of the most inventive elements of the novel and should be employed "openly and audaciously rather than shame-facedly ... In many of these passages lie some of Dreiser's best writing, which otherwise will be totally lost" (GSC, APS). The choice of Harry Brown as second screenwriter may have also been motivated by Moffat's wish to retain an inner voice for Clyde's deliberations. Brown's novel, *A Walk in the Sun*, incorporates monologue for several characters, and Robert Rossen's screenplay had employed the device in an opening narration by Burgess Meredith ("this book tells a story that happened long ago, way back in 1943"), a soldier's letters home, and other characters' soliloquies (some spoken, some voiced over) to unusual cinematic effect. In an effort to convince Stevens of the merits of this device, Moffat wrote a September 27 memo to Stevens (GSC, APS) in the form of an essay on cinematic narration. In this fascinating document he summarizes what he terms the *Our Town* narration (in which the narrator is a character in the story, but offers an objective narration in the past and present tense); the *Brief Encounter* narration (in which the narrator is a central protagonist giving a subjective narration in the past tense to support a flashback structure); the "literary" third-person narration, used to introduce a film or a scene within it; and the subjective "stream-of-consciousness" narration.

Recalling his own experiences writing documentary commentaries in wartime, Moffat points out the liabilities of, on the one hand, redundant verbiage and, on the other, departing so far 'from what was visible on screen that the audience could neither understand the words nor the image." To represent George's mental states, he suggests using both a third-person "literary" narration describing, for example, his daydreams at work ("Around him in the noisy room worked dozens of girls of all ages, all types ... and outside, beyond the windows, lay the river with its green banks and shady trees, inviting the imagination to wander ...") and a first-person narration voicing his emotional turmoil on the lake ("how could life be better after a wild brutal scheme like this—but how else? How? Go away—disappear like I came? Write letters to Mother from false places, using false names?"). Since such narration would not be recorded synchronously, the memo notes, it could be written after shooting.

A Meeting at the Movies

Stevens, meanwhile, had other worries about Wilson's draft screenplay. On August 18 he reluctantly sent it to Montgomery Clift's agent, Herman Citron of MCA, with a letter apologizing that although it represented the film's final structure, the characterizations were not yet realized. Stevens stressed that very little of this script would make it onto the screen, as the film ultimately proves. Brown's first draft, Wilson's second and a host of further rewrites and cuts were yet to come. Yet Wilson's initial screenplay does represent the film's major changes to Dreiser's characterizations: George is more decent and endearing than Clyde, Alice drabber and less dignified than Roberta, Angela more loving (and wittier) than Sondra, and Hannah Eastman more marginal than the novel's missionary mother. To further Stevens' vision of these characters, casting would matter as much as writing.

As we have seen, Montgomery Clift was Stevens' first casting decision, one clearly made on the basis of his physical resemblance to Dreiser's Clyde as well as the youth appeal of his modishly Method persona—intense, vulnerable, enigmatic. Commentators have richly described the yearning and sadness that Clift's characters exude, and the sexual complexities of their sensitivity and victimization. As with his predecessor Phillips Holmes, the veteran of cross-dressed roles in Princeton dramatics, Clift's slender, fine-boned appearance brings an androgynous quality to his characters, while his highly physical performance style can easily suggest psychological conflict or neurosis. But in the place of Holmes' WASP blondeness and irritable hauteur, Clift's dark looks and proletarian pronunciations (critics repeatedly note George's "yuh" for "you") facilitated Stevens' determination to make his protagonist ordinary, likeable and contemporary.

Having signed Clift, the director sought a romantic partner with comparative appeal. In a May 24, 1949 memo to a Paramount executive, he writes that Sondra

> must be a "dream girl," the kind of girl that a young man could see at first glance, and find his eyes so fixed upon her that his attention will not turn, nor can it be turned elsewhere … Her beauty and poise, as well as her wealth and background, must give to this young man the impression that she is unattainable, so that when he discovers that this is not so and that he can have her, he is willing to commit murder and does to bring this about.

Working ahead of Wilson, whose evocation of this character never satisfied him, Stevens stresses that she will be "fundamental" to the audience's engagement with the film, establishing "a frame of mind that is sympathetic to all that it portrays" (George Stevens memo to William Meiklejohn, May 24, 1949, GSC, APS). The only young star capable of creating this illusion, he concludes, is Elizabeth Taylor.

Then aged seventeen, the former child actress offered to American audiences the upper class connotations of "Englishness" via her birthplace, vocal inflections and roles in *Jane Eyre* (1943) and *National Velvet* (1945) as well as further "literary" prestige in films like *Little Women* (1949). In selecting her, Stevens departed sharply from Sternberg's casting of Sondra, played (as in Dreiser) as a flirtatious flapper by Frances Dee. Even more importantly, and again unlike Sternberg's pairing of the dark-haired Dee with the blonde Holmes, Taylor was a close visual match for Clift: a pale brunette with a high forehead, dark eyebrows and finely etched features. Their physical resemblance—particularly marked in profile—would be crucial to the film's love scenes and their combination of identification with desire.

Stevens' May memo also describes his conception of Roberta, and again it bears little resemblance to Dreiser's victim or Sternberg's. The novel remarks on her "wistfulness and wonder combined with a kind of self-reliant courage and determination" (*An American Tragedy*: 246), and Clyde is very taken with her prettiness, attributes that the Sternberg adaptation retained in casting Sylvia Sydney. But as Stevens frequently joked, this made Sternberg's Roberta far more sympathetic than Clyde or Sondra, sinking his film along with her. Where Dreiser's Roberta is twenty-two or twenty-three to Clyde's twenty, Stevens ordained that she should appear to be "26 and not too attractive." In pursuit of a suitable actress, the director considered thirty, including Jane Wyatt, June Lockhart, Barbara Bel Geddes, Angela Lansbury, Donna Reed, Barbara Lawrence and Gloria Grahame, before reluctantly considering Shelley Winters, then a sexy starlet at Universal. At her first appointment with the director, she wore drab clothing and sat in a corner of the hotel lobby, unnoticed by Stevens until he was finally about to leave the room. Her disguise would radically revise Dreiser's story and her own career.

Winters' test sequence was the lake scene from a version of the screenplay dated September 17, 1949 and headed "Harry Brown, An American Tragedy." Brown's services on the film officially commenced on August 12; Wilson's finished on September 23. Signing off the project, he left behind suggestions for further revision of the screenplay. These include greater development of the affair between George and Alice, to make loneliness and rejection his motivation, and to establish her love for him. Wilson also argues that George's uncle should not offer him promotion until his relationship with Angela signals his social acceptability. But first in Wilson's list for revision is the role of Hannah Eastman, who by this date is not seen with George until after his trial. To make good this deletion of his background, Wilson maintains that Hannah should appear as a character witness at his trial, testifying about her son's deprived background. In a related point, he also suggests that George and Alice could encounter a Salvation Army choir singing on a street corner after their first meeting outside the factory. The sight of this group could move George to confide his background and ambitions to Alice, establishing their intimacy and explaining her later sense of possessiveness.

How the two writers functioned together, whether they ever conferred or merely took individual instructions from Stevens and/or Moffat, is not clear from the extant documentation of the production. In an attempt to establish their respective contributions to the screenplay, Paramount issued an undated comparison of their two versions, extending as far as the scene—in Wilson's script— in which a depressed George rings the pregnant Alice to reassure her, followed by his elation at a telephoned invitation from Angela. (Brown's version of this scene has George bicker with Alice in her boarding house bedroom, as they do in Sternberg's adaptation.) Paramount's comparison and an incomplete draft by Brown dated September 1 suggest that the second writer varied more in regard to the staging of various key encounters, and the accompanying dialogue than in plot. As Moffat anticipated, the Harvard-educated Brown could write the wealthy characters' chat fluently, but little of it remains in the final film. His

September 1 draft has George's uncle expatiate at length on the power of advertising to sell bathing suits, and on the importance of efficiency in beating the competition. Angela spouts pages of arch Vassar dialogue, including a discarded description of the orchids in the conservatory where in this version she and George first kiss: "Horrible flowers. They practically have to be spoon-fed. And they're too intelligent for flowers. One of these days one is going to ask for a knife and fork and a piece of steak" (Harry Brown, Preliminary Draft, *A Modern Story*, September 1, 1949, GSC, APS).

But Brown's drafts of the film do offer one important difference from Wilson's: the setting of George and Alice's first encounter outside the factory. Wilson had followed the novel in having the two meet aquatically, with the town swimming pool replacing Dreiser's lake. But by September 21, Brown's sequence outline locates their meeting at the movies, where one evening a bored George takes a seat in the balcony and sees Alice close by: "They exchange whispered greetings and George moves over beside her. And there, in the half-darkness of the theater, reflections of the images on the screen flickering across their faces, their own whispered words mingling with those of the film, surrounded by couples engaged in love-making, they begin their ill-starred affair." Brown's staging of George and Alice's fateful meeting in a cinema distills Dreiser's multiple allusions to its influence on his characters into a single scene. It also establishes the film's second major visual motif—one that would importantly condition its photography and editing, as well as its relation to its medium.

One major element of the screenplay remained undecided until just prior to filming—its title. Through the preceding months, Stevens had considered a number of replacements for that of Dreiser's novel. Among those mentioned were *Now and Forever*, *The Lovers* and the working title of the script stage, *A Modern Story*. Still dissatisfied, the director offered the customary reward of 100 dollars for the right suggestion and Moffat won it. As he later explained, he had fallen asleep one evening in his office and woke up remembering a phrase of the Kaiser justifying his country's desire to expand its empire: "Germany needed its place in the sun" (Ivan Moffat, interview by Susan Winslow, April 1982, transcript, Filmmaker's Journey Collection, Margaret Herrick Library). Although the suitability of this title continued to be debated throughout the film's production, *A Place in the Sun* heads scripts from September 30, 1949.

If Moffat's much-mythologized story is true, his dream is one of the most overdetermined in Hollywood history. Dreiser sets Clyde's execution in mid-winter, although in the weeks leading to it he thinks sorrowfully of the end of "the beauty of the days—of the sun and rain" (*An American Tragedy* 864). Eisenstein transforms the season to spring, when Clyde's final plea to live echoes across "the bright sunlit courtyard of the prison, all in green and in flowers" (Montagu, 1969: 340). As the documentation of this film's writing demonstrates, Michael Wilson had Clyde take a sunlit walk to his execution in his first treatment, and Moffat himself had referred in his May 1949 script notes to the protagonist's search for "the place in the sun." (Here his renaming as "George *East*man" is also fitting.) Harry Brown's Second World War novel *A Walk in the Sun* had become a literary success in 1945 and a cinematic one in 1946. The speech that Moffat recalled (made by Wilhelm II in 1901) not only presses Germany's claim for colonial possessions "in order that the sun's rays may fall fruitfully upon our activity and trade in foreign parts," but also sets out his government's policy of naval development to secure them: "The more Germans go out upon the waters, whether it be in races or regattas, whether it be in journeys across the ocean, or in the service of the battle flag, so much the better for us" (Gauss, 1915: 182). In one marvelous feat of condensation, Moffat's dream links the film's title to its watery climax with the consequent extinction of the protagonist's life and to the origins of his own collaboration with Stevens, at war with a conquering Germany. His association of its theme of personal advancement with military aggression intimates the dark side of American ambition and its possible complicity with the enemy it had just defeated.[5] So doing, Moffat nominated this film as the war picture that Stevens had never been asked to make.

Headed "GEORGE STEVENS PRODUCTION OF A PLACE IN THE SUN / Based on Theodore Dreiser's 'An American Tragedy' / SCREENPLAY BY HARRY BROWN AND MICHAEL WILSON," a Final White Script dated September 30, 1949, signaled that shooting could begin, although Brown was retained for further revisions. Stevens once admitted that if he had to choose between pre-production, shooting and post-production, he would sacrifice shooting.[6] Certainly, compared to the writing period and the thirteen months of editing that would follow, filming on this project was comparatively rapid, constrained as it was by Taylor's two-months loan from her contract at MGM and the increasingly wintry weather at the film's Sierra locations. Studio memos indicate that shooting began with Clift, Taylor and Winters, with the supporting characters filmed afterwards. Anne Revere, who had played Taylor's mother in *National Velvet*, was a late signing to play Clift's, with a week's guaranteed filming and first billing among the featured players authorized on December 27.

The extant documentation of this period is largely retrospective, from interviews with Stevens and Moffat, as well as star biographies. It functions as much as a commentary on the final film as on the process of making it, varying with memory and affection. The Method-trained Winters' recollections are the most detailed among the actors, describing Stevens' "very unusual way of working" (Winters, 1980: 276). Winters recalls that before filming Stevens would discuss the scene to be shot, but not its individual lines, and then film the second or third rehearsal to achieve "an almost improvisatory quality." Then, while having that take printed for later viewing, he would rehearse the scene minutely and film it again. According to the actress, Stevens occasionally rehearsed scenes silently, to achieve the non-verbal style that he, as a veteran of the pre-sound era, regarded as the true language of the cinema. This emphasis on physical performance accorded with Clift's training, and may explain Stevens' tactful handling of the presence on the set of his acting coach, Mira Rostova, whose interventions sometimes extended into the shot, ruining the take. And while Rostova coached Clift, Clift coached Taylor, stressing the importance of embodied emotion and occasionally offering readings of her lines. Although such latitude was unusual, Clift did not recall it later, criticizing Stevens' direction as manipulative and inflexible: "George preconceives everything through a viewfinder" (Kashner and MacNair, 2002: 181).

Stevens would certainly have needed to do so since the film's deep focus shots, its closely choreographed long takes from fixed positions and the extended footage necessary for its overlapping dissolves all required careful planning. Mellor's photography is one of the its most noted features, beginning with the very deliberate choice of black and white to avoid what Stevens called the "Oh, What a Beautiful Morning" effect of Technicolor.[7] If the argument of *A Place in the Sun* is that moral responsibility is best illustrated in shades of gray, its contrasts are nonetheless precise, with rich blacks, brilliant whites and good visibility even in low-light sequences. With many of its scenes set outdoors, or in indoor settings with classical ornaments or printed textiles and furnishings, the result is not so much a desaturation of hues as an intensification of outlines and tonalities, a sort of screen effect. Here, Michael O'Pray's observation that "the presence of light and its blocking (as opposed to color film) in black-and-white film is close to the material heart of film, its conditions of existence" (O'Pray, 2004: 211) is an apposite commentary on its contribution to this film's striking reflexivity.

It's an Eastman

A Place in the Sun opens as the Paramount logo dissolves with a drum roll over the names of the film's three stars, superimposed upon the figure of a hitchhiker seen at the side of a highway. Like Sternberg's Clyde Griffiths so often does, he faces away from the spectator as Franz Waxman's main romantic theme begins to play—here in a "jazzy-bluesy rendition" (Darby and Du Bois, 1990: 142) of what will become a romantic string orchestration. The credits continue to dissolve into each other as the hitchhiker backs towards the camera, only turning when the final credit, "Produced and Directed by George Stevens" has faded out. As the camera closes in tightly on the hitchhiker's face, framing it between neck and hairline, he looks towards the roadside. A reverse shot reveals a large billboard on which a pretty brunette reclines in a one-piece bathing suit against a painted sky. The advertisement proclaims, "It's an Eastman." As the hitchhiker gazes up at it, a horn sounds from the highway behind him and he turns again to see an open-topped Cadillac with another brunette at the wheel speed past him. Turning back a third time he discovers a battered junk truck has stopped at the summons of his still raised thumb and covering his look of dismay (and also his nose) he climbs into the front seat.

This famous opening is structured by a series of questions, answers and further questions, beginning with the film's credits ("Who is responsible for this?") and their climax at Stevens' name as producer and director. Only then does the mysterious hitchhiker turn and reveal himself, a revelation that is further delayed by the camera's measured movement to the close-up of his face. But the hitchhiker's concentrated gaze only provokes further curiosity, with the reverse shot of the model both an answer and a further question. ('What is an Eastman?') Denied a close-up of this elevated figure, the spectator turns with the hitchhiker to the speeding convertible, whose driver's face is also not discernible, becoming even less visible as her car, in a reversal of the camera's move forward to Clift's face, drives away.

Not surprisingly, this enigmatic opening has provoked extensive commentary. Considering it in the light of Clift's sexually ambiguous star persona, Steven Cohan claims that the combination of his "trademark rebel uniform"—leather jacket, jeans and a white T-shirt—with his avid pose exploits his ability to excite "the intense desire of his fans, male and female." From the film's outset, George Eastman's longings seem as complex as the combination of sexual and consumer aspirations solicited by the billboard. As he watches the convertible disappear down the highway, it is not clear whether he is admiring the car or its driver, both becoming "an elusive, blurred object in the distance" (Cohan, 1997: 229–30).

Following Cohan, Sam Girgus maps the relay of the camera's look through the hitchhiker's focused expression to the model in the advertisement. The height and size of this smiling woman, and the angling of the billboard towards his face, enables this male look to be returned with interest, since hers coincides with the turning of his back to the camera. The dominating power of the billboard's East*man* is argued to feminize further the fine featured traveler beneath her, eliciting "awe, admiration and identification" (Girgus, 1998: 195) rather than sexual desire. Moreover, she names him in the series of revelations that structure the scene. Turned once, twice, three times by the succession of objects which attract his attention (the billboard, the Cadillac, the junk truck), reduced to riding in the ancient vehicle to his uncle's factory, the hitchhiker's passivity is further evidence of a femininity that will lead him both to identify with and become the erotic object of two differently dominating female figures.

To Cohan's queer and Girgus's psychoanalytic readings of George Eastman's ambiguity, Stevens' biographer Marilyn Moss adds a third, emphasizing his national significance as the anti-hero of a mobile post-war America. Stressing George's social and class instability, Moss first mentions his encounter with another Eastman—not the female one on the billboard but the male cousin (now aristocratically named 'Earl') with whom he is framed as he steps into the elevator at the Eastman factory. In another moment of doubling, the resemblance of two dark haired men succeeds that of the women in the previous scene. George's refracted images in this hall of mirrors are represented by the multiplication of his family name. By the end of the film's second scene it has appeared on the billboard, the façade of the factory, his uncle's business card, the door of his office and a check from Eastman Industries to the Internal Revenue for the then immense sum of $100,000.

With its unmistakably cinematic namesake, and its multiple and spectacular repetitions, "It's an Eastman" will increasingly be legible across this film as a reference to the cinema itself: "It's a movie." Immediately succeeding the opening credits, the name might have been included among them. The billboard on which it appears extends virtually to the width of the frame, matching it with the screen. In identifying this family name with film, the hitchchiker's interpellation as an Eastman will link his social and economic aspirations with cinematic fantasy. Throughout the ensuing scenes screens and screen surrogates abound, while the name Eastman is seen and spoken incessantly.

Riding into his uncle's city (identified on the check as Carthage, a suitably classical equivalent for Dreiser's Lycurgus) in the junk truck, George Eastman is filmed through its rectangular windscreen, which again extends to the full width of the frame. At the gate of the Eastman factory, he produces his uncle's business card and is directed to his office. En route he enters an elevator, whose doors fleetingly frame him and Earl Eastman (Keefe Brasselle), matching the two cousins who have not yet met. In the reception area outside his uncle's office, a secretary inquires "Mr Eastman?" At George's "Yes," she apologizes, "I'm awfully sorry but *our* Mr Eastman isn't here today." Learning that George is a nephew of the company president, she invites him into his executive office to telephone his home. There, sitting in his uncle's large leather chair, George receives an invitation to the Eastman mansion before noticing the $100,000 check made out to the Internal Revenue. A dissolve links his fantastical enthronement (exorbitantly signified in a long pull back across the immense office) to another screen-like image, of a cheap tweed suit displayed in a shop window. This $35 garment is linked with a cut to the dinner jacket worn by Earl, framed in a mirror adjusting his tie. Struck by his resemblance to his cousin, Charles Eastman (Herbert Heyes) announces George's imminent visit and new job at the factory to his disapproving family. Then George himself arrives in the ill-fitting suit, symmetrically posed beneath a series of classical arches as he advances down the mansion's long hall.

Questioned about his previous employment and widowed mother, George hesitantly attempts to explain as the horn from the previous scene sounds outside and the Cadillac's driver arrives in a white evening gown and fur stole. Addressed affectionately by Earl as "Vickers," Angela banters with the Eastmans while George—in the scene's only close-up—watches with fascination. Only then is she given her own middle close-up, as George looks on from a distance, unintroduced. Asked about her family's new vacation house at the lake, she pronounces it "a dream palace. I'm going to end my days there'" and sweeps out with Earl (who includes his cousin in his goodbyes with a curt "Eastman"). Afterward George is awkwardly ushered out by his uncle and aunt, who reprovingly exclaims "Charles Eastman!" A dissolve links this scene to the two cousins walking past the factory showroom the next morning, with Earl warning George that "You've got to be aware every minute, whatever your job is, that you're an Eastman and you're expected to act accordingly." As George turns to look at a swimsuit model pirouetting before yet another Eastman insignia, Earl sternly informs him that socializing with the firm's women employees is not permitted— a prohibition underlined by their passage past a sign warning FACTORY EMPLOYEES FORBIDDEN BEYOND THIS POINT. George is then taken to the mill's packaging room, where the mostly female workforce sit at a conveyor belt putting suits into boxes. [8] Above them, in a set design clearly based on Moffat's description of the Jantzen factory, large posters display models clad in Eastman swimwear.

Greeted by a wolf whistle and watched closely by one young employee, George is introduced to his female supervisor and put to work on the production line. Unlike Sternberg, whose film follows Dreiser in making Clyde the supervisor of the women in the collar stamping room, dressed in his own collar and tie at a desk to the side of the frame, Stevens puts his protagonist in the middle of the packaging room as "one of the girls" (Girgus, 1998: 199). So doing he reduces both the class and the gender hierarchies of Dreiser's novel, while elaborating the egalitarian significance of sportswear. To the bustling musical theme introducing Alice Tripp, a series of overlapping images dissolve George's image into those of various tough-looking women workers, the bathing beauties above them and a calendar marking, as it did in Sternberg's film, the passage of time. Divested of his tweed suit, George's physique, like that of the models, is on display in his white T-shirt, contrasting the slender youth with the burly women on the line. There he stands (Figure 4.1), boxing swimwear in the repetitive rhythm of mass production, enacting the oxymoron that Adorno found so indicative of the American culture of this period: "the leisure industry."[9] The montage concludes with a friendly exchange of looks between him and the young woman who watched his arrival, and she lingers in the room at closing time.

From the outset, *A Place in the Sun* frequently employs the dissolve for its most conventional narrative purpose—to indicate the passage of time. Formally, such editing establishes a fluidity intensified by Stevens' extensive use of music. But, as in the Sternberg version, longer and more conspicuous dissolves and superimpositions are also used to draw parallels and point out contrasts, as well, eventually, as to suggest intention and inevitability, the uncanny powers of desire and fate. Partly planned at the shooting stage but intensified in editing, these dissolves became the alternative to Dreiser's internal monologues, effectively operating to "photograph a thought" and to perform another function, one not sought in the Sternberg film or in Eisenstein's treatment. Their length give them "face," as Adrian Miles says of those exceptional moments of cinematic linkage in which its usually "incorporeal" transformations exceed their narrative utility and become visible (Miles, 1999: 217–26). These foregrounded signifiers of film editing, like the reflexively chosen name "Eastman," work to associate George's place in the sun with his place on the screen.

Another dissolve reveals George in his boarding house bedroom at night, laboriously writing a proposal to speed up production in a bid for promotion.

Figure 4.1 George (Montgomery Clift) packs bathing suits with Alice (Shelley Winters) in *A Place in the Sun*, Paramount 1951 (Kobal Collection).

Through his rectangular window, the Vickers factory sign flashes in the darkness as a clarinet sounds its siren call and George rises to go out. As he heads for the door he passes another rectangular image on his bedroom wall, a print of John Everett Millais' 1851–2 painting of the dead Ophelia. As Girgus (1998: 201) observes, the print functions as a film citation in its own right, of Olivier's 1948 *Hamlet*, with its own hesitating hero and his lover's drowning. (As noted already, it also echoes Eisenstein's reference to Ophelia's burial in his earlier adaptation, as well as the Victorian theme of female victimization which Eisenstein quotes from Tennyson.) The Oedipal dynamics of the play may have had an additional resonance for Stevens. In his interview with Robert Hughes he recalled that his father had played Hamlet and his "mother's mother played Ophelia with [the celebrated Victorian actor Edwin] Booth when she was eighteen years old" (February–March 1967, GSC). A cut then reveals a third screenlike image, a nearly full frame insert of a photograph in the local paper showing Angela and two other young socialites invited to a dance that evening at the Eastman mansion. George is next seen in the dark outside the gates of the Eastman estate, which open to admit Angela in her convertible and then close against his troubled features. Another cut to a wide shot shows him approaching the town cinema, whose marquee displays the title *Now and Forever*. As George walks past a poster for the film, its writer-director is identified as one "Ivan Moffat."

Entering the crowded balcony of the cinema, George discovers Alice sitting nearby, surrounded by spectators who watch the film's unseen romance. (Obscured by their noise, its soundtrack includes the line "Vicki, do you really think we could be happy there, perhaps never seeing anyone again?" pronounced in a stagey English accent.) Spying George, the delighted Alice exclaims "Small world" and is derided by the spotty youth beside her, a sailor wearing service ribbons who loudly replies, "That's what *you* think." After George moves to sit next to her the scene dissolves to the conclusion of the evening's program. Now the balcony is revealed to be almost empty, its three remaining couples embracing or asleep. Only George and Alice sit upright, facing the screen (and us, their actual spectatorial counterparts) in some embarrassment.

This scene, which, as indicated, was written by Harry Brown in the later stages of scripting, fulfills a number of functions in the film. On the most basic narrative level, it establishes George's loneliness as the proximate cause for his involvement with Alice, with his exclusion from the Eastman party demonstrating his family's rejection. (This motivation was important to the film's writers, who sought to exculpate George from any suggestion of casual promiscuity.) Secondly, the cinema itself offers the opportunity for George and Alice to get together away from the factory, where a social encounter would be impossible. Tonally, the scene provides a brief moment of humor in the film, both in the couple's rueful realization of the few oblivious spectators at the film's end and those spectators' derisive response earlier to its love scene. (Over what sounds like a screen kiss, several emit loud squelching sounds, while others jeer.) Moreover, as in the junk truck and the factory, it enables George to be contrasted with the comic proletariat (the implicitly malodorous truck, the hatchet-faced garment workers, the spotty sailor). His first question to Alice, in regard to the latter, is a sardonic "Who's your friend?" Her relation to this background, typically rendered in medium tones rather than the striking black and whites of the wealthy settings, is less certain. Throughout the film the mousey-haired Alice is costumed in beiges and grays but she is more attractive than her counterparts in the packaging room and she is alone at the cinema. By the scene's end, she and George are conspicuously isolated from the working-class audience who earlier filled the balcony.

The title of the mock film that George and Alice watch was actually considered for *A Place in the Sun*. Like that chosen, *Now and Forever* is highly ambiguous, suggesting both eternal love and the two romances conducted by George, one temporary and one that will last until the end of his life. (Another suggested title, *The Lovers*, offers the same multiple meanings, as the plural might include more than one couple.) Ivan Moffat's credit on the poster was evidently Stevens' practical joke, and the director actually posed for photographs sitting beneath it dressed as a beggar selling pencils. Given Moffat's extensive contributions to the conception and production of *A Place in the Sun*, the joke may have included more than an element of due recognition. But it also works at Moffat's expense: with the possible exception of George and Alice, the audience of *Now and Forever* doesn't like it. They laugh at its love scene, fall asleep or leave before its conclusion.

There is a clear precedent for all this in a film with which Brown, Moffat and Stevens were undoubtedly familiar. Released four years before their film's scripting, it too features an illicitly meeting couple who watch a movie from a cinema balcony and later share a rowboat. The film they see is deemed "terribly bad" and the pair (like the spectators surrounding George and Alice) leave early to go boating in the park. Unlike the actual films-within-films celebrated by Rachel Moore (2004: 1–11) for their stimulation of intimacy and love between their diegetic spectators, the mock movie in *Brief Encounter* (1945) functions in contrast to its love story. Alec (Trevor Howard) and Laura (Celia Johnson) watch the preview of *Flames of Passion* at their first visit to the Palladium, where the trailer for the jungle romance "coming soon" is comically followed by an advertisement for (again significantly) a baby carriage. Later they attend the actual feature, but the premature ending of their own romance is presaged by their departure before its conclusion. The difference between love in a cold climate, whose only flames are those in Laura's hearth, and the torrid embrace of the Victor Mature/Debra Paget types parodied in the trailer is emphatically asserted.

But as a later scene dramatizing Laura's thoughts on the train home reveals, her fantasies are conventionally cinematic. That afternoon she and Alec have confessed their feelings for each other and the elated housewife sits in the commuter carriage gazing through her reflected image at the landscape passing outside its window, gazing—so to speak—into her own head. Her voice over the scene (a narration which Moffat's earlier memo to Stevens had explicitly discussed) recalls, "I imagined being with him in all sorts of glamorous circumstances. It was one of those absurd fantasies just like one has when one is a girl, of being wooed and married by the ideal of one's dreams." At this point the camera moves right, aligning the film frame with the train window, in which a series of romantic images of Laura and Alec together (notably, dancing in formal clothes beneath chandeliers and riding in an open-topped car) dissolve over her reflection. These images, and their use of conspicuous overlapping dissolves, will also figure in *A Place in the Sun*.

We never see *Now and Forever*. It is, in the terminology Michel Chion borrows from Pierre Schaeffer, an acousmatic presence, a sound without a visible source. When such an unvisualized sound is the voice of an offscreen character, Chion observes, the unseen source "remains liable to appear in the visual field at any moment," for film offers the possibility of "play with showing, partially showing, and not showing" (Chion, 1999: 21). Unlike that of the commentator, the source of such a voice is within the story, haunting the space of the screen. Immaterial and non-localized, its restless liminality disturbs and entices the spectator, inviting *"the loss of self, to desire and fascination"* (Chion, 1999: 24) with the play of presence and absence particular to cinematic representation. The voice without a place threatens the spectator with a return to an infantile state of sensory delirium and rampant idealization, and it is this fantasmatic state that will become identified with George Eastman's place in the sun.

After the lights come up in the cinema, George walks Alice home. En route she raises his status as "the boss's nephew" and he replies "I'm in the same boat as the rest of you." But Alice demurs: "Pretty soon they'll move you up to a better job and first thing you know you'll find yourself in the front office. And that's the last we'll see of George Eastman." Meanwhile, George's distance from his wealthy relations is illustrated by images from his past. The couple passes a pool hall, and then a Salvation Army choir singing on the sidewalk. This brings George to a halt and he glances with silent recognition at a young boy in the group. After another dissolve he puts his arm around Alice's shoulder and suggestively asks whether she's "lonely all of the time," to which her characteristically plaintive reply is that she's too busy putting bathing suits into boxes six days a week to be lonely then. But when he asks whether she ever puts herself into a bathing suit, she confesses that she can't swim: "I was even scared of the duck pond when I was a kid." By the time the two reach Alice's address ("4433 ½ Elm Avenue" she notes helpfully) she has described the rural poverty that brought her to the Eastman factory.

George offers to escort Alice into the lodging house, but she warns him of the ferocity of her landlady. Obscured by the darkness, they kiss. Despite his pleas to stay outside, she goes into her room and stands in its window as George looks at her from below—in roughly the same position in which he first beheld the Eastman billboard. A cut then matches its dark rectangle with the daylit one at the factory's exit, as the two leave after work. To Alice's anxious question about why he wasn't returning her glances in the packaging room, George replies that he's been thinking about his efficiency plan. At this moment the two see Angela, parked in her convertible on the street outside the factory. She is greeted warmly by Charles Eastman, but neither notice George. Later at a bar Alice tells him that she's glad that he hasn't been moved upward, that it's better for him than "running around with those Eastmans" and—again offering his loneliness to explain his deepening relationship with Alice—George declares that he's only been invited once to their home. At this point a drunk collapses onto their table and the two leave. Seeking privacy in a parking spot frequented by local couples, they are again interrupted, by a policeman who finds them kissing and sends them away.

When the two finally arrive at Alice's lodging house it's raining and she apologizes that she can't invite him in. Assuring her that he doesn't want to cause difficulties, George reaches through the open window and switches on her radio. As Alice tries to turn it down, she accidentally moves the dial and the soft rhumba changes into a loud march. George races into her room to retune it, occupying the position within the frame he has repeatedly gazed at, and jokingly echoes Alice's words to him, "I wish I could ask you in, but ..." Then Alice joins him and the two dance to the sound of the rhumba in the dark bedroom. As she murmurs "Oh George" the camera pans discreetly right to the window, through which we see him leave as the dawn fades up. Now he is really framed, taking up Alice's lines and the place of the female figure with which he has been identified from the billboard's slogan onward. This is not the last we'll see of George Eastman.

A Perfect Match

As the couple quietly greet each other the next day in the packaging room, Charles Eastman and Earl pass by with a management detail. Surprised to see his nephew in such lowly work, Eastman hails George, claims that he's been "keeping on eye on" him and offers a position of greater responsibility. At George's query about his production report, his uncle suggests discussing it at a family party the next month. Afterward the disappointed Alice, who definitely has been keeping an eye on George during this exchange, complains that she'd hoped to spend that evening celebrating his birthday at "our little party." George assures her that he'll just pay his respects and then be over. "You'd better be," she smiles.

To the sounds of a waltz, George enters the Eastman party through its arched hallway, again wrongly dressed in a business suit for the black tie affair. Ignored by the guests surrounding him, he takes refuge in the empty billiard room. There, holding the cue behind his back, he sinks an elegant three-banked shot to the audible admiration of the passing Angela. That this shot is actually performed by Clift while smoking a cigarette rather complicates the feminine passivity attributed to him by some readers of this scene. Here, in Wilson's revised conception, the character's (and the actor's) visible skill seems to offer a raffish masculinity, albeit one which re-establishes his position as the object of the female gaze. "I see you had a misspent youth," Angela opens and asks why he's alone: "Being exclusive, being dramatic, being blue?" George replies that he's just fooling around and invites her to play, proffering the cue. She elects to watch him and lounges against the English hunting prints lining the wall until he's forced to admit that she's making him nervous. The two then introduce themselves, with George declaring that he saw her there the previous spring. "I don't remember seeing you," Angela replies but quickly follows with an acknowledgement that she sees him now. As George regards her eagerly, she says "You look unusual." Yet in this continual exchange of gendered positions it is Angela who—in a return to cinematic convention—is now given the close-up, its soft focus suggesting the romantic haze of his perception.

Just then Charles Eastman enters and insists that George telephone his mother to announce his promotion to department head. "Smart boy," he tells Angela. The embarrassed nephew places a call to the Bethal Independent Mission in Kansas City, where Hannah Eastman—presiding over a soup kitchen—answers anxiously. As he reassures his "Mama" that he's not ill, and has won a promotion that will enable him to send her more money, Angela draws near and hears her wish him happy birthday. Jealous of the attention paid to this rival, she fidgets with the phallic regalia of cue ball and champagne cork (Figure 4.2), whose explosive pop makes Hannah ask who's there. Bending toward the phone, Angela teasingly calls out "It's me, Mama." As George tries to explain her away as "just a girl," Angela, now occupying the center of the frame, raises her eyebrows in protest. With clear amusement she watches him collapse into acquiescence at his mother's catechizing. Exhausted by this ordeal, he hangs up and lowers his head, while Angela teases "Did you promise to be a good boy? Not to waste your time on girls?" But again the power relations between them shift as George replies sexily, "I don't *waste* my time." Responding to this challenge, Angela once again takes the initiative and George's hand, briskly leading her "blue boy" to the entrance of the ballroom. With the camera remaining at a distance, the couple halt, pause for a beat, and whirl into a waltz in the style imagined by Laura in *Brief Encounter*. Then they dance through the classical doorway into the unseen room.

A second montage now proceeds, superimposing long shots of the party over a middle close-up of Hannah meditatively touching the phone much as

Figure 4.2 George (Montgomery Clift) telephones his "Mama" as Angela (Elizabeth Taylor) looks on in *A Place in the Sun*, Paramount 1951 (Kobal Collection).

Sternberg superimposed Mrs Griffiths' image over Clyde's departing train. Unlike the factory montage, these images are fluent and dynamic, concluding with an extended version of the traveling shot in Sternberg's party scene—down a corridor, past abandoned drinks and cigarettes, through a doorway into the nearly empty ballroom, where a dissolve to a close-up reveals Angela nestled dreamily on George's shoulder, as the two continue to dance. Stevens stressed this sequence's contrast of the poverty of the mission with the grandeur of the mansion, but the dissolve through Hannah's worried face also suggests that it represents her fears, of losing George to a life of luxury. Like Alice and Angela, she too is seeing him, albeit in her mind's eye. George's evening in this setting, with its theatrical columns and arches, its sweeping camera and swelling strings, evokes "glamor" as a highly cinematic phenomenon—spectacular, illusory, fantasmatic. Yet, unlike Laura's imaginings, these scenes are actually happening. He dances the night away with Angela, until another dissolve takes him apologetically back to 4433 ½ Elm Avenue, where the waiting Alice has fallen asleep.

This is only the second time we have seen George inside Alice's lodgings, so her bitter tone when she asks why he didn't telephone seems gratingly possessive. Now filmed in the light, the small room is crammed with furniture and its lodger, her waist size emphasized by a black belt round her midriff, looms large in the foreground. As Stevens later claimed, his Alice was "the kind of girl a man could be all mixed up with in the dark, but come the morning wonder how the hell he got into this" (Hughes, 2004: 70). To emphasize this diminution in George's desire, the script now has him use her masculine nickname, "Al." She questions him closely about the pretty girls at the party, Angela Vickers in particular, until he gives up trying to reassure her. Then Alice begins to cry and miserably announces that they are "in trouble." Shot over her shoulder and across a table laid with pathetic birthday treats, George is already at a distance as she recalls "Remember the first night you came here? Oh, I'm so worried." Here, as Stevens admitted, the dice are loaded against Alice. Unlike Sternberg's Roberta—who in Sylvia Sidney's incarnation is more beautiful and sympathetic than Frances Dee's Sondra—Winters' Alice is increasingly presented as a depressed nag. Her Oscar-nominated performance invokes the Jewish stereotype that she would reprise for an Academy Award as Mrs Von Daan in *The Diary of Ann Frank* (1959). (In the latter film, Stevens acceded to contemporary prejudice by casting a non-Jew, Millie Perkins, in the title role.)

A dissolve to the factory shows Alice despondently packing in the foreground as George, enclosed in the department head's glass office, paces nervously in the background. At the shift's end she walks past his window and waves feebly. The sense of distance is maintained when, back in his boarding house with the Vickers sign flashing through his window, he is seen ringing her from the hall telephone in a static long shot. With his back to the camera, as Sternberg so often filmed Holmes, he confesses that he hasn't found "any doctor yet" but still attempts to reassure her. Immediately afterward, a ring brings him back to the telephone in the same long shot, but this time his hunched back straightens as he accepts an invitation from Angela. Returning to his room he sits contemplatively at his table, and behind him looms the print of the drowned Ophelia, temptation approaching the unaware. The dissolve to George's pensive expression as Angela drives him to the party suggests its unconscious persistence.

At the party the couple, now perfectly matched in dark formal wear, sweep in past Angela's surprised parents and dance cheek to cheek in a series of very large close-ups, dissolving from her face to his to hers again. Finally, Angela asks her silent partner if he's unhappy: "You seem so strange, so deep and far away, as though you were holding something back." Recalled from thought, he rests his forehead against hers, their faces uncannily fitting together. Here the characteristics that Freud perceived in the uncanny are clearly identifiable, as the scene intensifies the novel's thematics of doubling (Figure 4.3), oedipal longing and strange familiarity. Thus, confessing his feelings, George concludes "I guess maybe I loved you even before I saw you." Attempting to respond, Angela

Figure 4.3 The matching profiles of Elizabeth Taylor and Montgomery Clift in *A Place in the Sun*, Paramount 1951 (Kobal Collection).

suddenly turns away to ask "Are they watching us?" and then pulls him out to the tree shadowed terrace. There, in another series of huge close-ups, she pledges her love in return. In response to his fears that she will disappear for the summer vacation, she assures him that they can spend weekends together at the lake, offering to fetch him from the factory: "You'll be my pickup." As she tenderly holds his face in her hands, the overcome George exclaims, "'If I could only tell you how much I love you." "Tell Mama, tell Mama all," she replies, and their unseen mouths draw together in a kiss (Figure 4.4).

Much has been made of this love scene, with its reversal of the conventionally gendered co-ordinates of activity and passivity, the surprised intensity of its declarations and the extraordinary closeness of its framing. The finished scene is the consequence of several factors, beginning with a passage from the novel that Stevens had marked, of Clyde thinking "of the shadow which lay so darkly" between him and Sondra and feverishly declaring "If you only knew how much I love you! If you only knew! I wish I could tell you *all*. I wish I could" (*An American Tragedy*: 483) The dialogue was rewritten the night before shooting to

Figure 4.4 The kiss "on everyone's lips" in *A Place in the Sun*, Paramount 1951 (Kobal Collection).

take Angela "beyond her sophistication at the time," as Stevens later put it. "I explained I'd like them to get it in their heads, rehearse it off-screen, then get them in there and throw them at one another" in order to achieve "the excitement of a preordained meeting" (American Film Institute 2004: 103). To film very close, William Mellor used then-rare six-inch lenses, employing three cameras to maintain spontaneity. At the editing stage, Stevens characteristically used a screening room instead of a movieola, with the actors' close-ups projected side by side and then cut so that each face dissolved into the other. Finally, to comply with the Production Code Administration's insistence that the kissing "throughout the story, should not be unduly passionate, prolonged, or open-mouth" (letter from Joseph J. Breen to Luigi Luraschi, Paramount Pictures, November 1, 1949, APS file, PCA archive), the shot selected masks the actors' lips with Clift's shoulder, making their kiss both visible and invisible, absent and present.

The effect is that of a fantasmatic fusion, an imaginary union inaugurated with the vertiginous dissolves between the matched faces of the dancing couple and culminating in the blurred intensity of the very close kiss. For George this fusion will be fatal. Steven Cohan remarks on the "self-consuming negation of his individuality," so like an infant's engagement with its mother, overwhelming "a stable subject/object relation" (Cohan, 1997: 230–1). Sam Girgus echoes this analysis to stress his "identification with the imaginary closeness and security of the feminine as opposed to classic Oedipal distancing" (Girgus, 1998: 206) and his consequent "free-fall" (Girgus, 1998: 193) into the desire and fascination that Michel Chion might have predicted. For Angela, protected by the material realities of wealth and position, this union will also be transformative, changing a debutante into a postulant by the film's conclusion. But Angela and George are not the only parties to this love scene. When she turns away from him to ask, "Are they watching us?" she is ostensibly referring to her parents, whose curiosity about her new escort has been voiced. Yet she turns to look directly into the camera, fleetingly acknowledging the presence of other spectators, those in the film's audience. In the moments that follow, those spectators are drawn into the lovers' embrace by the immense lenses with which it is filmed. As Paramount's publicists would later proclaim, "The effect is so realistic that most spectators feel they are actually participating in the happy event" (Paramount Showmanship Manual, 1951, Publicity: A Place in the Sun, Core Collection, Academy of Motion Picture Arts and Sciences Library, Los Angeles).

Murder at Loon Lake?

A black interval fades up to George consulting a telephone directory, dissolves to his departure from a drugstore with a package and dissolves again to him waiting outside a doctor's surgery. Inside, Alice claims to be a recently married woman who can't afford a child. When the doctor tries to console her by recalling his own marital worries, she breaks down and admits that she has no husband. Stiffening at her revelation, he sternly refuses "advice on material and financial problems which I can't help." Returning to George's car, Alice wryly observes, "He thought I ought to make a very healthy mother," and then insists "You just gotta marry me—family or no family, this future of yours or no future."

Just as they had 20 years earlier, the Production Code administrators stipulated "that we cannot accept any suggestion of the subject of abortion" (Joseph I. Breen to Luigi Luraschi, Paramount Pictures, November 14, 1949, APS file, PCA archive). Throughout scripting, PCA head Joe Breen had vetoed lines such as Alice's "You said nothing would happen—remember? Well—it's happened," and George's "There must be someone—some place you can go" (Joseph I. Breen to Luigi Luraschi, Paramount Pictures, September 30, 1949, APS file, PCA archive). But even without such dialogue the abortion references in the completed film are wholly intelligible, as they were in the 1931 adaptation. Indeed, *Variety* would report that the "Breen office has been astonishingly cooperative" (July 18, 1951) in regard to the film's sexual content. As in the Sternberg version, the inefficacy of the methods attempted is effectively demonstrated, but that may not have been the only reason for the PCA's sanction of these scenes. Their reversal of the film's title is all too apparent, with the visits to the drugstore and the doctor taking place at night. The resulting *noir* atmosphere of transgression and menace reaches its peak in the darkened car, when Alice insists that they marry during George's September holiday and he, illumined only by his match lighting a rare cigarette, argues and then agrees.

A dissolve takes George, still smoking, back to his room, where he tears a calendar from the wall and circles Friday, September 1. As he does so, his radio announces a series of summer fatalities. Backed by a crescendo of thumping strings, the report mentions five drownings and the danger of unpatrolled beaches: "Make your holiday death's holiday too." Here, in one of the scenes most indebted to the Sternberg adaptation, temptation arrives in the form of a news report, albeit on the radio rather than in a newspaper. Having adopted Clyde's cigarette, George also imitates his darting eyes as he considers the import of what he hears. But, unlike Clyde, who mercilessly proceeds to the hotel to collect the fatal travel brochures, he throws himself to his bed in horror.

Just then, the sound of Angela's horn is heard at his window and the lovers are tenderly reunited in her parked convertible. In a radical departure from this tragedy's predecessors, she brings the prospect of potential parental acceptance: George is invited to spend his holiday with her family. When he hastily lies that he has been invited to spend it with the Eastmans, she assures him that they will be joining them at the lake. Once more in the driver's seat, Angela throws back her head to rhapsodize about the vacation pleasures that await them—swimming, sunbathing, riding. When George marvels, "And you love me?" her assent brings his head to her shoulder. A dissolve from their blissful faces to Alice's boarding house shows her summoned in her dressing gown to the telephone, where she reluctantly concedes to George's request for a week's delay of their wedding, in order that he may secure a bonus from his uncle at the lake.

Alice's despondent face now dissolves into two images, of white sails on the lake superimposed over Angela waterskiing behind a boat driven by George—a leisured plenitude that corresponds to Eisenstein's montaged "dream of the joys of sport and the bright outdoors" (Montagu, 1969: 283). This imagery is singled out in Raymond Chandler's famous dismissal of the film's "portrayal of how the lower classes think the upper classes live ... They ought to have called it Speedboats for Breakfast" (Hiney and Macshane, 2000: 179). But Chandler's objections seem crucially misconceived as the film continually uses the introductory dissolve from character to scene objectively *and* subjectively, to represent such visions as both diegetically "real" and fantasmatic. The effect is to represent George's visit to the Vickers' "dream palace" as precisely a "dream holiday." The scene dissolves to Angela's parents standing before yet another screen-like expanse, the large glass doors of their new lakeside home. There her mother (Frieda Inescort) explains that her invitation to George is a test to "see him set down 24 hours a day with people Angela knows," to make him an object of continuous surveillance at their place in the sun.

A further dissolve reveals the young couple riding horses to a forested lakeshore, where Angela plunges in shrieking at the water's chill. Toweling down afterwards, she identifies this remote place as Loon Lake, with only a lodge and "crumbly old boats" at its other end. Drawing the recumbent George closer, her upright back centered against the sublime prospect she claims as her own discovery, she relates the story of a couple drowning there the previous summer— with the man's body never found. A loon's eerie call punctuates her tale as George's eyes move in thought. Again, Angela asks what he's thinking, and he evades her by laying his head in her lap, assuming with his virgin "Mama" the pose of a pieta. When her attempt to reassure him about her parents' eventual approval provokes him to propose marriage, she suddenly rises to her feet, asking "Haven't I told you? I intend to." The scene ends with George, filmed from behind looking into the lake as a very long and highly prophetic dissolve overlaps its waters with an image of Alice.[10] Now visibly pregnant, she walks slowly to her mailbox and discovers a photograph in the local paper of George and Angela boating together. The next dissolve is to flames.

The fire is for a Hawaiian *luau* hosted by the Vickers. (In a 1950s update of the floral motifs in the Sternberg version, the diners wear enormous *leis*.) As George's uncle praises his ability to "meet people" and suggests a transfer to the front office, a uniformed black maid brings a telephone to the other "Mr Eastman." This reminder of the social hierarchy that George seeks to surmount is followed by the image of a furious Alice. She has arrived at the local bus station and loudly announces her intention to come and "tell them everything" unless George picks her up. Pleading his mother's illness, George excuses himself from the party, assuring the perturbed Angela that he will return as soon as he can, and quickly kisses her goodbye.

At the station a bus driver turns to listen as Alice loudly threatens to expose George to the newspapers and kill herself unless they marry immediately. To the sound of church bells the scene dissolves to the next morning as the couple arrives at the local court house, where a sign on the door for the portentously named Registry of Births, Marriages and Deaths announces its closure for the Labor Day holiday (Figure 4.5). A relieved George suggests a prenuptial picnic at Loon Lake and the surprised Alice agrees. As they pass the empty courtroom, he stands with his back to its entrance and the camera lingers on the judge's bench, which ominously dissolves over the couple's approach to the lake. Near the launch, George pulls the clutch, declares that they've run out of gas and suggests a boat trip before he goes to get more. The boatman remarks on the unusual name he offers, "Gilbert Edwards," and looks up as Alice shrieks when she stumbles getting into the dinghy. "Don't worry," she assures him, "my husband is a very good swimmer."

As George rows, the remoteness of the dark lake is revealed in intermittent high angled long shots through the trees. Sweating with tension, he glares at the unwitting figure before him as Alice babbles about their future and the "little

Figure 4.5 George (Montgomery Clift) and Alice (Shelley Winters) at the Registry Office in *A Place in the Sun*, Paramount 1951 (Kobal Collection).

things" that compensate for poverty. Eventually he claims to be out of breath and she suggests that they just drift—"After all, we're not going anywhere." Then, as night falls, she exclaims "Look behind you," and childishly intones "Star light, star bright, first star I see tonight, wish me luck, wish me light, make my wish come true tonight." At this George softens and his face becomes thoughtful. When Alice asks what he wished, he first replies with a curt "nothing" but then apologizes, promising to "stick by her." Apparently resigned to doing so, he leans back in the bow as she continues her projection of a life "just like any other old married couple ... content with what you've got." But as she prattles on about their future, happily scrimping and saving together, he finally shouts "Stop it" into her baleful face. Chastened, she asks if he had wished her dead and George furiously denies it. As he collapses back into his seat, she looms forward in distorted close-up to apologize, lurches sideways and upsets the boat. A last long shot shows them falling into the water, and then only the upturned boat on the lake's surface as the shot dissolves into the skeletal branches of a dead tree.

A loon sounds its lonely call as George is seen staggering to the shore. He walks through the forest by moonlight, stumbling on a group of campers who tell him the way to the road. A dissolve through the trees to the morning light reveals a snarling police dog being quieted by its master, a large man with a cane. District Attorney Frank Marlow (Raymond Burr) limps into the courthouse and answers a telephone call from the coroner. Again as in the Sternberg version, he repeats his announcement of a couple drowning in the lake. The scene dissolves to George parking at the Vickers house, where the maid greets him with concern and asks if he's ill. As he pours himself a whisky, Angela arrives in tennis clothes, hears that his mother is much better and tells him that he's winning his parents over with "his boyish charm." When she mentions the likelihood of a Christmas engagement, he urges her to run away and marry immediately. But Angela enthuses about a big wedding—"all girls want one." As George gulps down his drink, the scene dissolves to the lake, where Marlow learns that the victim carried an Eastman employee's card and that someone drove away from the boathouse late that night. At the Vickers' house George is greeted by Angela's friends, who tease him about having "another woman stashed around some-place." When the couple seek seclusion in the speedboat, her friends pile in as they roar away from the dock, where—in a montage effect remarkably like that which Eisenstein sought—a deep focus shot contrasts their sport with news of Alice's drowning broadcast from a forgotten portable radio in the foreground. [11]

This time the lake's waters dissolve over George, now sitting exhausted on the Vickers' patio, where Earl Eastman arrives brandishing a newspaper report of suspected murder. Taking refuge indoors, George is startled by a summons from the Vickers' butler to report to Angela's father. As George approaches, Mr Vickers (Sheppard Strudwick) is also reading a paper, on which the briefly glimpsed headline reads "MURDER AT LOON LAKE?" Their chat begins ominously, with Vickers warning that he will be "a little bit personal." As Angela enters surreptitiously, George answers his questions about his background in a concise version of the declamatory speech in Wilson's preliminary screenplay. "Very poor people," he explains, "religious work ... sidewalk services ... no training, no education," in the sole concession—apart from the brief glimpse of the street singers after the movie—to the novel's first book. As George continues, the angle changes from a mid-shot of him looking away from the camera to a close-up of open-eyed sincerity. He protests his love for Angela and his willingness to do anything to make her happy—"even if it's right that I shouldn't see her anymore." Vickers is moved and so is his daughter, who drives George away to be alone with him. Her convertible dissolves to Alice's room, where the landlady tells the police that she had been seeing "an Eastman." As an officer telephones the District Attorney, a siren indicates that the exuberant Angela and terrified George are being pursued by a motorcycle patrolman. For the second time in the film, the law interrupts him with a woman in a car, to issue Angela a speeding ticket. Afterwards George collapses onto her shoulder and murmurs in his sleep as the dusk brings the sound of more sirens (Figure 4.6).

Figure 4.6 An exhausted George (Montgomery Clift) collapses on Angela (Elizabeth Taylor) in *A Place in the Sun*, Paramount 1951 (Kobal Collection).

Guilty of Desire

Waking with a start, George is told by Angela that he's been protesting "not my fault ... don't hate me." Echoing her opening allusion to dreams, she insists it's all a "bad dream ... a false dream" and promises that she'll always love him.

When they return to the house, George sees a police car parked in the drive and desperately embraces her once more. Now dressed against the chill in a white scarf wound round her head like a veil, she tells him "Every time you leave me for a minute, it's like goodbye. I like to believe it's because you can't live without me." After she enters the house, George escapes into the woods where—like Sternberg's Clyde—he hurries straight to the waiting deputies. He is turned over to Marlow with a curt, "Here's your baby." Denying murder, he begs not to be questioned at the Vickers' home and is taken to jail. But Marlow goes to their house and in a fixed long shot paces with his cane as he questions all present about their knowledge of George's "double life." This is the reference that confirms Steven Cohan's queer reading of Clift's character in the film. As he points out, the star's intensity feeds into the complex combination of desire and identification by which George androgynously doubles Angela while double crossing Alice. In Cohan's view, Alice's power to blackmail George is strong enough to suggest a greater transgression than that of heterosexual fornication and their furtive meetings take place in settings appropriate to 1950s homosexual encounters. But although George's impetus to infancy rather than fatherhood is—moderately, by the standards of 1950s American masculinity—perverse, his erotic energy is directed at the socially idealized Angela, not the "queer" figure of "Al." The desire he will reluctantly confess in court is to rid himself of his backstreet lover. If transgression dooms George, it is the transgression of attempting to possess a hypernormative ideal, setting in motion the inevitable loss (of the object or his life) that Angela blithely lyricizes in her echo of Cole Porter. The traditional identification of the double with the soul of the deceased that Freud discusses in "The Uncanny" underscores the intimation of mortality.

As the District Attorney offers to ensure her anonymity, Angela is taken upstairs in a forlorn bridal procession, flanked by Mrs Vickers and the maid, both also dressed in nuptial white. (Here the film's renaming of the site of the Vickers' vacation house "Bride's Lake" designates it as the site of her fantasmatic wedding, long desired but realized only as premature widowhood. Recall Laura's voice over her reflection in the train window in *Brief Encounter*: "those absurd fantasies just like one has when one is a girl, of being wooed and married by the ideal of one's dreams"; and Angela's description of the lake house: "a dream palace. I'm going to end my days there.") Entering her bedroom Angela pauses, also reflected in the giant rectangular mirror that extends across an entire wall and nearly all the frame. Seeing herself in that screen space, she faints to the floor. A dissolve to George's cell shows him back in his workaday white T-shirt, being told by his lawyers that she will be kept out of the trial. The defense team is convinced by his claim that he was unable to go through with the murder at the lake but a newspaper headline records Marlow's vow to send him to the electric chair. After reading it, Mrs Vickers throws the paper—its full-page photograph of George confirming his fatal transformation to a media spectacle—into the fire. As the flames dissolve into Angela's picture window, she turns from it to watch the image burn.

A further dissolve through the flames reveals the now abandoned holiday house and another shows Marlow opening the prosecution's case by questioning Alice's landlady, a factory employee and the doctor. (Despite the District Attorney's ferocity, this is not a show trial in the Sternberg style. The courtroom is much smaller and without a raked gallery.) A camper, the bus driver and the boatman fill out the later stages of the story while the coroner claims evidence of a blow to Alice's head. As the court stenographer prints out several days' of testimony against George, his attorney begins the case for the defense: "This boy is on trial for the act of murder, not for the thought of murder … And if you find this boy guilty of desire but not guilty in deed, then he must walk out of this courtroom as free as you or I." Stressing the absence of prosecution witnesses to the events on the lake, he calls George to the stand.

To the sound of the loon's cry, the defendant admits that "In the back of my mind was the thought of drowning her—but I didn't want to think such things." Out on the lake, George explains, he realized that he couldn't go through with it. He recalls Alice's accusation of him wanting her dead, but protests that he no longer did so. Asked what he was thinking about, he replies "I was thinking of somebody else." Clearly leading him, the defense attorney elaborates, "Another girl. You were thinking that this other girl and her world were lost to you forever." When the boat capsized, George continues, he was stunned, perhaps as a result of a blow to his head as he fell in. By the time he swam round the boat, Alice had gone down.

Marlow's cross-examination begins by reiterating the defense attorney's elegiac summation of George's feelings on leaving the Vickers' barbecue to meet Alice: "Up there on that terrace in the moonlight you left behind, didn't you, the girl you loved, and with her your hopes, your ambitions, your dreams." His argument, however, is that George intended to return, and lied repeatedly in order to do so. Another dissolve seems to float the fatal vessel into the courtroom. Like Sternberg, Stevens retains this scene from the novel, with George also asked to sit in the boat and go through the drowning (Figure 4.7). Challenged on the distance between him and Alice on surfacing, he literally trips on a rope tied to the bow when trying to explain how he could fail to swim such a short way. In a final gesture of condemnation, Marlow swaps his threatening cane for an oar, crashing it down to demonstrate the blow to Alice. As George attempts to steady himself after this barrage, his seat in the witness box dissolves to Angela's in a lecture hall, where a teacher is describing the adolescent's transition from "sheltered immaturity" to "the responsibilities of adult life." In the light of the subsequent blacklisting of two of this film's leading figures, his remarks on the "adoption of an extreme belief or creed" as evidence of immaturity now have a startling resonance. But Angela is not listening. Instead, she draws back her notebook to read a newspaper whose headline is "EASTMAN JURY OUT."

Another dissolve returns the jury to the courtroom, where they pronounce George guilty of murder in the first degree. To the flashes of press cameras he shakily writes "Mother, I am convicted." Arriving at the death house, down a cor-

Figure 4.7 The District Attorney (Raymond Burr) makes George (Montgomery Clift) re-enact the drowning in *A Place in the Sun*, Paramount 1951 (Kobal Collection).

ridor hung with plants and a caged bird—pathetic reminders of the natural world now barred to George—Hannah Eastman is led into his cell. There she is greeted by the prison chaplain and her son—uniformed, hunched, crewcut—like the GI he was initially conceived to be, like "a poetic ghost inside his grey death-clothes" (Capote, 2001: 104). In Wilson's revision of Dreiser and Eisenstein's indictment of religion, George is informed that the Governor has refused a reprieve *before* the chaplain (Paul Frees) asks what he was actually thinking as he surfaced on the lake. The benumbed prisoner slumps on his cot as the minister, mouthing the period's pop psychology, suggests that he may have "hidden the full truth of this even from yourself." When George indicates that at the moment he found himself unable to save Alice he was thinking of Angela, the chaplain quietly declares him guilty of murder "in your heart." So doing, this pseudo-analyst unwittingly affirms the very superstition that Eisenstein derided and Freud sought to analyze: "As soon as something actually happens in our lives which seems to confirm the old, discarded beliefs we get a feeling of the uncanny; it is as though we were making a judgement something like this: 'So, after all, it is *true* that one can kill a person by the mere wish!'" (Freud, 1985: 371).

As Angela's theme plays over George's examination of conscience, the close-up of her face at their first kiss dissolves into his, a vivid use of the optical effect to "let the audience see his desire," as Stevens later told the American Film Institute. Significantly, the director continued, "They have to know his need for the thing that—even accidentally—traps him. So how do you do those things? Cinema, at its most effective, is one scene effectively superseded by the next. Isn't that it? The hatchet on the rope and the guillotine falls in the next cut" (American Film Institute, 2004: 103–4).

A further dissolve reveals an equally close shot of the prisoner looking yearningly through the bars. Then, in apparent confirmation of the imputed efficacy of thought that has convicted him before man and God, the next dissolve brings Angela to his cell. In a long black dress with a high white collar and a close fitting hat obscuring her hair, she now resembles a novice in a religious order. Viewed once more from behind, George beholds this apparition, as cinema spectators must, without moving or speaking. Finally, he chokingly confesses that he now realizes he's "guilty of a lot of things—most of what they say of me," but Angela pledges the lifelong love that is the price of his extinction. They kiss gently and she is led away, marveling that they "spend the best part of [their] time together just saying goodbye."

The final scene of *A Place in the Sun* was originally edited to show George looking through the window of the execution chamber at the electric chair. A close-up of him yielded to a flashback of moments from the film, "about 8 frames each," spooling backwards to "a wailing infant's face" (George Stevens interviewed by Robert Hughes, February–March 1967, GSC). But this vision of the condemned man's life passing before him was deemed labored and Stevens sought an alternative. An ending showing George walking toward the chamber in a sudden shaft of bright sunlight was test screened, but the director later complained that "the audience didn't get that purged feeling, that tragic release that I'd hoped they would get there; in fact, they looked at it and they were down." Ultimately, Stevens chose the vision from George's past that he had already repeated in the cell, his first kiss with Angela. As George walks to his execution, Angela's rapt countenance is again superimposed over his own, now not as evidence of criminal intent but as compensation for its punishment. (His last walk, not filmed to support a lengthy superimposition, had to be extended by step-printing.) In this highly reflexive image (by now an image of an image) the audience sees George's desire for what it is—a dissolution into cinematic fantasy that is as consequential as the executioner's blow.

Stevens hailed this conclusion as a realization of his film's tragic import, combining the classical principles of magnitude, catharsis and recognition. As he told interviewer Robert Hughes, to achieve "in the most glamorous form—the girl, the money, the success, and what you've never hoped to gain, is an extraordinary experience, even if it's only envisaged; but to envisage it, to live it, and then be tortured by it in actuality is expanding the opportunity for life's awareness to an extraordinary degree" (February–March 1967, GSC). If Eisenstein's adaptation of Dreiser's ambiguous novel is a melodramatic appeal against American injustice and Sternberg's an indictment of its protagonist *and* his society, Stevens' upholds tragedy's reconciliation to the penalty exacted for transgressive desire.

Ecstasy and Brutality

Described like this, *A Place in the Sun* seems vulnerable to the criticisms it has subsequently received, notably Ivan Moffat's complaint to a 1975 American Film Institute seminar that "Stevens was a romantic, so the bleak social picture painted by Dreiser took second place to the steamy love affair between George and Angela" (Moffat, 2004: 255). Certainly the film's ill-starred romance became the theme of its publicity campaign, as Paramount executive Russell Holman had pleaded after viewing early rushes of Clift and Taylor's scenes together. (On October 27, 1949, Holman sent a teletype to Stevens urging that the film be titled *The Lovers*, "since both script and footage indicate primary motivating force of whole drama is love between Clift and Taylor. This will also be picture's primary interest for world audience both before and when they see it" (GSC).) After a series of previews for critics and journalists in spring 1951, their praise for the love scenes headed the publicity for its September release. In Britain, the June 19 issue of *Picture Post* led its preview (Birch and Hutton, 1951: 35) with a page-wide close-up of the couple's first kiss. The illustration's caption, "The Whole Screen Is Filled With Ecstasy" was then quoted in a studio advertisement for "the picture with the kiss that already is being talked about from one end of the world to the other," again with an immense close-up.

As the studio advised exhibitors to "capitalize on the kiss angle" by giving away candy kisses and small cards printed with a woman's pursed lips and the slogan "THE GREAT NEWS IS ON EVERYONE'S LIPS—A PLACE IN THE SUN" (Paramount Showmanship Manual, 1951, Core Collection, Publicity: A Place in the Sun, Academy of Motion Pictures Arts and Sciences Library, Los Angeles), *Look* magazine featured stills of the film's love scenes in an article in which RKO producers Jerry Wald and Norman Krasna claimed that film kisses were getting "bigger than ever" (Wald and Krasna, September 1, 1951: 36).[12] The following month saw *Photoplay* feature sequential sets of frames from three scenes in which the couple kisses—on the terrace, after the *luau* and just before George's arrest—which the magazine's editors claimed to have had copied directly from a print screened in Paramount's projection room. This device, and its claim to reveal the actual film rather than posed publicity stills, became a dominant feature of the studio's advertising, most strikingly on its lobby card, which borders a posed photograph of Clift and Taylor cheek to cheek with a celluloid ribbon, its perforations clearly showing, featuring frames of George and Angela's first kiss. Clichéd though this may seem a half-century later, it is difficult to imagine a more reflexive image of the film *as* a film than that ribbon, invented by its hero's namesake.

This emphasis was borne out in the film's initial reception, in which its cinematic technique was a major topic. As a review of the film's premiere in the Los Angeles *Daily News* (Smith, 1951) put it, "Ardent students of the cinema will spend long hours discussing certain scenes. Over beer, pretzels, martinis and canapés, they will talk with awe about the way Stevens handled his people and his ideas." Although the widespread coverage of the film's close-ups[13] was often offered as an equivalent of Mellor's six-inch lenses, to facilitate imaginary access to romantic ecstasy, it also worked in reverse, to identify the film with the production of such fantasies by Hollywood's "dream factory."[14] Notable in this respect is an (undated) quote from *Life* magazine in a Paramount advertisement: "The cinematic kiss—that long, tender, graceful swoop and strain which most Americans try to duplicate more or less successfully in their daily lives—is handled with proper reverence in 'A PLACE IN THE SUN.'"

If these abundant allusions to the role of the American cinema in Stevens' American tragedy conform to one theme in Dreiser's novel, the film's softening of its class conflict is better remembered in the aftermath of its release. While editing commenced on *A Place in the Sun*, Stevens commissioned Michael Wilson to write an outline for an adaptation of Jack Shaefer's novella *Shane*. By March 1950, when Wilson submitted his seventeen-page outline, the "Hollywood Ten"[15] had lost their appeals and begun serving prison sentences for refusing to testify about their political affiliations to the House Un-American Activities Committee. Later that year a conservative faction of the Directors Guild led by Cecil B. De Mille marshaled the passage of a mandatory loyalty oath for the Guild's membership in the absence of its liberal president, Joseph Mankiewicz. When, in October 1950, Mankiewicz called a meeting to reconsider the oath, De Mille denounced him as a fellow traveler and attempted to oust him from the presidency. Stevens led the move to defend Mankiewicz, resigning from the Guild's board and challenging De Mille on the capital gains he'd amassed while his colleagues were serving in the war. The Guild's right wing was defeated, but HUAC launched a new wave of hearings. Wilson received his subpoena in the spring of 1951, when *A Place in the Sun* began to be previewed. In March he wrote Stevens after a screening, admitting his disappointment with the film's climax, but congratulating the director on "the totality of the piece and its input. You have given it the compassion of true tragedy. It is a deeply pro-human picture—an inadequate word to describe a crucial quality in a time when our culture is being de-humanized and brutalized" (March 26, 1951, GSC, APS).

Wilson appeared before HUAC in September 1951, the month of *A Place in the Sun's* national release. Asked if he were a member of the Communist Party, he claimed Fifth Amendment protection against self-incrimination and escaped jail, but not the studios' blacklist of those believed to support this particular "extreme belief." *Shane* (1953) would be written by A. B. Guthrie, Jr., although the emphasis on the class conflict between the ranchers and the smallholders in Wilson's outline was retained. In spring 1952, *A Place in the Sun* won five

Academy Awards, for its direction, photography, editing, music and screenplay. It was the last such award Wilson would be able to claim. When *Friendly Persuasion* was belatedly filmed by William Wyler in 1956, Wilson went uncredited, despite the screenplay's Academy Award nomination. *The Bridge on the River Kwai* (1957) won a screenplay Oscar for Wilson and his fellow blacklistee, Carl Foreman, but both were denied credit and only received their Awards posthumously, in 1984. Wilson's contribution to another Oscar nominated screenplay, for *Lawrence of Arabia* (1962), was acknowledged even later by the Academy Board of Directors.

Another veteran of *A Place in the Sun*, actress Anne Revere, also became blacklisted. Named to the Committee as a left winger by one of her oldest friends in the industry, actor Lee J. Cobb, she appeared before HUAC on May 25, 1951. There she was shown a photocopy of her alleged Communist Party registration card and asked if she recognized it. Revere later declared that the unsigned card in the photocopy was a fake, but she refused to answer the Committee's questions, saying "I regard any questions on politics or religious views as violating the rights of citizens" (*Variety*, September 13, 1974). The actress was an Academy Award winner herself, for her supporting role as Taylor's mother in *National Velvet*, and treasurer of the Screen Actors Guild. But after refusing to testify she did not appear in another film until 1970. She bitterly believed that after her "testimony before HUAC, Paramount, in a fit of 'patriotism,' cut my part to the bone. Stevens fought for me, but his hands were tied, contractually" (Frey, 1970: 30). "And the sloppy love scene at the end of the film was a real tip-off of the times. It was a cover-up of the real story" (Taylor, 1967: 20).

As the film's documentation demonstrates, by the time Wilson completed his contribution to the screenplay, Hannah Eastman was not seen with George until after his trial. The September 30, 1949 White Script retains George's telephone call to her and two scenes together after his conviction. A December 27, 1949 casting memorandum records Revere's contract for one week's shooting with another week's option, and photography was concluded on January 3. The omitted material she refers to is presumably the dialogue in the White Script in which George's mother appeals to him, as in the novel, to issue a public statement "that could be a guide to other young men in the future who might be misled. You could leave a light burning." In a subsequent scene George protests "You taught me the Christian way of life, Mama. But wasn't I also taught to be ambitious? To climb the ladder of success? How do you square that?"

"I taught you that you cannot serve both God and Mammon," she replies. When George asks if his statement should warn others that "it's a sin to try to get ahead," she answers "Give them faith, George. Give them this simple truth. It is all I have lived by—it is all you have to say."

Stevens later recalled that after the film's editor William Hornbeck gave him a four-and-a-half hour rough cut at the end of January 1950, he took over the supervision of its cutting, editing and scoring, as per his usual practice of directorial control. This process was interrupted by the shooting of his next picture, *Something to Live For* (1952), but by the first preview of *A Place in the Sun* on November 8, 1950 the running time had been reduced to two-and-a-half hours. The sixth preview was held in February 1951. Significantly, Stevens kept a February 1, 1951 letter from Paul MacNamara of Famous Artists congratulating him after a screening, but criticizing his ending:

> it might be a good idea to shorten it if possible so that people could come out of the theater having experienced a real emotional jolt ... If I might make a suggestion, I think that the character of Clift's mother and the part of the story she has to play is not too important and I felt the business about the letter and the long scene in the cell with her takes away from that part of the picture ... somehow I don't think the average guy in that situation would be concerned with trying to leave a message. (GSC)

The Release Dialogue Script of *A Place in the Sun* is dated February 21, 1951. Although a seventh preview of a slightly modified final version was held in May, Hannah's sermon against Mammon was almost certainly eliminated before its speaker's fateful appointment with HUAC on the 25th of that month.

Afterimages

In 1965, Paramount licensed the telecast rights of *A Place in the Sun* to the National Broadcasting Company (NBC), for screening in its "Saturday Night at the Movies" slot. Warned by his attorney that the agreement between the companies permitted NBC to show commercials during the program, Stevens applied for a Los Angeles Superior Court injunction against any such transmission of his film. In a remarkable repetition of Dreiser's suit against Paramount, the director argued that interference with its editing would violate the editorial control vested in him by his original contract with Liberty[16] as well as the "moral message" of both the novel and the film:

> "AN AMERICAN TRAGEDY" is an extraordinarily moral story. It has all the essential elements we associate with classic Greek tragedy including the ultimate destruction of the man who believes he can abandon—can defy—fundamental moral concepts. This is not a story that can be told in bits and pieces. This is a story that depends both for its dramatic impact and for what it has to say—on its flow, on the continuity of its action without distraction ...
> To interrupt "A PLACE IN THE SUN" 10, 20, or 30 times during the course of its presentation is to cut and edit it as to destroy almost entirely its effectiveness. It now becomes a series of filmed episodes interspersed with a variety of other filmed episodes which tell stories of body odor, beer, cigarettes, ketchup, automobile tires, cough drops, anti-freeze, cigars, shavers, tooth paste, etc., skillfully contrived to rivet the viewer's attention upon what they are selling ...

(George Stevens, Declaration on Application for Temporary Injunction to Superior Court of the State of California for the County of Los Angeles, *George Stevens Plaintiff v. National Broadcasting Company*, Defendants, January 31, 1966, GSC, APS)

In February 1966, a preliminary injunction was issued restraining NBC from cutting or editing *A Place in the Sun* for the purposes of inserting "other material which will so alter, adversely effect or emasculate the artistic or pictorial quality of said motion picture as to destroy or distort materially or substantially the mood, effect or continuity of said motion picture as produced and directed by the plaintiff" (Preliminary Injunction awarded by Judge Ralph H. Nutter, February 15, 1966, GSC). But on March 12, the network went ahead with its telecast, interrupting the film nine times for a total of forty-two color advertisements. The fortieth commenced after the film's somber conclusion with a jingle for Granny Goose corn chips:

> Put a little snap in your life ...
> Have yourself a fiesta.
> A corn fiesta by Granny, Granny Goose.
> They're roasted uniquely, flavored just right.
> They're different completely, thin, golden and light.

Even more galling to Stevens was the re-editing of his film to accommodate these interruptions. The frequent dissolves posed a particular problem for NBC. To avoid cutting away from or returning to the film during superimpositions, it was interrupted at the end of the preceding shot and the transition changed to a fade-out. Thirty seconds of Stevens' dissolves were thus eliminated and with them their accompanying dialogue and music bridges. Thus, for example, George's aunt's reproving "Charles Eastman" to her husband for hiring his poor relation was simply cut out to obviate the dissolve to the Eastman factory. In other cases, NBC's editors added film footage from another print to support dialogue. This tactic was employed in the transition between Alice's agreement to a delay in the wedding and George's visit to the lake. The original dissolve between her final "I'll wait here," the long shot of Bride's Lake dotted with sailboats and the one of Angela waterskiing behind a boat driven by George, was changed to a fade-out. To avoid leaving Alice's speech over a blank screen, NBC extended the shot of her on the telephone. To facilitate a return to the film after the commercials, the network eliminated the long shot of the lake that Stevens had dissolved between Alice and the couple waterskiing. As he complained, "I had included this scene for the specific purpose of contrasting the natural beauty and peace of the lake with the ugliness and squalor of Alice's rooming house. This mood NBC completely destroyed." Stevens' defense of his film's transitions form a major part of his declaration to the Los Angeles Superior Court that NBC's transmission of *A*

Place in the Sun violated the terms of its preliminary injunction. His 27-page statement to the court offers an exemplary discussion of the differences between the cut, the fade-out and the dissolve. It stresses the importance of the last for the purpose of contrasting

> George's lonely, desperate affair with his co-worker at the Eastman factory, Alice Tripp, and his fantasy-come-true romance with Angela Vickers, the glitteringly beautiful daughter of a wealthy, patrician family ... I made extensive use of the technique of superimposition of images from George's yearned-for world of luxury in scenes depicting his real world of poverty to show his drives toward success, achievement and the possession of things seemingly beyond his reach. (George Stevens, Declaration in Support of Order to Show Cause in Re: Contempt, *George Stevens, Plaintiff, v. National Broadcasting Company*, Defendants, April 1, 1966, GSC)

On June 3, Judge Richard L. Wells issued a decision entirely in keeping with the ironies that characterize the extraordinary history of Dreiser's novel and its film adaptations. While agreeing that NBC's commercial interruptions effectively weakened the "mood, effect or continuity, and the audience involvement; and therefore, some of the artistry of the film," he ruled that "the film was so dramatic, strong, exciting, romantic, tragic, interesting and artistic that it prevailed over the commercial interruptions" (Richard L. Wells, Judge of the Superior Court of the State of California for the County of Los Angeles, Memorandum Decision in Re: Contempt, *George Stevens, Plaintiff vs. National Broadcasting Company*, Defendants, June 3, 1966, GSC). Stevens appealed, supported by film critic Arthur Knight, who testified that commercial breaks damaged the film, and opposed by the legendary producer Jack Warner, who maintained that they did not. But on May 23, 1967, Superior Court Judge Ben Koenig concluded that NBC's commercial interruptions did not diminish the film's drama and artistry and that, in any case, the final-cut clause in his contract did not pertain to them. The judge did concede that "distorted or truncated versions" of televised films could compromise a director's credit, an acknowledgement that Stevens saluted "in recognition that tv 'may not cut and butcher films as, unhappily, has been the practice in the past'" (Murphy, 1967: 4).

Twenty-one years later, the case of the dissolves in *A Place in the Sun* was reopened by Jean-Luc Godard. In a controversial sequence of the 1988 "Toutes Les Histoires" chapter of his video meditation on film and twentieth century history, *Histoire(s) du cinéma*, he considers "(19)39–44, martyrdom and resurrection of the documentary." A lengthy series of artistic allusions, including Rembrandt's *Self-Portrait: Wide-Eyed*, yield to Picasso's *Guernica* and Goya's *Disasters of War*, apparently invoked to criticize cinema's failure to see and to "testify to [the] presence," in Jacques Rancière's (2002: 218) phrase, of the Holocaust. But Hollywood is then said to offer an afterimage of that notoriously unrepresentable event in what Godard later described as the "shadowed happiness" (Daney, 1991: 165) of Elizabeth Taylor in *A Place in the Sun*.

This argument is conducted by a series of superimpositions, proceeding from Stevens' footage of a freight car filled with corpses as Godard intones "And if George Stevens hadn't been the first to use the first 16 mm color film in Auschwitz and Ravensbruck ..."[17] This image then dissolves into Angela cradling George's head in her lap at the deadly lake as his voice-over continues "... Elizabeth Taylor's happiness might never have found *A Place in the Sun*." In a video re-edit of the moment at which Angela kisses her lover and rises to declare her intention to marry him, a further dissolve encircles her head with the descending hands of Mary Magdalene from Giotto's Arena frescoes at Padua. As these images are reviewed in slow and stop motion, Godard recites "O what wonder to look at what one cannot see/sweet wonder of our blind eyes."

Defending this juxtaposition, Alan Wright argues that in combining these apparently antithetical images with the saint forbidden to touch the body of the resurrected Christ, this sequence brilliantly reveals the imperceptible trauma at the heart of ecstasy, the deadly stillness inside moving pictures.[18] Unlike the synthetic montage pioneered by Eisenstein, the oppositions here remain in conflict: "By presenting a fleeting glimpse of happiness and the deadly grip of terror within the same frame, he attempts to document that which can only obtain expression at the extreme limits of comprehension."

If Wright (2000: 54) is categorical on the contraries that Godard dissolves into "unbearable proximity", the attribution of the two female figures in his montage has been subjected to debate. Jacques Rancière identifies Angela, "the rich heiress" (Rancière, 2002: 117), with the cinema, raised by the literal icon descending from above. But, as he admits, this dissolve requires the inversion of the Magdalene's position in Giotto's fresco. There the saint grounded by her carnality kneels at the feet of the risen Christ, who turns away from her touch. Tony Wood adheres to a longer tradition in proposing this sanctified prostitute as Hollywood—the commodified cinema redeemed "in the name of the immortal powers of the image" (Wood, 2002: 146).

But what of the doomed figure cradled in the pieta at Loon Lake? The "East" man who would rise to his angelic "Mama," the fatal object of desire? Both saint and angel draw us away from Godard's other object of interest, the 16-mm Kodachrome on which Stevens bore witness to the Holocaust, the technical achievement of the cinema pioneer after whom he named his hero. Shadowed by successive superimpositions of the very celluloid his namesake devised, it is George Eastman who is martyred to redeem the Hollywood to which its director returned. Real and fantasmatic, deadly and sublime, his tragic search for *A Place in the Sun* continues as an allegory of film itself.

Notes

1. See also, R. Hughes (2004), "Getting the Belly Laugh," in P. Cronin (ed.), *George Stevens: Interviews*, Jackson, MS: University Press of Mississippi, p. 66.
2. See J. McBride (1991), *Frank Capra: The Catastrophe of Success*, London: Faber & Faber, p. 514 and M. A. Moss (2004), *Giant: George Stevens, A Life in Film, Madison*, Wisconsin: University of Wisconsin Press, p. 155.
3. Eisenstein himself had declared in 1926, in regard to Mack Sennett's Bathing Beauties, "America is possessed by the ideal of the petty-bourgeois 'Bathing Girl'"—Eisenstein, S. (1988a), "However Odd—Khoklova!" in R. Taylor (ed.), *S. M. Eisenstein: Selected Works, Volume I, Writings 1922–34*, London: British Film Institute, p. 71.
4. Echoing this name, that of one of the attorneys in the film will be changed from Dreiser's Jephson to Jansen.
5. In his 1967 interview with Robert Hughes, Stevens underlines this implication when he recalls that another title under consideration was borrowed from a biography of Mussolini, *Disappointed Dream*: "he was preparing Italy for its place in the sun, you know" (GSC).
6. Ivan Moffat, interview by George Stevens Jr, June 1982, transcript, Filmmaker's Journey Collection, Margaret Herrick Library.
7. George Stevens, Jr. comments thus on his father's avoidance of color on the DVD commentary of *A Place in the Sun*, Paramount Pictures, 2001.
8. The factory's resemblance to the one where George has been created as a film character is suggested by Edmund Wilson's 1958 commentary on Dreiser's suit against Paramount: "The truth is that Hollywood at present is very much like a mill-town. The writers, shut up by day in small cells in large buildings, which, like mills, have armed guards at the doors, compelled to collaborate in twos just as a pair of weavers is given so many looms and reporting like schoolchildren to supervisors who commend or suppress or censor, display, even outside the studios, a psychology of mill-hands or children. They have no choice about the nature of their subjects and no influence on the quality of their products; and once having foregone the right to express their own tastes and beliefs, they are disturbed at seeing anybody fight for it"—Wilson, E. (1958), "Eisenstein in Hollywood," in *The American Earthquake: A Documentary of the Twenties and Thirties*, Garden City, New York: Doubleday Anchor Books, p. 399.
9. See Adorno, T. (1991), "Free Time," in J.M. Bernstein (ed.), *The Culture Industry: Selected Essays on Mass Culture*, London: Routledge, p. 164: "Just as the term 'show business' is taken today taken utterly seriously, the irony in the expression 'leisure industry' has now been quite forgotten."
10. Watson, W. (1984), *Cinema Program Notes: A Place in the Sun*, Austin: Cinema Texas, University of Texas at Austin, p. 31 describes this effect as "almost Eisensteinian," combining, as in his montages, two images to generate a third distinct meaning, that of Alice's drowning.

11. In a sound effect also reminiscent of the overtonal montages in Eisenstein's treatment, Stevens replaced the noise of the motorboat engine with that of a German Stuka bomber, "the ones that used to dive on the people on the road when they were trying to get out of France ... a vicious sound that they might associate with other things"—Hughes, R. (2004), "Getting the Belly Laugh," *George Stevens: Interviews*, Jackson, MS: University Press of Mississippi, p. 71.

12. As Wald and Krasna pointed out, such kissing scenes still had to contend with Production Code restrictions on their length (no more than twenty seconds) and execution (the actors were required to be fully clothed, in a vertical position and making no suggestive movements).

13. See Crowther, B. (1951), "Seen in Close-Up," *New York Times*, September 23, II, 1.

14. Hortense Powdermaker's much discussed study of Hollywood and the Production Code, *The Dream Factory: An Anthropologist Looks at the Movie-Makers* (1950), Boston: Little, Brown & Co, had been published in the year before *A Place in the Sun* was released.

15. The "Hollywood Ten" comprised screenwriters Ring Lardner, John Howard Lawson, Dalton Trumbo, Albert Maltz, Alvah Bessie, Lester Cole, Samuel Ornitz, screenwriter/producer Adrian Scott, and directors Edward Dmytryk and Herbert Biberman.

16. The fact that Stevens' Liberty contract was agreed in 1946, prior to the licensing of films for TV broadcast, potentially offered him rights denied to Otto Preminger in his 1965 suit against the TV editing of *Anatomy of a Murder* (1959), produced after such licensing became a common practice.

17. The footage shown is actually from Dachau. Stevens didn't film at Auschwitz or Ravensbruck, although the documentaries he worked on for the Nuremberg trials include film of several concentration camps.

18. See, notably on Rancière's discussion of *Histoire(s) de Cinéma*, Mulvey, L. (2006), *Death 24x a Second: Stillness and the Moving Image*, London: Reaktion Books.

Epilogue

In 1926, Theodore Dreiser proclaimed:

The movies are America's ra-tat-ta, the calliope ahead of the circus. The movies are doing the utmost to spread our American psychology and the world seems ready for it ... No other people have ever dreamed such riotous dreams. We go all over the world with our shout of "take a chance," that success is in money, in big buildings, that there is love for everyone, a swell time for everyone. (Carples, 1926: 107)

If *An American Tragedy* was the writer's warning against the illusory nature of "our success dreams and our love dreams'" (Carples, 1926: 107), Hollywood's dream machine was the obvious instrument of their dramatization. But could the hucksters of shadowland dispel their own illusions? Could Hollywood ever bear witness to the nation's systemic injustice, coercive ideologies, unhappy endings?

In its indictment of the American fantasy of success (an indictment as ambiguous as Clyde's guilt, as so many commentators have observed) Dreiser's novel presented an undeniable challenge to Hollywood adaptation. The sheer complexity of its charges confounds narrative causality as well as the conventional time constraints of the Hollywood feature. Clyde's story is told and retold in almost rebarbitive detail. His culpability is considered from perspectives as varied as the neurologist's laboratory, the psychoanalytic couch and the Catholic confessional. To complicate this complexity, its author's views moved considerably leftward between the novel's writing and its cinematic adaptation.

To this challenge Eisenstein responded with a melodrama of Jazz Age beauty denied – the bright lights that dazzle a poor boy are extinguished forever by a ruthless system that punishes the very desire it has incited. Yet even Eisenstein cannot refrain from accusing his hapless protagonist of murder. Determined to eschew determinism, Sternberg attempted to represent the obliquity of Clyde's motivations. But, in turning him so often away from view, he redirects the spectator's attention to the milieu that surrounds him, and its complicity in the crime he both confesses and denies. Hugely praised on its release, Stevens' adaptation—whose star-crossed (and very starry) lovers keep faith with the fantasies of Hollywood infatuation—has been subsequently condemned as a romanticization of the cruel realities of class in the United States. But in shifting the blame from the country's economic system to its popular culture, *A Place in the Sun*, with its deliberately idealized casting, is the adaptation that most seeks to represent the American dream as a cinematic production.

Dreiser accused the movies of complicity in his tragedy and dared them to confess. He could imagine a cinema that would "make art enjoyable and yet critically reject the world presented by it," but he would not have concurred with this description of Sternberg's *Tragedy*. That adaptation won this praise from Herbert Ihering because "the social structure in which the crime takes place is shown clearly" (Ihering, 1980: 26–7). To represent the overwhelming influence of that structure, Eisenstein whirls Clyde in a vortex of temptation, superimposing his distracted movements on the social background that brings him to the brink of murder. In Stevens' version of the story, George Eastman is "framed" by the cinema itself, becoming both the personification and the victim of its celluloid illusions.

Each adaptation of Dreiser's novel measures the defendant's guilt and that of America differently and not always as its makers intended. But all three acknowledge some connection between individual tragedy and the national conviction that "our success dreams and our love dreams" will come true. The conscious intention of this study is to reconsider Hollywood's adherence to such beliefs. But it too has complex motives. In recounting this film history at a dark time in the nation's own, this book looks forward to happier endings.

Bibliography

Adorno, T. (1991), "Free Time," in J.M. Bernstein (ed.), *The Culture Industry: Selected Essays on Mass Culture*, London: Routledge.

Allen, M. (1999), *Family Secrets: The Feature Films of D.W. Griffith*, London: British Film Institute.

American Film Institute (2004), "George Stevens," in P. Cronin (ed.), *George Stevens: Interviews*, Jackson, MS: University Press of Mississippi.

Baxter, J. (1971), *The Cinema of Josef von Sternberg*, London: A. Zwemmer.

Baxter, P. (1993), *Just Watch! Sternberg, Paramount and America*, London: British Film Institute.

Behlmer, R. (ed.) (1972), *Memo. from David O. Selznick*, New York: Viking Press.

Bergen, R. (1999), *Eisenstein: A Life in Conflict*, Woodstock, NY: Overlooks Press.

Birch, L. and Hutton, K. (1951), "The Best Film Ever Made," *Picture Post*, 19 June.

Bordwell, D. (1988), "The Classical Hollywood Style—1917–1960," in D. Bordwell, J. Staiger and K. Thompson, *The Classical Hollywood Cinema*, London: Routledge.

Bowers, C. (1962), *My Life*, New York: Simon & Schuster.

Boyle, H. (2004), "George Stevens Puts Art Business Together," in P. Cronin (ed.), *George Stevens: Interviews*, Jackson, MS: University Press of Mississippi.

Brill, A. A. (1914), *Psychanalysis [sic], Its Theory and Practical Applications*, Philadelphia: W. B. Saunders.

Buckley, J. H. (ed.) (1958), *Poems of Tennyson*, Cambridge: Riverside Press.

Bulgakowa, O. (2001), "The Evolving Eisenstein," in A. La Valley and B. P. Scherr (eds), *Eisenstein at 100: A Reconsideration*, New Brunswick, NJ: Rutgers University Press.

Capote, T. (2001) *Answered Prayers*, London: Penguin Classics.

Carples, E. (1926), "The Story That Cost $93,000," *Motion Picture Magazine*, August vol. XXXI.

Carr, H. (1930), "The Lancer," *Los Angeles Times*, October 13.

Chion, M. (1999), *The Voice in the Cinema*, (ed. and trans. C. Gorbman), New York: Columbia University Press.

Clover, C. (2000), "Judging Audiences: The Case of the Trial Movie," in C. Gledhill and L. Williams (eds), *Reinventing Film Studies*, London: Arnold.

Cohan, S. (1997), *Masked Men: Masculinity and Movies in the Fifties*, Bloomington: Indiana University Press.

Cohen, K. (1977), "Eisenstein's Subversive Adaptation," in G. Peary and R. Shatzkin (eds), *The Classic American Novel and the Movies*, New York: Frederick Ungar Publishing Company.

Cronin, P. (2004), "Introduction," in P. Cronin (ed.), *George Stevens: Interviews*, Jackson, MS: University Press of Mississippi.

Crowther, B. (1951), "Seen in Close-Up," *New York Times*, September 23.

Daney, S (1991), "Godard Makes (Hi) Stories," in R. Bellour and M. L. Bandy (eds), *Jean-Luc Godard: Son + Image, 1974–1991*, New York: Museum of Modern Art.

Darby, W. and Du Bois, J. (1990), *American Film Music*, Jefferson, NC: McFarland & Company.

De Grazia, E. (1991), *Girls Lean Back Everywhere: The Law of Obscenity and the Assault on Genius*, New York: Random House.

Denby, D. (2003), "The Cost of Desire," *New Yorker*, April 21 and 28.

Denby, D. (2004), *American Sucker*, New York: Viking.

Dreiser, T. (1919), *The Long Long Trail*, manuscript, Dreiser Collection, Annenberg Rare Book and Manuscript Library, Van Pelt-Dietrich Library, University of Pennsylvania.

Dreiser, T. (1920), *Lady Bountiful, Jr.*, manuscript, Dreiser Collection, Annenberg Rare Book and Manuscript Library, Van Pelt-Dietrich Library, University of Pennsylvania.

Dreiser, T. (1921), "Hollywood Now," *McCall's Magazine*, September.

Dreiser, T. (1948), *An American Tragedy*, Cleveland: World Publishing Company.

Dreiser, T. (1987), "Hollywood: Its Morals and Manners," in A. K. Sterling (ed.), *The Best of Shadowland*, Metuchen, NJ: Scarecrow Press.

Dreiser, T. (1991), *Newspaper Days*, in T. D. Nostwich (ed.), Philadelphia: University of Pennsylvania Press.

Eisenstein, S. (1933), "The Cinema in America: Some Impressions of Hollywood" (trans S. D. Kogan), *International Literature*, no. 3, July.

Eisenstein, S. (1976), "Notes for a Film of Capital," *October*, 2, Summer.

Eisenstein, S. (1977), *Film Form*, (ed. and trans. J. Leyda), New York: Harvest.

Eisenstein, S. (1983), *Immoral Memories: An Autobiography* (trans. H. Marshall), Boston: Houghton Mifflin.

Eisenstein, S. (1987), *Nonindifferent Nature: Film and the Structure of Theory* (trans. H. Marshall), Cambridge: Cambridge University Press.

Eisenstein, S. (1988a), "However Odd—Khoklova!" in R. Taylor (ed.), *S. M. Eisenstein: Selected Works, Volume I, Writings 1922–34*, London: British Film Institute.

Eisenstein, S. (1988b), "Bela Forgets the Scissors," in R. Taylor (ed.), *S. M. Eisenstein: Selected Works, Volume I, Writings 1922–34*, London: British Film Institute.

Eisenstein, S. (1988c), "Literature and Cinema: A Reply to a Questionnaire," in R. Taylor (ed.), *S. M. Eisenstein: Selected Works, Volume I, Writings 1922–34*, London: British Film Institute.

Eisenstein, S. (1988d), "Statement on Sound" (co-signed by Vsevolod Pudovkin and Grigori Alexandrov), in R. Taylor (ed.), *S.M. Eisenstein Selected Works, Volume I, Writings 1922–34*, London: British Film Institute.

Eisenstein, S. (1988e), "The Form of the Script," in R. Taylor (ed.), *S. M. Eisenstein: Selected Works, Volume I, Writings 1922–34*, London: British Film Institute.

Eisenstein, S. (1988f), "The Dramaturgy of Film Form," in R. Taylor (ed.), *S. M. Eisenstein: Selected Works, Volume I, Writings 1922–34*, London: British Film Institute.

Eisenstein, S. (1988g), "The Principles of New Russian Cinema," in R. Taylor, *S.M. Eisenstein: Selected Works, Volume I, Writings 1922–34*, London: British Film Institute.

Eisenstein, S. (1988h), "Help Yourself!" in R. Taylor, *S. M. Eisenstein: Selected Works, Volume I, Writings 1922–34*, London: British Film Institute.

Eisenstein, S. (1988i), "An Attack by Class Allies," in R. Taylor, *S. M. Eisenstein: Selected Works, Volume I, Writings 1922–34*, London: British Film Institute.

Eisenstein, S. (1991a), "Montage and Architecture," in M. Glenny and R. Taylor (eds), *Selected Works, Volume II, Towards a Theory of Montage*, London: British Film Institute.

Eisenstein, S. (1991b), "Pushkin the Montageur," in M. Glenny and R. Taylor (eds), *Selected Works, Volume II, Towards a Theory of Montage*, London: British Film Institute.

Eisenstein, S. (1995), *Selected Works, Volume IV, Beyond the Stars: The Memoirs of Sergei Eisenstein*, R. Taylor (ed.), London: British Film Institute.

Eisenstein, S. (1996), "Speeches to the All-Union Creative Conference of Soviet Filmworkers," R. Taylor (ed.), *S. M. Eisenstein: Selected Works, Volume III, Writings 1934–1947*, London: British Film Institute.

Elias, R. H. (ed.) (1950), *Letters of Theodore Dreiser: A Selection, Volume I*, Philadelphia: University of Pennsylvania Press.

Elias, R. H. (ed.) (1959), *Letters of Theodore Dreiser: A Selection, Volume II*, Philadelphia: University of Pennsylvania Press.

Ellmann, R. (1982), *James Joyce*, New York: Oxford University Press.

Engels, F. (1968), "Socialism: Utopian and Scientific" (trans. Edward Aveling), in Karl Marx and Frederick Engels, *Selected Works*, London: Lawrence & Wishart.

Felman, S. (1977), "Turning the Screw of Interpretation," *Yale French Studies*, numbers 55–56.

Freud, S. (1985), "The 'Uncanny'", in *Art and Literature*, volume 14, the Pelican Freud Library, Harmondsworth: Penguin Books.

Frey, R. (1970), "Anne Revere Begins Again," *After Dark*, December.

Gauss, C (1915), *The German Kaiser as Shown in His Public Utterances*, New York: Charles Scribner's Sons.

Girgus, S. (1998), *The Cinema of Democracy in the Era of Ford, Capra and Kazan*, Cambridge: Cambridge University Press.

Goodwin, J. (1993), *Eisenstein, Cinema and History*, Urbana: University of Illinois Press.

Goodwin, J. (2001), "Eisenstein: Lessons with Hollywood," in A. La Valley and B. P. Scherr (eds), *Eisenstein at 100: A Reconsideration*, New Brunswick, NJ: Rutgers University Press.

Hall, M. (1931a), "Fictional Espionage," *New York Times*, March 15.

Hall, M. (1931b), "The Screen: Mr Dreiser's Famous Story," *New York Times*, August 6.

Hankins, L. K. (1993), "'Across the Screen of My Brain': Virginia Woolf's 'The Cinema' and Film Forums of the Twenties," in D. F. Gillespie (ed.), *The Multiple Muses of Virginia Woolf*, Columbia, MO: University of Missouri Press.

Hansen, M. (1991), *Babel to Babylon: Spectatorship in America*, Cambridge, MA: Harvard University Press.

Hansen, M. (2000), "The Mass Production of the Senses: Classical Cinema as Vernacular Modernism," in C. Gledhill and L. Williams (eds), *Reinventing Film Studies*, London: Arnold.

Higashi, S. (2002), "The New Woman and Consumer Culture," in J. M. Bean and D. Negra (eds), *A Feminist Reader in Early Cinema*, Durham, NC: Duke University Press.

Hiney, T. and Macshane, F. (eds) (2000), *The Raymond Chandler Papers*, New York: Atlantic Monthly Press.

Hughes, R. (2004), "Getting the Belly Laugh," *George Stevens: Interviews*, Jackson, MS: University Press of Mississippi.

Hussman, L. (1995), "Squandered Possibilities: The Film Versions of Dreiser's Novels," in M. Gogol (ed.), *Theodore Dreiser: Beyond Naturalism*, New York: New York University Press.

Ihering, H. (1980), "The Blue Angel and An American Tragedy" (trans. Maarat Koskinen), in P. Baxter (ed.), *Sternberg*, London: British Film Institute.

Jacobs, L. (1995), "An American Tragedy: A Comparison of Film and Literary Censorship," *Quarterly Review of Film and Video*, 15(4).

James, H. (1986), "Preface," *The Aspern Papers and The Turn of the Screw*, (ed. A. Curtis), London: Penguin.

Jameson, F. (1991), *Postmodernism, or the Cultural Logic of Late Capitalism*, Durham, NC: Duke University Press.

Joyce, J. (1993) *Ulysses* (ed. J. Johnson), Oxford: Oxford University Press.

Kadir, D. (2003), "Introduction: America and its Studies", *PMLA*, 118(1).

Kashner, S. and MacNair, J. (2002), *The Bad and The Beautiful: A Chronicle of Hollywood in the Fifties*, London: Little, Brown & Company.

Kearney, P. (1926), *An American Tragedy*, undated manuscript, George Stevens

Collection, Margaret Herrick Library, Academy of Motion Picture Arts and Sciences.

Kenaga, H. (2006), "Making the 'Studio Girl,'" *Film History*, 18.

Kirschner, W. (2004), "Conversation with George Stevens", in P. Cronin (ed.), *George Stevens: Interviews*, Jackson, MS: University Press of Mississippi.

Klimans, B. (1977), "An American Tragedy: Novel, Scenario, and Films," *Literature/Film Quarterly*, 5(3), Summer.

Klumph, H. (1926), "Miss La Plante Sees New York," *Los Angeles Times*, March 28.

Koszarski, R. (1990), *History of the American Cinema, Volume 3, An Evening's Entertainment, 1915–1928*, New York: Charles Scribner's Sons.

Kracauer, S. (1995), *History: The Last Things Before the Last*, Princeton: Markus Wiener Publishers.

Krasna, N. and Wald, J. (1951), "Hollywood Kiss," *Look*, September 1.

Laplanche, J. and Pontalis, J.-B. (1986), "Fantasy and the Origins of Sexuality," in V. Burgin, J. Donald and C. Kaplan (eds) *Formations of Fantasy*, London: Methuen.

Lasky, J. (with Don Weldon) (1957), *I Blow My Own Horn*, Garden City, New York: Doubleday.

Leyda, J. and Voynow, Z. (1982), *Eisenstein at Work*, New York: Pantheon Books, Museum of Modern Art.

Lingeman, R. (1990), *Theodore Dreiser: An American Journey, 1908–1945*, New York: G.P. Puttnam's Sons.

Loeb, J. (1901), *Comparative Physiology of the Brain and Comparative Psychology*, London: John Murray.

Loving, J. (2005), *The Last Titan: A Life of Theodore Dreiser*, Berkeley: University of California Press.

Marchant, R. (2006), "Century-old Hollywood Battle Retrieved from Archives," www.thejournalnews.com/apps/pbcs.dll/article?AID=20060824/NEWS02/6082403 (accessed October 9, 2006).

Martin, Q. (1927), "The Magic Lantern: A Book That Would Make a Great Film," *New York World*, March 7.

McBride, J. (1991), *Frank Capra: The Catastrophe of Success*, London: Faber & Faber.

Mencken, H. L. (1948), "Introduction," in T. Dreiser, *An American Tragedy*, Cleveland and New York: World Publishing Company.

Merck, M. (2007), "Introduction," *America First: Naming the Nation in US Film*, London: Routledge.

Michaels, W. B. (1987), *The Gold Standard and the Logic of Naturalism: American Literature at the Turn of the Century*, Berkeley: University of California Press.

Miles, A. (1999), "Cinematic Paradigms for Hypertext," *Continuum: Journal of Media and Cultural Studies*, 13.2.

Moers, E. (1969) *Two Dreisers*, New York: Viking Press.

Moffat, I. (2004) *The Ivan Moffat File* (ed. G. Lambert), New York: Pantheon Press.

Montagu, I. (1969), *With Eisenstein in Hollywood* (including the texts of S. M. Eisenstein, G. V. Alexandrov and I. Montagu, *Sutter's Gold* and *An American Tragedy*), New York: International Publishers.

Moss, M. A. (2004), *Giant: George Stevens, A Life in Film*, Madison, WI: University of Wisconsin Press.

Mulvey, L. (2006), *Death 24x a Second: Stillness and the Moving Image*, London: Reaktion Books.

Murphy, A. D. (1967), "Stevens Loses 'Sun' Spots Suit Vs. Par-NBC," *Variety*, May 24.

Nowell-Smith, G. (1991), "Eisenstein on Montage," in M. Glenny and R. Taylor (eds), *S. M. Eisenstein, Selected Works, Volume II, Toward a Theory of Montage*, London: British Film Institute.

O'Pray, M. (2004), *Film, Form and Phantasy: Adrian Stokes and Film Aesthetics*, Basingstoke: Palgrave.

Penn Warren, R. (1971), *Homage to Theodore Dressier*, New York: Random House.

Petri, B. (1987), *A Theory of American Film: The Films and Techniques of George Stevens*, New York: Garland.

Phillips, W. L. (1963), "The Imagery of Dreiser's Novels," *PMLA*, December.

Potamkin, H. (1977), "Novel into Film: A Case Study of Current Practice," in L. Jacobs (ed.), *The Compound Cinema: The Film Writings of Harry Alan Potamkin*, New York: Teachers College Press, Teachers College, Columbia University.

Powdermaker, H. (1950), *The Dream Factory: An Anthropologist Looks at the Movie-Makers*, Boston: Little, Brown & Company.

Rancière, J. (2002), "The Saint and the Heiress: A propos of Godard's Histoire(s) du Cinéma," *Discourse*, 24(1) (Winter).

Riggio, T. P. (ed.) (1982), *Theodore Dreiser's American Diaries, 1902–1926*, Philadelphia: University of Pennsylvania Press.

Riggio, T. P. and West, J. III (1996), *Dreiser's Russian Diary*, Philadelphia: University of Pennsylvania Press.

Ryan, E. M. (2004) "Cruel Words, Theodore Dreiser!" *Los Angeles Sunday Times*, in F. E. Rusch and D. Pizer (eds), *Theodore Dreiser: Interviews*, Urbana: University of Illinois Press.

Salt, B. (1980), "Sternberg's Heart Beats in Black and White," in P. Baxter, *Sternberg*, London: British Film Institute.

Schallert, E. (1926), "The Hero of the 'Tragedy,'" *Los Angeles Times*, July 25.

Schatz, T. (1996), *The Genius of the System: Filmmaking in the Studio Era*, New York: Holt.

Scheuer, P. (1930), "Russian Film Genius Here," *Los Angeles Times*, June 22.

Schulberg, B. (1981), *Moving Pictures: Memories of a Hollywood Prince*, New York: Stein & Day.

Seltzer, M. (1992), *Bodies and Machines*, New York: Routledge.

Seton, M (1952) *Sergei M. Eisenstein*, New York: A.A. Wyn.

Smith, D. (1951), "Film Review: A Place In the Sun", Los Angeles *Daily News*, August 15.

Sternberg, J. (1966), *Fun in a Chinese Laundry*, London: Secker & Warburg.

Strychacz, T. (1993), *Modernism, Mass Culture, and Professionalism*, Cambridge: Cambridge University Press.

Swanberg, W. A. (1965), *Dreiser*, New York: Charles Scribner's Sons.

Taylor, C. (1967), "Blacklist—Horror Role for Anne Revere," *Los Angeles Times*, June 20.

Taylor, R. (2002), *October*, London: British Film Institute.

Thompson, K. (1988) "The Formation of the Classical Narrative", in D. Bordwell, J. Staiger and K. Thompson, *The Classical Hollywood Cinema*, London: Routledge.

Watson, J. B. (1913), "Psychology as the Behaviorist Views It," *Psychological Review*, 20.

Watson, W. (1984), *Cinema Program Notes: A Place in the Sun*, Austin: Cinema Texas, University of Texas at Austin.

Williams, L. (1998), "Melodrama Revised," in N. Browne (ed.), *Refiguring American Film Genres: Theory and History*, Berkeley: University of California Press.

Wilson, E. (1958), "Eisenstein in Hollywood," in *The American Earthquake: A Documentary of the Twenties and Thirties*, Garden City, NY: Doubleday Anchor Books.

Winters, S. (1980), *Shelley—Also Known as Shirley*, New York: William Morrow.

Wood, T. (2002), "The Ecstatic Spiral," *New Left Review*, 18, November/ December.

Wright, A. (2000) "Elizabeth Taylor at Auschwitz," in Michael Temple and James B. Williams, *The Cinema Alone—Essays on the Work of Jean-Luc Godard 1985–2000*, Amsterdam: Amsterdam University Press.

Yutkevich, S. and Eisenstein, S. (1988), "The Eighth Art. On Expressionism, America and, of course, Chaplin", in R. Taylor (ed.), *S. M.Eisenstein: Selected Works, Volume I, Writings 1922–23*, London: British Film Institute.

Index

[Note: Italic page numbers indicate images. "n" indicates a reference in a footnote.]